THE NORMAL

The Normal Christian Life

WATCHMAN NEE

Victor®

The Bible Teacher's Teacher

KINGSWAY COMMUNICATIONS LTD
Eastbourne, England
COOK COMMUNICATIONS MINISTRIES
Colorado Springs, Colorado • Paris, Ontario

ISBN 1 84291 237 2

Victor is an imprint of
KINGSWAY COMMUNICATIONS LTD
Lottbridge Drove, Eastbourne BN23 6NT, England.
Email: books@kingsway.co.uk

Printed in the U.S.A.

Contents

Scripture quotations are from the Revised Version
unless otherwise indicated.

Preface

THE ministry of Watchman Nee had been known in English only from transcriptions of his spoken messages in tracts and magazine articles when, in 1957, *The Normal Christian Life* was first published in Bombay and was at once accorded a widespread welcome. Compiled from such records and from private notebooks, this collection was edited in the author's absence, and is based upon addresses originally given by Mr. Nee during and shortly after a visit to Europe in 1938–39.

From the day in 1920 when, as a college student, he found the Lord Jesus Christ as his Saviour during the visit of a Chinese evangelist to his native city of Foochow, Nee To-sheng gave himself without reserve to God for work among his own people. Over the years he became widely known in China as a gifted preacher of the Gospel and an original expositor of the Word, whose ministry bore remarkable fruit in individuals and in many groups of spiritually virile Christians. This book sets forth something of his personal understanding of the Christian life towards the end of those first years of unrestricted service for his Lord.

In the years that have followed, the Church of God in China has passed through recurring periods of the severest testing with but brief interludes of respite, and the author, together with many of those associated with him in work and witness, has had his full share of these experiences right up to the present. It is perhaps not surprising therefore that his ministry should come to us today with freshness and power. Many have already testified to the transformation this book has wrought in their lives through new discoveries of the greatness of Christ and of His finished work on the cross.

The demand for a new edition made possible a further careful revision of the text in 1961. Readers are reminded that this is a compilation of spoken addresses and not, despite superficial appearances, a systematic treatise of Christian doctrine. It is to be approached not as an intellectual exercise but as a message to the heart. Read thus it will, I believe, speak as from the Spirit of God Himself, with challenging power.

ANGUS I. KINNEAR
London, 1961

1

The Blood of Christ

WHAT is the normal Christian life? We do well at the outset to ponder this question. The object of these studies is to show that it is something very different from the life of the average Christian. Indeed a consideration of the written Word of God—of the Sermon on the Mount for example—should lead us to ask whether such a life has ever in fact been lived upon the earth, *save only by the Son of God Himself*. But in that last saving clause lies immediately the answer to our question.

The apostle Paul gives us his own definition of the Christian life in Galatians 2. 20. It is 'no longer I, but Christ'. Here he is not stating something special or peculiar—a high level of Christianity. He is, we believe, presenting God's normal for a Christian, which can be summarized in the words: I live no longer, but Christ lives His life in me.

God makes it quite clear in His Word that He has only one answer to every human need—His Son, Jesus Christ. In all His dealings with us He works by taking *us* out of the way and substituting Christ in our place. The Son of God died instead of us for our forgiveness: He lives instead of us for

our deliverance. So we can speak of two substitutions—a
Substitute on the Cross who secures our forgiveness and a
Substitute within who secures our victory. It will help us
greatly, and save us from much confusion, if we keep constantly before us this fact, that God will answer all our questions in one way and one way only, namely, by showing us
more of His son.

Our dual problem: sins and sin

We shall take now as a starting-point for our study of the
normal Christian life that great exposition of it which we
find in the first eight chapters of the Epistle to the Romans,
and we shall approach our subject from a practical and
experimental point of view. It will be helpful first of all to
point out a natural division of this section of Romans into
two, and to note certain striking differences in the subject-
matter of its two parts.

The first eight chapters of Romans form a self-contained
unit. The four-and-a-half chapters from 1. 1 to 5. 11 form
the first half of this unit and the three-and-a-half chapters
from 5. 12 to 8. 39 the second half. A careful reading will
show us that the subject-matter of the two halves is not the
same. For example, in the argument of the first section we
find the plural word 'sins' given prominence. In the second
section, however, this is changed, for while the word 'sins'
hardly occurs once, the singular word 'sin' is used again and
again and is the subject mainly dealt with. Why is this?

It is because in the first section it is a question of the sins
I have committed before God, which are many and can be
enumerated, whereas in the second it is a question of sin as

a principle working in me. No matter how many sins I commit, it is always the one sin-principle that leads to them. I need forgiveness for my sins, but I need also deliverance from the power of sin. The former touches my conscience, the latter my life. I may receive forgiveness for all my sins, but because of my sin I have, even then, no abiding peace of mind.

When God's light first shines into my heart my one cry is for forgiveness, for I realize I have committed sins before Him; but when once I have received forgiveness of sins I make a new discovery, namely, the discovery of sin, and I realize not only that I have committed sins before God but that there is something wrong within. I discover that I have the nature of a sinner. There is an inward inclination to sin, a power within that draws to sin. When that power breaks out I commit sins. I may seek and receive forgiveness, but then I sin once more. So life goes on in a vicious circle of sinning and being forgiven and then sinning again. I appreciate the blessed fact of God's forgiveness, but I want something more than that: I want deliverance. I need forgiveness for what I have done, but I need also deliverance from what I am.

God's dual remedy: the blood and the cross

Thus in the first eight chapters of Romans two aspects of salvation are presented to us: firstly, the forgiveness of our sins, and secondly, our deliverance from sin. But now, in keeping with this fact, we must notice a further difference.

In the first part of Romans 1 to 8, we twice have reference to the Blood of the Lord Jesus, in chapter 3. 25 and in chapter 5. 9. In the second, a new idea is introduced in chapter 6. 6, where we are said to have been 'crucified' with Christ. The argument of the first part gathers round that aspect of the work of the Lord Jesus which is represented by 'the Blood' shed for our justification through 'the remission of sins'. This terminology is, however, not carried on into the second section, where the argument centres now in the aspect of His work represented by 'the Cross', that is to say, by our union with Christ in His death, burial and resurrection. This distinction is a valuable one. We shall see that the Blood deals with what we have done, whereas the Cross deals with what we are. The Blood disposes of our sins, while the Cross strikes at the root of our capacity for sin. The latter aspect will be the subject of our consideration in later chapters.

The problem of our sins

We begin, then, with the precious Blood of the Lord Jesus Christ and its value to us in dealing with our sins and justifying us in the sight of God. This is set forth for us in the following passages:

'All have sinned' (Rom. 3. 23).

'God commendeth his own love toward us, in that, while we were yet sinners, Christ died for us. Much more then, being now justified by his blood, shall we be saved from the wrath of God through him' (Rom. 5. 8, 9).

'Being justified freely by his grace through the redemption that is in Christ Jesus: whom God set forth to be a propitiation, through faith, by his blood, to shew his righteousness, because of the passing over of the sins done aforetime, in

the forbearance of God; for the shewing, I say, of his righteousness at this present season: that he might himself be
just, and the justifier of him that hath faith in Jesus' (Rom.
3. 24–26).

We shall have reason at a later stage in our study to look
closely at the real nature of the Fall and the way of recovery. At this point we will just remind ourselves that when
sin came in it found expression in an act of disobedience to
God (Rom. 5. 19). Now we must remember that whenever
this occurs the thing that immediately follows is guilt.

Sin enters as disobedience, to create first of all a separation between God and man whereby man is put away from
God. God can no longer have fellowship with him, for there
is something now which hinders, and it is that which is
known throughout Scripture as 'sin'. Thus it is first of all
God who says, 'They are all under sin' (Rom. 3. 9). Then,
secondly, that sin in man, which henceforth constitutes a
barrier to his fellowship with God, gives rise in him to a
sense of guilt—of estrangement from God. Here it is man
himself who, with the help of his awakened conscience,
says, 'I have sinned' (Luke 15. 18). Nor is this all, for sin also
provides Satan with his ground of accusation before God,
while our sense of guilt gives him his ground of accusation
in our hearts; so that, thirdly, it is 'the accuser of the
brethren' (Rev. 12. 10) who now says, 'You have sinned'.

To redeem us, therefore, and to bring us back to the purpose of God, the Lord Jesus had to do something about
these three questions of sin and of guilt and of Satan's
charge against us. Our sins had first to be dealt with, and
this was effected by the precious Blood of Christ. Our guilt
has to be dealt with and our guilty conscience set at rest by

showing us the value of that Blood. And finally, the attack of the enemy has to be met and his accusations answered. In the Scriptures the Blood of Christ is shown to operate effectually in these three ways, Godward, manward and Satanward.

There is thus an absolute need for us to appropriate these values of the Blood if we are to go on. This is a first essential. We must have a basic knowledge of the fact of the death of the Lord Jesus as our Substitute upon the Cross, and a clear apprehension of the efficacy of His Blood for our sins, for without this we cannot be said to have started upon our road. Let us look then at these three matters more closely.

The Blood is primarily for God

The Blood is for atonement and has to do first with our standing before God. We need forgiveness for the sins we have committed, lest we come under judgment; and they are forgiven, not because God overlooks what we have done but because He sees the Blood. The Blood is therefore not primarily for us but for God. If I want to understand the value of the Blood I must accept God's valuation of it, and if I do not know something of the value set upon the Blood by God I shall never know what its value is for me. It is only as the estimate that God puts upon the Blood of Christ is made known to me by His Holy Spirit that I come into the good of it myself and find how precious indeed the Blood is to me. But the first aspect of it is Godward. Throughout the Old and New Testaments the word 'blood' is used in connection with the idea of atonement, I think over a hundred times, and throughout it is something for God.

In the Old Testament calender there is one day that has a great bearing on the matter of our sins and that day is the Day of Atonement. Nothing explains this question of sins so clearly as the description of that day. In Leviticus 16 we find that on the Day of Atonement the blood was taken from the sin offering and brought into the Most Holy Place and there sprinkled before the Lord seven times. We must be very clear about this. On that day the sin offering was offered publicly in the court of the tabernacle. Everything was there in full view and could be seen by all. But the Lord commanded that no man should enter the tabernacle itself except the high priest. It was he alone who took the blood and, going into the Most Holy Place, sprinkled it there to make atonement before the Lord. Why? Because the high priest was a type of the Lord Jesus in His redemptive work (Heb. 9. 11, 12), and so, in figure, he was the one who did the work. None but he could even draw near to enter in. Moreover, connected with his going in there was but one act, namely, the presenting of the blood to God as something He had accepted, something in which He could find satisfaction. It was a transaction between the high priest and God in the Sanctuary, away from the eyes of the men who were to benefit by it. The Lord required that. The Blood is therefore, in the first place, not for ourselves but for Him.

Earlier even than this there is described in Exodus 12. 13 the shedding of the blood of the passover lamb in Egypt for Israel's redemption. This is again, I think, one of the best types in the Old Testament of our redemption. The blood was put on the lintel and on the door-posts, whereas the meat, the flesh of the lamb, was eaten inside the house; and

God said: 'When I see the blood, I will pass over you.' Here we have another illustration of the fact that the blood was not meant to be presented to man but to God, for the blood was put on the lintel and on the door-posts, where those feasting inside the house would not see it.

God is satisfied

It is God's holiness, God's righteousness, which demands that a sinless life should be given for man. There is life in the Blood, and that Blood has to be poured out for me, for my sins. God is the One who requires it to be so. God is the One who demands that the Blood be presented, in order to satisfy His own righteousness, and it is He who says: '*When I see the blood*, I will pass over you.' The Blood of Christ wholly satisfies God.

Now I desire to say a word at this point to my younger brethren in the Lord, for it is here that we often get into difficulties. As unbelievers we may have been wholly untroubled by our conscience until the Word of God began to arouse us. Our conscience was dead, and those with dead consciences are certainly of no use to God. But later, when we believed, our awakened conscience may have become acutely sensitive, and this can constitute a real problem to us. The sense of sin and guilt can become so great, so terrible, as almost to cripple us, by causing us to lose sight of the true effectiveness of the Blood. It seems to us that our sins are so real, and some particular sin may trouble us so many times, that we come to the point where to us our sins loom larger than the Blood of Christ.

Now the whole trouble with us is that we are trying to

sense it; we are trying to feel its value and to estimate subjectively what the Blood is for us. We cannot do it; it does not work that way. The Blood is first for God to see. We then have to accept God's valuation of it. In doing so we shall find our salvation. If instead we try to come to a valuation by way of our feelings we get nothing; we remain in darkness. No, it is a matter of faith in God's Word. We have to believe that the Blood is precious to God *because He says it is so* (1 Peter 1. 18, 19). If God can accept the Blood as a payment for our sins and as the price of our redemption, then we can rest assured that the debt has been paid. If God is satisfied with the Blood, then the Blood must be acceptable. Our valuation of it is only according to His valuation— neither more nor less. It cannot, of course, be more, but it must not be less. Let us remember that He is holy and He is righteous, and that a holy and righteous God has the right to say that the Blood is acceptable in His eyes and has fully satisfied Him.

The believer's access to God

The Blood has satisfied God; it must satisfy us also. It has therefore a second value that is manward, in the cleansing of our conscience. When we come to the Epistle to the Hebrews we find that the Blood does this. We are to have 'hearts sprinkled from an evil conscience' (Heb. 10. 22).

This is most important. Look carefully at what it says. The writer does not tell us that the Blood of the Lord Jesus cleanses our hearts, and then stop there in his statement. We are wrong to connect the heart with the Blood in quite that way. It may show a misunderstanding of the sphere in which the Blood operates to pray, 'Lord, cleanse my heart from sin by Thy Blood'. The heart, God says, is 'desperately sick' (Jer. 17. 9), and He must do something more funda-mental than cleanse it: He must give us a new one. We do not wash and iron clothing that we are going to throw away. As we shall shortly see, the 'flesh' is too bad to be cleansed; it must be crucified. The work of God within us must be something wholly new. 'A new heart also will I give you, and a new spirit will I put within you' (Ezek. 36. 26).

No, I do not find it stated that the Blood cleanses our hearts. Its work is not subjective in that way, but wholly objective, before God. True, the cleansing work of the Blood is seen here in Hebrews 10 to have reference to the heart, but it is in relation to the conscience. 'Having our hearts sprinkled from an evil conscience.' What then is the mean-ing of this?

It means that there was something intervening between myself and God, as a result of which I had an evil conscience whenever I sought to approach Him. It was constantly reminding me of the barrier that stood between myself and Him. But now, through the operation of the precious Blood, something new has been effected before God which has removed that barrier, and God has made that fact known to me in His Word. When that has been believed in and accepted, my conscience is at once cleared and my sense of guilt removed, and I have no more an evil conscience towards God.

Every one of us knows what a precious thing it is to have a conscience void of offence in our dealings with God. A heart of faith and a conscience clear of any and every accusation are both equally essential to us, since they are interdependent. As soon as we find our conscience is uneasy, our faith leaks away, and immediately we know we cannot face God. In order therefore to keep going on with God we must know the up-to-date value of the Blood. God keeps short accounts, and we are made nigh by the Blood every day, every hour and every minute. It never loses its efficacy as our ground of access if we will but lay hold upon it. When we enter the Most Holy Place, on what ground dare we enter but by the Blood?

But I want to ask myself, am I really seeking the way into the presence of God by the Blood or by something else? What do I mean when I say, 'by the Blood'? I mean simply that I recognize my sins, that I confess that I have need of cleansing and of atonement, and that I come to God on the basis of the finished work of the Lord Jesus. I approach God through His merit alone, and never on the basis of my attainment; never, for example, on the ground that I have been extra kind or patient today, or that I have done something for the Lord this morning. I have to come by way of the Blood every time. The temptation to so many of us when we try to approach God is to think that because God has been dealing with us—because He has been taking steps to bring us into something more of Himself and has been teaching us deeper lessons of the Cross—He has thereby set before us new standards, and that only by attaining to these can we have a clear conscience before Him. No! A clear conscience is *never* based upon our attainment; it can only be based on the work of the Lord Jesus in the shedding of His Blood.

I may be mistaken, but I feel very strongly that some of

us are thinking in terms such as these: 'Today I have been a little more careful; today I have been doing a little better; this morning I have been reading the Word of God in a warmer way, so today I can pray better!' Or again, 'Today I have had a little difficulty with the family; I began the day feeling very gloomy and depressed; I am not feeling too bright now; it seems there must be something wrong; therefore the way is not clear for me to approach God.'

What, after all, is your basis of approach to God? Do you come to Him on the uncertain ground of your feeling, the feeling that you may have achieved something for God today? Or is your approach based on something far more secure, namely, the fact that the Blood has been shed, and that God looks on that Blood and is satisfied? Of course, were it conceivably possible for the Blood to suffer any change, the basis of your approach to God might be less trustworthy. But the Blood has never changed and never will. Your approach to God is therefore always in boldness; and that boldness is yours through the Blood and never through your personal attainment. Whatever be your measure of attainment today or yesterday or the day before, as soon as you make a conscious move into the Most Holy Place, immediately you have to take your stand upon the safe and only ground of the shed Blood. Whether you have had a good day or a bad day, whether you have consciously sinned or not, your basis of approach is always the same—the Blood of Christ. God's acceptance of that Blood is the ground upon which you may enter, and there is no other.

As with many other facets of our Christian experience, this matter of access to God has two phases, an initial and a progressive one. The former is presented to us in Ephesians

2 and the latter in Hebrews 10. Initially, our standing with God was secured by the Blood, for we are 'made nigh in the blood of Christ' (Eph, 2. 13). But thereafter our ground of continual access is still by the Blood, for the apostle exhorts us: 'Having therefore . . . boldness to enter into the holy place by the blood of Jesus . . . let us draw near' (Heb. 10. 19, 22). To begin with I was made nigh by the Blood, and to continue in that new relationship I come through the Blood every time. It is not that I was saved on one basis and that I now maintain my fellowship on another. You say, 'That is very simple; it is the A.B.C. of the Gospel.' Yes, but the trouble with many of us is that we have moved away from the A.B.C. We have thought we had progressed and so could dispense with it, but we can never do so. No, my initial approach to God is by the Blood, and every time I come before Him it is the same. Right to the end it will always and only be on the ground of the precious Blood.

This does not mean at all that we should live a careless life, for we shall shortly study another aspect of the death of Christ which shows us that anything but that is contemplated. But for the present let us be satisfied with the Blood, that it is there and that it is enough.

We may be weak, but looking at our weakness will never make us strong. No trying to feel bad and doing penance will help us to be even a little holier. There is no help there, so let us be bold in our approach because of the Blood: 'Lord, I do not know fully what the value of the Blood is, but I know that the Blood has satisfied Thee; so the Blood is enough for me, and it is my only plea. I see now that whether I have really progressed, whether I have really attained to something or not, is not the point. Whenever I come before Thee, it is always to be on the ground of the precious Blood.' Then our conscience is really clear before God. No conscience could ever be clear apart from the Blood. It is the Blood that gives us boldness.

'No more conscience of sins': these are the tremendous words of Hebrews 10. 2. We are cleansed from every sin; and we may truly, with Paul, echo the words of David: 'Blessed is the man to whom the Lord will not reckon sin' (Rom. 4. 8).

Overcoming the accuser

In view of what we have said we can now turn to face the enemy, for there is a further aspect of the Blood which is Satanward. Satan's most strategic activity in this day is as the accuser of the brethren (Rev. 12. 10) and it is as this that our Lord confronts him with His special ministry as High Priest 'through his own blood' (Heb. 9. 12).

How then does the Blood operate against Satan? It does so by putting God on the side of man against him. The Fall brought about a state of affairs in man which gave Satan a footing within him, with the result that God was compelled to withdraw Himself. Man is now outside the garden— beyond reach of the glory of God (Rom. 3. 23)—because he is inwardly estranged from God. Because of what man has done, there is that in him now which, until it is removed, renders God morally unable to defend him. But the Blood removes that barrier, and restores man to God and God to man. Man is in favour now, and because God is on his side he can face Satan without fear.

You remember that verse in John's first Epistle—and this

is the translation of it I like best: 'The blood of Jesus his Son cleanses us from *every* sin.'[1] It is not exactly 'all sin' in the general sense, but *every* sin, every item. What does it mean? Oh, it is a marvellous thing! God is in the light, and as we walk in the light with Him everything is exposed and open to that light, so that God can see it all—*and yet* the Blood is able to cleanse from every sin. What a cleansing! It is not that I have not a profound knowledge of myself, nor that God has not a perfect knowledge of me. It is not that I try to hide something, nor that God tries to overlook something. No, it is that He is in the light and I too am in the light, and that *there* the precious Blood cleanses me from every sin. The Blood is enough for that!

Some of us, oppressed by our own weakness, may at times have been tempted to think that there are sins which are almost unforgivable. Let us remember the word: 'The blood of Jesus Christ his Son cleanses us from every sin.' Big sins, small sins, sins which may be very black and sins which appear to be not so black, sins which I think can be forgiven and sins which seem unforgivable, yes, *all* sins, conscious or unconscious, remembered or forgotten, are included in those words: 'every sin'. 'The blood of Jesus his Son cleanses us from every sin', and it does so because in the first place it satisfies God.

Since God, seeing all our sins in the light, can forgive them on the basis of the Blood, what ground of accusation has Satan? Satan may accuse us before Him, but, 'If God is for us, who is against us?' (Rom. 8. 31). God points him to the Blood of His dear Son. It is the sufficient answer against

---

[1] 1 John 1. 7: Marginal reading of New Translation by J. N. Darby.

which Satan has no appeal. 'Who shall lay anything to the charge of God's elect? It is God that justifieth; who is he that shall condemn? It is Christ Jesus that died, yea rather, that was raised from the dead, who is at the right hand of God, who also maketh intercession for us' (Rom. 8. 33, 34). Thus God answers his every challenge.

So here again our need is to recognize the absolute sufficiency of the precious Blood. 'Christ having come a high priest . . . through his own blood, entered in once for all into the holy place, having obtained eternal redemption' (Heb. 9. 11, 12). He was Redeemer once. He has been High Priest and Advocate for nearly two thousand years. He stands there in the presence of God, and 'he is the propitiation for our sins' (1 John 2. 1, 2). Note the words of Hebrews 9. 14; '*How much more* shall the blood of Christ . . . cleanse your conscience'. They underline the sufficiency of His ministry. *It is enough for God.*

What then of our attitude to Satan? This is important, for he accuses us not only before God but in our own conscience also. 'You have sinned, and you keep on sinning. You are weak, and God can have nothing more to do with you.' This is his argument. And our temptation is to look within and in self-defence to try to find in ourselves, in our feelings or our behaviour, some ground for believing that Satan is wrong. Alternatively we are tempted to admit our helplessness and, going to the other extreme, to yield to depression and despair. Thus accusation becomes one of the greatest and most effective of Satan's weapons. He points to our sins and seeks to charge us with them before God, and if we accept his accusations we go down immediately.

Now the reason why we so readily accept his accusations

is that we are still hoping to have some righteousness of our own. The ground of our expectation is wrong. Satan has succeeded in making us look in the wrong direction. Thereby he wins his point, rendering us ineffective. But if we have learned to put no confidence in the flesh, we shall not wonder if we sin, for the very nature of the flesh is to sin. Do you understand what I mean? It is because we have not come to appreciate our true nature and to see how helpless we are that we still have some expectation in ourselves, with the result that, when Satan comes along and accuses us, we go down under it.

God is well able to deal with our sins; but He cannot deal with a man under accusation, because such a man is not trusting in the Blood. The Blood speaks in his favour, but he is listening instead to Satan. Christ is our Advocate, but we, the accused, side with the accuser. We have not recognized that we are unworthy of anything but death; that, as we shall shortly see, we are only fit to be crucified anyway. We have not recognized that it is God alone that can answer the accuser, and that in the precious Blood He has already done so.

Our salvation lies in looking away to the Lord Jesus and in seeing that the Blood of the Lamb has met the whole situation created by our sins and has answered it. That is the sure foundation on which we stand. Never should we try to answer Satan with our good conduct but always with the Blood. Yes, we are sinful, but, praise God! the Blood cleanses us from every sin. God looks upon the Blood whereby His Son has met the charge, and Satan has no more ground of attack. Our faith in the precious Blood and our refusal to be moved from that position can alone silence his charges and put him to flight (Rom. 8. 33, 34); and so it will be, right on to the end (Rev. 12. 11). Oh, what an emancipation it would be if we saw more of the value in God's eyes of the precious Blood of His dear Son!

2

The Cross of Christ

WE have seen that Romans 1 to 8 falls into two
sections, in the first of which we are shown
that the Blood deals with what we have done,
while in the second we shall see that the Cross deals with
what we are. We need the Blood for forgiveness; we need
also the Cross for deliverance. We have dealt briefly above
with the first of these two and we shall move on now to the
second; but before we do so we will look for a moment at a
few more features of this passage which serve to emphasize
the striking difference of theme and subject-matter between the two halves.

Some further distinctions

Two aspects of the resurrection are mentioned in the two
sections, in chapters 4 and 6. In Romans 4. 25 the resurrection of the Lord Jesus is mentioned in relation to our
justification: 'Jesus our Lord . . . was delivered up for our
trespasses, and was raised for our justification.' Here the
matter in view is that of our standing before God. But in

Romans 6. 4 the resurrection is spoken of as imparting to us new life with a view to a holy walk: 'That like as Christ was raised from the dead . . . so we also might walk in newness of life.' Here the matter before us is behaviour.

Again, peace is spoken of in both sections, in the fifth and eighth chapters. Romans 5 tells of peace with God which is the effect of justification by faith in His Blood: 'Being therefore justified by faith, we have peace with God through our Lord Jesus Christ' (5. 1 mg.). This means that, now that I have forgiveness of sins, God will no longer be a cause of dread to me. I who was an enemy to God have been 'reconciled . . . through the death of his Son' (5. 10). I very soon find, however, that I am going to be a great cause of trouble to myself. There is still unrest within, for within me there is something that draws me to sin. There is peace with God, but there is no peace with myself. There is in fact civil war in my own heart. This condition is well depicted in Romans 7 where the flesh and the spirit are seen to be in deadly conflict within me. But from this the argument leads in chapter 8 to the inward peace of a walk in the Spirit. 'The mind of the flesh is death', because it 'is enmity against God', but 'the mind of the spirit is life and peace' (Rom. 8. 6, 7).

Looking further still we find that the first half of the section deals generally speaking with the question of justification (see, for example, Romans 3. 24–26; 4. 5, 25), while the second half has as its main topic the corresponding question of sanctification (see Rom. 6. 19, 22). When we know the precious truth of justification by faith we still know only half of the story. We still have only solved the problem of our standing before God. As we go on, God has something more to offer us, namely, the solution of the problem of our conduct, and the development of thought in these chapters serves to emphasize this. In each case the second step follows from the first, and if we know only the first, then we are still leading a sub-normal Christian life. How then can we live a normal Christian life? How do we enter upon it? We must, of course, initially have forgiveness of sins, we must have justification, we must have peace with God: these are our indispensable foundation. But with that basis truly established through our first act of faith in Christ, it is yet clear from the above that we must move on to something more.

So we see that objectively the Blood deals with *our sins*. The Lord Jesus has borne them on the Cross for us as our Substitute and has thereby obtained for us forgiveness, justification and reconciliation. But we must now go a step further in the plan of God to understand how He deals with *the sin principle in us*. The Blood can wash away my sins, but it cannot wash away my 'old man'. It needs the Cross to crucify me. The Blood deals with the *sins*, but the Cross must deal with the *sinner*.

You will scarcely find the word 'sinner' in the first four chapters of Romans. This is because there the sinner himself is not mainly in view, but rather the sins he has committed. The word 'sinner' first comes into prominence only in chapter 5, and it is important to notice how the sinner is there introduced. In that chapter a sinner is said to be a sinner because he is born a sinner; not because he has committed sins. The distinction is important. It is true that often, when a Gospel worker wants to convince a man in the street that he is a sinner, he will use the favourite verse

Romans 3. 23, where it says that 'all have sinned'; but this use of the verse is not strictly justified by the Scriptures. Those who so use it are in danger of arguing the wrong way round, for the teaching of Romans is not that we are sinners because we commit sins, but that *we sin because we are sinners*. We are sinners by constitution rather than by action. As Romans 5. 19 expresses it: 'Through the one man's disobedience the many were made [or 'constituted'] sinners.'

How were we constituted sinners? By Adam's disobedience. We do not become sinners by what we have done but because of what Adam has done and has become. I speak English, but I am not thereby constituted an Englishman. I am in fact a Chinese. So chapter 3 draws our attention to what we have done—'all have sinned'—but it is nevertheless not because we have done it that we become sinners.

I once asked a class of children, 'Who is a sinner?' and their immediate reply was, 'One who sins.' Yes, one who sins is a sinner, but the fact that he sins is merely the evidence that he is already a sinner; it is not the cause. One who sins is a sinner, but it is equally true that one who does not sin, if he is of Adam's race, is a sinner too, and in need of redemption. Do you follow me? There are bad sinners and there are good sinners, there are moral sinners and there are corrupt sinners, but they are all alike sinners. We sometimes think that if only we had not done certain things all would be well; but the trouble lies far deeper than in what we do: it lies in what we are. A Chinese may be born in America and be unable to speak Chinese at all, but he is a Chinese for all that, because he was born a Chinese. It is birth that counts. So I am a sinner because I am born in Adam. It is a matter not of my behaviour but of my heredity, my parentage. I am not a sinner because I sin, but I sin because I come of the wrong stock. I sin because I am a sinner.

We are apt to think that what we have done is very bad, but that we ourselves are not so bad. God is taking pains to show us that we ourselves are wrong, fundamentally wrong. The root trouble is the sinner; he must be dealt with. Our sins are dealt with by the Blood, but we ourselves are dealt with by the Cross. The Blood procures our pardon for what we have done; the Cross procures our deliverance from what we are.

Man's state by nature

We come therefore to Romans 5. 12–21. In this great passage, grace is brought into contrast with sin and the obedience of Christ is set against the disobedience of Adam. It is placed at the beginning of the second section of Romans (5. 12 to 8. 39) with which we shall now be particularly concerned, and its argument leads to a conclusion which lies at the very heart of our further meditations. What is that conclusion? It is found in verse 19 already quoted: 'For as through the one man's disobedience the many were made sinners, even so through the obedience of the one shall the many be made righteous.' Here the Spirit of God is seeking to show us first what we are, and then how it was we came to be what we are.

At the beginning of our Christian life we are concerned with our doing, not with our being; we are distressed rather by what we have done than by what we are. We think that if only we could rectify certain things we should be good Christians, and we set out therefore to change our actions.

But the result is not what we expected. We discover to our dismay that it is something more than just a case of trouble on the outside—that there is in fact more serious trouble on the inside. We try to please the Lord, but find something within that does not want to please Him. We try to be humble, but there is something in our very being that refuses to be humble. We try to be loving, but inside we feel most unloving. We smile and try to look very gracious, but inwardly we feel decidedly ungracious. The more we try to rectify matters on the outside the more we realize how deep-seated is the trouble. Then we come to the Lord and say, 'Lord, I see it now! Not only what I have *done* is wrong; *I* am wrong.'

The conclusion of Romans 5. 19 is beginning to dawn upon us. We are sinners. We are members of a race of people who are constitutionally other than what God intended them to be. By the Fall, a fundamental change took place in the character of Adam whereby he became a sinner, one constitutionally unable to please God; and the family likeness which we all share is no merely superficial one but extends to our inward character also. We have been 'constituted sinners'. How did this come about? 'By the disobedience of one,' says the apostle. Let me try to illustrate this by a simple analogy.

My name is Nee. It is a fairly common Chinese name. How did I come by it? I did not choose it. I did not go through the list of possible Chinese names and select this one. That my name is Nee is in fact not my doing at all, and, moreover, nothing I can do can alter it. I am a Nee because my father was a Nee, and my father was a Nee because my grandfather was a Nee. If I act like a Nee I am a Nee, and if

I act unlike a Nee I am still a Nee. If I become President of the Chinese Republic I am a Nee, or if I become a beggar in the street I am still a Nee. Nothing I do or refrain from doing will make me other than a Nee.

We are sinners, not because of ourselves but because of Adam. It is not because I individually have sinned that I am a sinner, but because I was in Adam when he sinned. Because by birth I come of Adam, therefore I am a part of him. What is more, I can do nothing to alter this. I cannot, by improving my behaviour, make myself other than a part of Adam, and so a sinner.

In China I was once talking in this strain and remarked, 'We have all sinned in Adam.' A man said, 'I don't understand,' so I sought to explain it in this way. 'All Chinese trace their descent from Huang-ti,' I said. 'Over four thousand years ago he had a war with Si-iu. His enemy was very strong, but nevertheless Huang-ti overcame and slew him. After this Huang-ti founded the Chinese nation. Four thousand years ago therefore our nation was founded by Huang-ti. Now, what would have happened if Huang-ti had not killed his enemy, but had been himself killed instead? Where would you be now?' 'There would be no me at all,' he answered. 'Oh, no! Huang-ti can die his death and you can live your life.' 'Impossible?' he cried. 'If he had died, then I could never have lived, for I have derived my life from him.'

Do you see the oneness of human life? Our life comes from Adam. If your great-grandfather had died at the age of three, where would you be? You would have died in him! Your experience is bound up with his. And in just the same way, the experience of every one of us is bound up with that of Adam. None can say, 'I have not been in Eden,' for potentially we all were there when Adam yielded to the serpent's words. So we are all involved in Adam's sin, and by being born 'in Adam' we receive from him all that he became as a result of his sin—that is to say, the Adam-nature which is the nature of a sinner. We derive our existence from him, and because his life became a sinful life, a sinful nature, therefore the nature which we derive from him is also sinful. So, as we have said, the trouble is in our heredity, not in our behaviour. Unless we can change our parentage there is no deliverance for us.

But it is in this very direction that we shall find the solution of our problem, for that is exactly how God has dealt with it.

As in Adam so in Christ

In Romans 5. 12–21 we are not only told something about Adam; we are told also something about the Lord Jesus. 'As through the one man's disobedience the many were made sinners, even so through the obedience of the one shall the many be made righteous.' In Adam we receive everything that is of Adam; in Christ we receive everything that is of Christ.

The terms 'in Adam' and 'in Christ' are too little understood by Christians, and, at the risk of repetition, I wish again to emphasize by means of an illustration the hereditary and racial significance of the term 'in Christ'. This illustration is to be found in the letter to the Hebrews. Do you remember that in the earlier part of that letter the writer is trying to show that Melchizedek is greater than Levi? You recall that the point to be proved is that the priesthood of Christ is greater than the priesthood of Aaron who was of the tribe of Levi. Now, in order to prove that, he has first to prove that the priesthood of Melchizedek is greater than the priesthood of Levi, for the simple reason that the priesthood of Christ is 'after the order of Melchizedek' (Heb. 7. 14–17), while that of Aaron is, of course, after the order of Levi. If the writer can demonstrate to us that in the eyes of God Melchizedek is greater than Levi, then he has made his point. That is the issue, and he proves it in a remarkable way.

He tells us in Hebrews chapter 7 that one day Abraham, returning from the battle of the kings (Gen. 14), offered a tithe of his spoils to Melchizedek and received from him a blessing. Inasmuch as Abraham did so, Levi is therefore of less account than Melchizedek. Why? Because the fact that Abraham offered tithes to Melchizedek means that Isaac 'in Abraham' offered to Melchizedek. But if that is true, then Jacob also 'in Abraham' offered to Melchizedek, which in turn means that Levi 'in Abraham' offered to Melchizedek. It is evident that the lesser offers to the greater (Heb. 7. 7). So Levi is less in standing than Melchizedek, and therefore the priesthood of Aaron is inferior to that of the Lord Jesus. Levi at the time of the battle of the kings was not yet even thought of. Yet he was 'in the loins of his father' Abraham, and, 'so to say, through Abraham', he offered (Heb. 7. 9, 10).

Now this is the exact meaning of 'in Christ'. Abraham, as the head of the family of faith, includes the whole family in himself. When he offered to Melchizedek, the whole family offered in him to Melchizedek. They did not offer separately as individuals, but they were in him, and therefore in making his offering he included with himself all his seed.

So we are presented with a new possibility. In Adam all was lost. Through the disobedience of one man we were all constituted sinners. By him sin entered and death through sin, and throughout the race sin has reigned unto death from that day on. But now a ray of light is cast upon the scene. Through the obedience of Another we may be constituted righteous. Where sin abounded grace did much more abound, and as sin reigned unto death, even so may grace reign through righteousness into eternal life by Jesus Christ our Lord (Rom. 5. 19–21). Our despair is in Adam; our hope is in Christ.

The divine way of deliverance

God clearly intends that this consideration should lead to our practical deliverance from sin. Paul makes this quite plain when he opens chapter 6 of his letter with the question: 'Shall we continue in sin?' His whole being recoils at the very suggestion. 'God forbid!' he exclaims. How could a holy God be satisfied to have unholy, sin-fettered children? And so 'how shall we any longer live therein?' (Rom. 6. 1, 2). God has surely therefore made adequate provision that we should be set free from sin's dominion.

But here is our problem. We were born sinners; how then can we cut off our sinful heredity? Seeing that we were born in Adam, how can we get out of Adam? Let me say at once, the Blood cannot take us out of Adam. There is only one way. Since we came in by birth we must go out by death. To do away with our sinfulness we must do away

with our life. Bondage to sin came by birth; deliverance
from sin comes by death—and it is just this way of escape
that God has provided. Death is the secret of emancipation.
'We . . . died to sin' (Rom. 6. 2).

But how can we die? Some of us have tried very hard to
get rid of this sinful life, but we have found it most tena-
cious. What is the way out? It is not by trying to kill ourselves, but by recognizing that *God has dealt with us in Christ.*
This is summed up in the apostle's next statement: 'All we
who were baptized into Christ Jesus were baptized into his
death' (Rom. 6. 3).

But if God has dealt with us 'in Christ Jesus' then we
have got to *be* in Him for this to become effective, and that
now seems just as big a problem. How are we to 'get into'
Christ? Here again God comes to our help. We have in fact
no way of getting in, but, what is more important, we need
not try to get in, for we *are* in. What we could not do for
ourselves, God has done for us. *He has put us into Christ.* Let
me remind you of 1 Corinthians 1. 30. I think that is one of
the best verses of the whole New Testament: 'Ye are in
Christ.' How? 'Of him [that is, 'of God'] are ye in Christ.'
Praise God! it is not left to us either to devise a way of entry
or to work it out. We need not plan how to get in. God has
planned it; and He has not only planned it but He has also
performed it. *Of him* are ye in Christ Jesus.' We are in; therefore we need not try to get in. It is a divine act, and it is
accomplished.

Now if this is true, certain things follow. In the illustration from Hebrews 7 which we considered above we saw
that 'in Abraham' all Israel—and therefore Levi who was
not yet born—offered tithes to Melchizedek. They did not

offer separately and individually, but they were in Abraham when he offered, and his offering included all his seed. This, then, is a true figure of ourselves as 'in Christ'. When the Lord Jesus was on the Cross all of us died—not individually, for we had not yet been born—but, being in Him, we died in Him. 'One died for all, therefore all died' (2 Cor. 5. 14). When He was crucified all of us were crucified there with Him.

Many a time when preaching in the villages of China one has to use very simple illustrations for deep divine truth. I remember once I took up a small book and put a piece of paper into it, and I said to those very simple folk, 'Now look carefully. I take a piece of paper. It has an identity of its own, quite separate from this book. Having no special purpose for it at the moment I put it into the book. Now I do something with the book. I post it to Shanghai. I do not post the paper, but the paper has been put into the book. Then where is the paper? Can the book go to Shanghai and the paper remain here? Can the paper have a separate destiny from the book? No! Where the book goes the paper goes. If I drop the book in the river the paper goes too, and if I quickly take it out again I recover the paper also. Whatever experience the book goes through the paper goes through with it, for it is still there in the book.'

'Of him are ye in Christ Jesus.' The Lord God Himself has put us in Christ, and in His dealing with Christ, God has dealt with the whole race. Our destiny is bound up with His. What He has gone through we have gone through, for to be 'in Christ' is to have been identified with Him in both His death and resurrection. He was crucified: then what about us? Must we ask God to crucify us? Never! When Christ was crucified we were crucified; and His crucifixion is past, therefore ours cannot be future. I challenge you to find one text in the New Testament telling us that our crucifixion is in the future. All the references to it are in the Greek aorist, which is the 'once-for-all' tense, the 'eternally past' tense. (See: Rom. 6. 6; Gal. 2. 20; 5. 24; 6. 14.) And just as no man could ever commit suicide by crucifixion, for it were a physical impossibility to do so, so also, in spiritual terms, God does not require us to crucify ourselves. We were crucified when Christ was crucified, for God put us there in Him. That we have died in Christ is not merely a doctrinal position, it is an eternal and indisputable fact.

His death and resurrection representative and inclusive

The Lord Jesus, when He died on the Cross, shed His Blood, thus giving His sinless life to atone for our sin and to satisfy the righteousness and holiness of God. To do so was the prerogative of the Son of God alone. No man could have a share in that. The Scripture has never told us that we shed our blood with Christ. In His atoning work before God He acted alone; no other could have a part. But the Lord did not die only to shed His Blood: He died that *we* might die. He died as *our* Representative. In His death He included *you and me*.

We often use the terms 'substitution' and 'identification' to describe these two aspects of the death of Christ. Now many a time the use of the word 'identification' is good. But identification would suggest that the thing begins from our side: that I try to identify myself with the Lord. I agree that the word is true, but it should be used later on. It is better to begin with the fact that the Lord included me in His death. It is the 'inclusive' death of the Lord which puts me in a position to identify myself, not that I identify myself in order to be included. It is God's inclusion of me in Christ that matters. It is something God has done. For that reason those two New Testament words 'in Christ' are always very dear to my heart.

The death of the Lord Jesus is inclusive. The resurrection of the Lord Jesus is alike inclusive. We have looked at the first chapter of 1 Corinthians to establish the fact that we are 'in Christ Jesus'. Now we will go to the end of the same letter to see something more of what this means. In 1 Corinthians 15. 45, 47 two remarkable names or titles are used of the Lord Jesus. He is spoken of there as 'the last Adam' and He is spoken of too as 'the second man.' Scripture does not refer to Him as the second Adam but as 'the last Adam'; nor does it refer to Him as the last Man, but as 'the second man'. The distinction is to be noted, for it enshrines a truth of great value.

As the last Adam, Christ is the sum total of humanity; as the second Man He is the Head of a new race. So we have here two unions, the one relating to His death and the other to His resurrection. In the first place His union with the race as 'the last Adam' began historically at Bethlehem and ended at the cross and the tomb. In it He gathered up into Himself all that was in Adam and took it to judgment and death. In the second place our union with Him as 'the second man' begins in resurrection and ends in eternity— which is to say, it never ends—for, having in His death done away with the first man in whom God's purpose was frustrated, He rose again as Head of a new race of men, in whom that purpose will at length be fully realized.

When therefore the Lord Jesus was crucified on the cross, He was crucified as the last Adam. All that was in the first Adam was gathered up and done away in Him. We were included there. As the last Adam He wiped out the old race; as the second Man He brings in the new race. It is in His resurrection that He stands forth as the second Man, and there too we are included. 'For if we have become united with him by the likeness of his death, we shall be also by the likeness of his resurrection' (Rom. 6. 5). We died in Him as the last Adam; we live in Him as the second Man. The Cross is thus the mighty act of God which translates us from Adam to Christ.

3

The Path of Progress: Knowing

OUR old history ends with the Cross; our new history begins with the resurrection. 'If any man is in Christ, he is a new creature: the old things are passed away; behold they are become new' (2 Cor. 5. 17). The Cross terminates the first creation, and out of death there is brought a new creation in Christ, the second Man. If we are 'in Adam' all that is in Adam necessarily devolves upon us; it becomes ours involuntarily, for we have to do nothing to get it. There is no need to make up our minds to lose our temper or to commit some other sin; sin comes to us freely and despite ourselves. In a similar way, if we are 'in Christ' all that is in Christ comes to us by free grace, without effort on our part but on the ground of simple faith.

But to say that all we need comes to us in Christ by free grace, though true enough, may seem unpractical. How does it work out in life? How does it become real in our experience?

As we study chapters 6, 7 and 8 of Romans we shall discover that the conditions of living the normal Christian life are fourfold. They are: (*a*) Knowing, (*b*) Reckoning, (*c*)

Presenting ourselves to God, and (*d*) Walking in the Spirit, and they are set forth in that order. If we would live that life we shall have to take all four of these steps; not one nor two nor three, but all four. As we study each of them we shall trust the Lord by His Holy Spirit to illumine our understanding; and we shall seek His help now to take the first big step forward.

Our death with Christ a historic fact

Romans 6. 1–11 is the passage before us now. In these verses it is made clear that the death of the Lord Jesus is representative and inclusive. In His death we all died. None of us can progress spiritually without seeing this. Just as we cannot have justification if we have not seen Him bearing *our sins* on the Cross, so we cannot have sanctification if we have not seen Him bearing *us* on the Cross. Not only have our sins been laid on Him but we ourselves have been put into Him.

How did you receive forgiveness? You realized that the Lord Jesus died as your Substitute and bore your sins upon Himself, and that His Blood was shed to cleanse away your defilement. When you saw your sins all taken away on the Cross, what did you do? Did you say, 'Lord Jesus, please come and die for my sins'? No, you did not pray at all; you only thanked the Lord. You did not beseech Him to come and die for you, for you realized that He had already done so.

But what is true of your forgiveness is also true of your deliverance. The work is done. There is no need to pray, but only to praise. God has put us all in Christ, so that when Christ was crucified, we were crucified also. Thus there is no need to pray. 'I am a very wicked person; Lord, please crucify me.' That is all wrong. You did not pray about your sins; why pray now about yourself? Your sins were dealt with by His Blood, and you were dealt with by His Cross. It is an accomplished fact. All that is left for you to do is praise the Lord that when Christ died you died also; you died for Him. Praise Him for it, and live in the sight of it. 'Then believed they his words: they sang his praise' (Psalm 106. 12).

Do you believe in the death of Christ? Of course you do. But the same Holy Scripture that says He died for us says also that we died with Him. Look at it again: 'Christ died for us' (Rom. 5. 8). That is the first statement, and that is clear enough; but is this any less clear? 'Our old man was crucified with him' (Rom. 6. 6). 'We died with Christ' (Rom. 6. 8).

When are we crucified with Him. What is the date of our old man's crucifixion? Is it tomorrow? Yesterday? Today? In order to answer this it may help us if for a moment I turn Paul's statement round and say, 'Christ was crucified with [i.e. *at the same time as*] our old man.' Some of you came here in twos. You travelled to this place together. You might say, 'My friend came here with me', but you might just as truly say, 'I came here with my friend.' Had one of you come three days ago and the other only today you could not possibly say that; but having come together you can make either statement with equal truth, because both are statements of fact. So also in historic fact we can say, reverently but with equal accuracy, 'I was crucified when Christ was crucified' or 'Christ was crucified when I was crucified', for they are not two historical events, but one. My crucifixion was 'with him'.[1] Has Christ been crucified? Then can I be otherwise? And if He was crucified nearly two thousand years ago, and I with Him, can my crucifixion be said to take place tomorrow? Can His be past and mine present or future? Praise the Lord, when He died on the Cross I died with Him. He not only died in my stead, but He bore me with Him to the Cross, so that when He died I also died. And if I believe in the death of the Lord Jesus, then I can believe in my own death just as surely as I believe in His.

Why do you believe that the Lord Jesus died? What is your ground for that belief? Is it that you *feel* He has died? No, you have never felt it. You believe it because the Word of God tells you so. When the Lord was crucified, two thieves were crucified at the same time. You do not doubt that they were crucified with Him, either, because the Scripture says so quite plainly.

You believe in the death of the Lord Jesus and you believe in the death of the thieves with Him. Now what about your own death? Your crucifixion is more intimate than theirs. They were crucified at the same time as the Lord but on different crosses, whereas you were crucified on the selfsame cross as He, for you were in Him when He died. How can you know? You can know for the one sufficient reason that God has said so. It does not depend on your feelings. If you feel that Christ has died, He has died; and if you do not feel that He has died, He has died. If you feel that you have died, you have died; and if you do not

---

[1] The expression 'with him' in Romans 6. 6 carries of course a doctrinal as well as a historical (or temporal) sense. It is only in the historical sense that the statement is reversible.—W. N.

feel that you have died, you have nevertheless just as surely died. These are divine facts. That Christ has died is a fact, that the two thieves have died is a fact, and that you have died is a fact also. Let me tell you, *You have died*! You are done with! You are ruled out! The self you loathe is on the Cross in Christ. And 'he that is dead is freed from sin' (Rom. 6. 7, A.V.). This is the Gospel for Christians.

Our crucifixion can never be made effective by will or by effort, but only by accepting what the Lord Jesus did on the Cross. Our eyes must be opened to see the finished work of Calvary. Some of you, prior to your salvation, may have tried to save yourselves. You read the Bible, prayed, went to Church, gave alms. Then one day your eyes were opened and you saw that a full salvation had already been provided for you on the Cross. You just accepted that and thanked God, and peace and joy flowed into your heart. And now the good news is that sanctification is made possible for you on exactly the same basis as that initial salvation. You are offered deliverance from sin as no less a gift of God's grace than was the forgiveness of your sins.

For God's way of deliverance is altogether different from man's way. Man's way is to try to suppress sin by seeking to overcome it; God's way is to remove the sinner. Many Christians mourn over their weakness, thinking that if only they were stronger all would be well. The idea that, because failure to lead a holy life is due to our impotence, something more is therefore demanded of us, leads naturally to this false conception of the way of deliverance. If we are pre-occupied with the power of sin and with our inability to meet it, then we naturally conclude that to gain the victory over sin we must have more power. 'If only I were stronger,' we say, 'I could overcome my violent outbursts of temper,' and so we plead with the Lord to strengthen us that we may exercise more self-control.

But this is altogether a fallacy; it is not Christianity. God's means of delivering us from sin is not by making us stronger and stronger, but by making us weaker and weaker. That is surely rather a peculiar way of victory, you say; but it is the divine way. God sets us free from the dominion of sin, not by strengthening our old man but by crucifying him; not by helping him to do anything but by removing him from the scene of action.

For years, maybe, you have tried fruitlessly to exercise control over yourself, and perhaps this is still your experience; but when once you see the truth you will recognize that you are indeed powerless to do anything, but that in setting you aside altogether God has done it all. Such a discovery brings human striving and self-effort to an end.

The first step: 'knowing this . . .'

The normal Christian life must begin with a very definite 'knowing', which is not just knowing something about the truth nor understanding some important doctrine. It is not an intellectual knowledge at all, but an opening of the eyes of the heart to see what we have in Christ.

How do you know your sins are forgiven? Is it because your pastor told you so? No, you just *know* it. If I ask you how you know, you simply answer, 'I know it!' Such knowledge comes by divine revelation. It comes from the Lord Himself. Of course the fact of forgiveness of sins is in the Bible, but for the written Word of God to become a living Word from God to you He had to give you 'a spirit of wisdom and revelation in the knowledge of him' (Eph. 1. 17). What you needed was to know *Christ* in that way, and it is always so. So there comes a time, in regard to any new apprehension of Christ, when you know it in your own heart, you 'see' it in your spirit. A light has shined into your inner being and you are wholly persuaded of the fact. What is true of the forgiveness of your sins is no less true of your deliverance from sin. When once the light of God dawns upon your heart you *see* yourself in Christ. It is not now because someone has told you, and not merely because Romans 6 says so. It is something more even than that. You know it because God has revealed it to you by His Spirit. You may not feel it; you may not understand it; but you know it, for you have seen it. Once you have seen yourself in Christ, nothing can shake your assurance of that blessed fact.

If you ask a number of believers who have entered upon the normal Christian life how they came by their experience, some will say in this way and some will say in that. Each stresses his own particular way of entering in and produces Scripture to support his experience; and unhappily many Christians are using their special experiences and their special scriptures to fight other Christians. The fact of the matter is that, while Christians may enter into the deeper life by different ways, we need not regard the experiences or doctrines they stress as mutually exclusive, but rather complementary. One thing is certain, that any true experience of value in the sight of God must have been reached by way of a new discovery of the meaning of the Person and work of the Lord Jesus. That is a crucial test and a safe one.

And here in our passage Paul makes everything depend upon such a discovery. 'Knowing this, that our old man was crucified with him, that the body of sin might be done away, that so we should no longer be in bondage to sin' (Rom. 6. 6).

Divine revelation essential to knowledge

So our first step is to seek from God a knowledge that comes by revelation—a revelation, that is to say, not of ourselves but of the finished work of the Lord Jesus Christ on the Cross. When Hudson Taylor, the founder of the China Inland Mission, entered into the normal Christian life it was thus that he did so. You remember how he tells of his long-standing problem of how to live 'in Christ', how to draw the sap out of the Vine into himself. For he knew that he must have the life of Christ flowing out through him and yet felt he had not got it, and he saw clearly enough that his need was to be found in Christ. 'I knew,' he said, writing to his sister from Chinkiang in 1869, 'that if only I could abide in Christ, all would be well, but I *could not*.'

The more he tried to get in the more he found himself slipping out, so to speak, until one day light dawned, revelation came and he saw. This is how he describes it.

'Here, I feel, is the secret: not asking how I am to get sap *out* of the Vine *into* myself, but remembering that Jesus *is* the Vine— the root, stem, branches, twigs, leaves, flowers, fruit, all indeed.'

Then, quoting a friend's words that had helped him, he continues:

'I have not got to *make* myself a branch. The Lord Jesus tells me I *am* a branch. I am *part of Him* and I have just to believe it and act upon it. I have seen it long enough in the Bible, but I *believe* it now as a living reality.'

It was as though something which had indeed been true all the time had now suddenly become true in a new way to him personally, and he writes to his sister again:

'I do not know how far I may be able to make myself intelligible about it, for there is nothing new or strange or wonderful— and yet, all is new! In a word, "whereas once I was blind, now I see." . . . I am dead and buried with Christ—aye, and risen too and ascended. . . . God reckons me so, and tells me to reckon myself so. He knows best. . . . Oh, the joy of seeing this truth— I do pray that the eyes of your understanding may be enlightened, that you may know and enjoy the riches freely given us in Christ.'[2]

Oh, it is a great thing to see that we are in Christ! Think of the bewilderment of trying to get into a room in which you already are! Think of the absurdity of asking to be put in! If we recognize the fact that we *are* in, we make no effort to enter. If we had more revelation, we should have fewer prayers and more praises. We spend so much time praying for ourselves just because we are blind to what God has done.

I remember one day in Shanghai I was talking with a brother who was very exercised concerning his spiritual

---

[2] The quotations are from *Hudson Taylor and the China Inland Mission* by Dr. and Mrs. Howard Taylor, Chapter 12, 'The Exchanged Life'. The whole passage should be read.—ED.

state. He said, 'So many are living beautiful, saintly lives. I am ashamed of myself. I call myself a Christian, and yet when I compare myself with others I feel I am not one at all. I want to know this crucified life, this resurrection life, but I do not know it, and I see no way of getting there.' Another brother was with us, and the two of us had been talking for two hours or so, trying to get the man to see that he could not have anything apart from Christ, but without success. Said our friend, 'The best thing a man can do is pray.' 'But if God has already given you everything, what do you need to pray for?' we asked. 'He hasn't,' the man replied, 'for I am still losing my temper, still failing constantly; so I must pray more.' 'Well,' we said, 'do you get what you pray for?' 'I am sorry to say that I do not get anything,' he replied. We tried to point out that, just as he had done nothing for his justification, so he need do nothing for his sanctification.

Just then a third brother, much used of the Lord, came in and joined us. There was a thermos flask on the table, and this brother picked it up and said, 'What is this?' 'A thermos flask.' 'Well, you just imagine for a moment that this thermos flask can pray, and that it starts praying something like this: "Lord, I want very much to be a thermos flask. Wilt Thou make me to be a thermos flask? Lord, give me grace to become a thermos flask. Do please make me one!" What will you say?' 'I do not think even a thermos flask would be so silly,' our friend replied. 'It would be nonsense to pray like that; it *is* a thermos flask!' Then my brother said, 'You are doing the same thing. God in times past has already included you in Christ. When He died, you died; when He lived, you lived. Now today you cannot say, "I want to die; I want to be crucified; I want to have resurrection life." The

Lord simply looks at you and says, "You *are* dead! You *have* new life!" All your praying is just as absurd as that of the thermos flask. You do not need to pray to the Lord for anything; you merely need your eyes opened to see that He has done it all.'

That is the point. We need not work to die, we need not wait to die, we *are* dead. We only need to recognize what the Lord has already done, and to praise Him for it. Light dawned for that man. With tears in his eyes he said, 'Lord, I praise Thee that Thou hast already included me in Christ. All that is His is mine!' Revelation had come, and faith had something to lay hold of; and if you could have met that brother later on, what a change you would have found!

The Cross goes to the root of our problem

Let me remind you again of the fundamental nature of that which the Lord has done on the Cross. I feel I cannot press this point too much for we *must* see it.

Suppose, for the sake of illustration, that the government of your country should wish to deal drastically with the question of strong drink and should decide that the whole country was to go 'dry', how could the decision be carried into effect? How could we help? If we were to search every shop and house throughout the land and smash all the bottles of wine or beer or brandy we came across, would that meet the case? Surely not. We might thereby rid the land of every drop of alcoholic liquor it contains, but behind those bottles of strong drink are the factories that produce them, and if we only deal with the bottles and leave the factories untouched, production will still continue and there is no permanent solution of the problem. No, the drink-producing factories, the breweries and distilleries throughout the land, must be closed down if the drink question is ever to be effectively and permanently settled.

We are the factory; our actions are the products. The Blood of the Lord Jesus dealt with the question of the products, namely, our sins. So the question of what we have done is settled, but would God have stopped there? What about the question of what we are? Our sins were produced by us. They have been dealt with, but how are *we* going to be dealt with? Do you believe the Lord would cleanse away all our sins and then leave us to get rid of the sin-producing factory? Do you believe that, having put away the goods produced, He would leave us to deal by ourselves with the source of production?

To ask this question is but to answer it. Of course He has not done half the work and left the other half undone. No, He has done away with the goods and also made a clean sweep of the factory that produces the goods.

The finished work of Christ really has gone to the root of our problem and dealt with it. There are no half measures with God. He has made full provision for sin's rule to be utterly broken.

'Knowing this,' says Paul, 'that our old man was crucified with him, that the body of sin might be done away, that so we should no longer be in bondage to sin' (Rom. 6. 6). '*Knowing this*'! Yes, but *do* you know it? 'Or are ye ignorant?' (Rom. 6. 3). May the Lord graciously open our eyes.

4

The Path of Progress: Reckoning

WE now come to a matter on which there has been some confusion of thought among the Lord's children. It concerns what follows this knowledge. Note again first of all the wording of Romans 6. 6: 'Knowing this, that our old man was crucified with him.' The tense of the verb is most precious, for it puts the event right back there in the past. It is final, once-for-all. The thing has been done and cannot be undone. Our old man has been crucified once and for ever, and he can never be un-crucified. This is what we need to know.

Then, when we know this, what follows? Look again at our passage. The next command is in verse 11: 'Even so reckon ye also yourselves to be dead unto sin.' This, clearly, is the natural sequel to verse 6. Read them together: '*Knowing* that our old man was crucified, . . . *reckon* ye yourselves to be dead.' That is the order. When we know that our old man has been crucified with Christ, then the next step is to reckon it so.

Unfortunately, in presenting the truth of our union with Christ the emphasis has too often been placed upon this second matter of reckoning ourselves to be dead, as though that were the starting point, whereas it should rather be upon *knowing* ourselves to be dead. God's Word makes it clear that 'knowing' is to precede 'reckoning'. 'Know this . . . reckon.' The sequence is most important. Our reckoning must be based on knowledge of divinely revealed fact, for otherwise faith has no foundation on which to rest. When we know, then we reckon spontaneously.

So in teaching this matter we should not over-emphasize reckoning. People are always trying to reckon without knowing. They have not first had a Spirit-given revelation of the fact; yet they try to reckon, and soon they get into all sorts of difficulties. When temptation comes they begin to reckon furiously. 'I am dead; I am dead; I am dead!' but in the very act of reckoning they lose their temper. Then they say, 'It doesn't work. Romans 6. 11 is no good.' And we have to admit that verse 11 *is* no good without verse 6. So it comes to this, that unless we know for a fact that we are dead with Christ, the more we reckon, the more intense will the struggle become, and the issue will be sure defeat.

For years after my conversion I had been taught to reckon. I reckoned from 1920 until 1927. The more I reckoned that I was dead to sin, the more alive I clearly was. I simply could not believe myself dead, and I could not produce the death. Whenever I sought help from others I was told to read Romans 6. 11, and the more I read Romans 6. 11 and tried to reckon, the further away death was: I could not get at it. I fully appreciated the teaching that I must reckon, but I could not make out why nothing resulted from it. I have to confess that for months I was troubled. I said to the Lord, 'If this is not clear, if I cannot be brought to see this which is so very fundamental, I will cease to do anything. I will not preach any more; I will not go out to serve Thee any more; I want first of all to get thoroughly clear here.' For months I was seeking, and at times I fasted, but nothing came through.

I remember one morning—that morning was a real morning and one I can never forget—I was upstairs sitting at my desk reading the Word and praying, and I said, 'Lord, open my eyes!' And then in a flash I saw it. I saw my oneness with Christ. I saw that I was in Him, and that when He died I died. I saw that the question of my death was a matter of the past and not of the future, and that I was just as truly dead as He was because I was in Him when He died. The whole thing had dawned upon me. I was carried away with such joy at this great discovery that I jumped from my chair and cried, 'Praise the Lord, I am dead!' I ran downstairs and met one of the brothers helping in the kitchen and laid hold of him. 'Brother,' I said, 'do you know that I have died?' I must admit he looked puzzled. 'What do you mean?' he said, so I went on: 'Do you not know that Christ has died? Do you not know that I died with Him? Do you not know that my death is no less truly a fact than His?' Oh it was so real to me! I longed to go through the streets of Shanghai shouting the news of my discovery. From that day to this I have never for one moment doubted the finality of that word: 'I have been crucified with Christ.'

I do not mean to say that we need not work that out. Yes, there is an outworking of the death which we are going to see presently, but this, first of all, its basis. I have been crucified: in Christ it has been done.

What, then, is the secret of reckoning? To put it in one

word, it is revelation. We need revelation from God Himself
(Matt. 16. 17; Eph. 1. 17, 18). We need to have our eyes
opened to the fact of our union with Christ, and that is
something more than knowing it as a doctrine. Such relevation is no vague indefinite thing. Most of us can remember the day when we saw clearly that Christ died for us, and
we ought to be equally clear as to the time when we saw
that we died with Christ. It should be nothing hazy, but
very definite, for it is with this as basis that we shall go on.
It is not that I reckon myself to be dead, and therefore I will
be dead. It is that, because I *am* dead—because I see now
what God has done with me in Christ—*therefore* I reckon
myself to be dead. That is the right kind of reckoning. It is
not reckoning *toward* death but *from* death.

The second step: 'even so reckon . . .'

What does reckoning mean? 'Reckoning' in Greek means
doing accounts, book-keeping. Accounting is the only thing
in the world we human beings can do correctly. An artist
paints a landscape. Can he do it with perfect accuracy? Can
the historian vouch for the absolute accuracy of any record,
or the map-maker for the perfect correctness of any map?
They can make, at best, fair approximations. Even in everyday speech, when we try to tell some incident with the best
intention to be honest and truthful, we cannot speak with
complete accuracy. It is mostly a case of exaggeration or
under-statement, of one word too much or too little. What
then can a man do that is utterly reliable? Arithmetic! There
is no scope for error there. One chair plus one chair equals
two chairs. That is true in London and it is true in Cape

Town. If you travel west to New York or east to Singapore it is still the same. All the world over and for all time, one plus one equals two. One plus one is two in heaven and earth and hell.

Why does God say we are to reckon ourselves dead? Because we *are* dead. Let us keep to the analogy of accounting. Suppose I have fifteen shillings in my pocket, what do I enter in my account-book? Can I enter fourteen shillings and sixpence or fifteen shillings and sixpence? No, I must enter in my account-book that which is in fact in my pocket. Accounting is the reckoning of facts, not fancies. Even so, it is because I am really dead that God tells me to account it so. God could not ask me to put down in my account-book what was not true. He could not ask me to reckon that I am dead if I am still alive. For such mental gymnastics the word 'reckoning' would be inappropriate; we might rather speak of 'mis-reckoning'!

Reckoning is not a form of make-believe. It does not mean that, having found that I have only twelve shillings in my pocket, I hope that by entering fifteen shillings incorrectly in my account-book such 'reckoning' will somehow remedy the deficiency. It won't. If I have only twelve shillings, yet try to reckon to myself: 'I have fifteen shillings; I have fifteen shillings; I have fifteen shillings', do you think that the mental effort involved will in any way affect the sum that is in my pocket? Not a bit of it! Reckoning will not make twelve shillings into fifteen shillings, nor will it make what is untrue true. But if, on the other hand, it is a fact that I have fifteen shillings in my pocket, then with great ease and assurance I can enter fifteen shillings in my account-book. God tells us to reckon ourselves dead, not that by the process of reckoning we may become dead, but because we are dead. He never told us to reckon what was not a fact.

Having said, then, that revelation leads spontaneously to reckoning, we must not lose sight of the fact that we are presented with a command: Reckon ye . . .'. There is a definite attitude to be taken. God asks us to do the account; to put down 'I have died' and then to abide by it. Why? Because it is a fact. When the Lord Jesus was on the Cross, I was there in Him. Therefore I reckon it to be true. I reckon and declare that I have died in Him. Paul said, 'Reckon ye also yourselves to be dead unto sin, but alive unto God.' How is this possible? 'In Christ Jesus.' Never forget that it is always and only true *in Christ*. If you look at yourself you will think death is not there, but it is a question of faith not in yourself but in Him. You look to the Lord, and know what He has done. 'Lord, I believe *in Thee*. I reckon upon the fact *in Thee*.' Stand there all the day.

The reckoning of faith

The first four-and-a-half chapters of Romans speak of faith and faith and faith. We are justified by faith in Him (Rom 3. 28; 5. 1). Righteousness, the forgiveness of our sins, and peace with God are all ours by faith, and without faith in the finished work of Jesus Christ none can possess them. But in the second section of Romans we do not find the same repeated mention of faith, and it might at first appear that the emphasis is therefore different. It is not really so, however, for where the words 'faith' and 'believe' drop out the word 'reckon' takes their place. Reckoning and faith are here practically the same thing.

What is faith? Faith is my acceptance of God's fact. It always has its foundations in the past. What relates to the future is hope rather than faith, although faith often has its object or goal in the future, as in Hebrews 11. Perhaps for this reason the word chosen here is 'reckon'. It is a word that relates *only* to the past—to what we look back to as settled, and not forward to as yet to be. This is the kind of faith described in Mark 11. 24: 'All things whatsoever ye pray and ask for, believe that ye have received them, and ye shall have them.' The statement there is that, if you believe that you already *have received* your requests (that is, of course, in Christ), then 'you shall have them'. To believe that you *may* get something, or that you *can* get it, or even that you *will* get it, is not faith in the sense meant here. This is faith—to believe that you have already got it. Only that which relates to the past is faith in this sense. Those who say 'God can' or 'God may' or 'God must' or 'God will' do not necessarily believe at all. Faith always says, 'God has done it.'

When, therefore, do I have faith in regard to my crucifixion? Not when I say God can, or will, or must crucify me, but when with joy I say, 'Praise God, in Christ *I am crucified*!'

In Romans 3 we see the Lord Jesus bearing our sins and dying as our Substitute that we might be forgiven. In Romans 6 we see ourselves included in the death whereby He secured our deliverance. When the first fact was revealed to us we believed on Him for our justification. God tells us to reckon upon the second fact for our deliverance. So that, for practical purposes, 'reckoning' in the second section of Romans takes the place of 'faith' in the first section. The emphasis is not different. The normal Christian life is lived progressively, as it is entered initially, by faith in divine fact: in Christ and His Cross.

Temptation and failure, the challenge to faith

For us, then, the two greatest facts in history are these: that all our sins are dealt with by the Blood, and that we ourselves are dealt with by the Cross. But what now of the matter of temptation? What is to be our attitude when, after we have seen and believed these facts, we discover the old desires rising up again? Worse still, what if we fall once more into known sin? What if we lose our temper, or worse? Is the whole position set forth above proved thereby to be false?

Now remember, one of the Devil's main objects is always to make us doubt the divine facts. (Compare Gen. 3. 4.) After we have seen, by relevation of the Spirit of God, that we are indeed dead with Christ, and have reckoned it so, he will come and say: 'There is something moving inside. What about it? Can you call this death?' When that happens, what will be our answer? The crucial test is just here. Are we going to believe the tangible facts of the natural realm which are clearly before our eyes, or the intangible facts of the spiritual realm which are neither seen nor scientifically proved?

Now we must be careful. It is important for us to recall again what are facts stated in God's Word for faith to lay hold of and what are not. How does God state that deliverance is effected? Well, in the first place, we are not told that sin as a principle in us is rooted out or removed. To reckon on that will be to miscalculate altogether and find ourselves in the false position of the man we considered earlier, who tried to put down the twelve shillings in his pocket as fifteen shillings in his account-book. No, sin is not eradicated. It is very much there, and, given the opportunity, will over-power us and cause us to commit sins again, whether con-sciously or unconsciously. That is why we shall always need to know the operation of the precious Blood.

But whereas we know that, in dealing with sins commit-ted, God's method is direct, to blot them out of remem-brance by means of the Blood, when we come to the principle of sin and the matter of deliverance from its power, we find instead that God deals with this indirectly. He does not remove the sin but the sinner. Our old man was crucified with Him, and because of this the body, which before had been a vehicle of sin, is unemployed (Rom. 6. 6).[1] Sin, the old master, is still about, but the slave who served him has been put to death and so is out of reach and his members are unemployed. The gambler's hand is un-employed, the swearer's tongue is unemployed, and these members are now available to be used instead 'as instru-ments of righteousness unto God' (Rom. 6. 13).

Thus we can say that 'deliverance from sin' is a more scriptural idea than 'victory over sin'. The expressions 'freed from sin' and 'dead unto sin' in Romans 6. 7 and 11 imply deliverance from a power that is still very present and

---

[1] The verb *katargeo* translated 'destroyed' in Romans 6. 6 (A.V.) does not mean 'annihilated', but 'put out of operation', 'made ineffective'. It is from the Greek root *argos*, 'inactive', 'not working', 'unprofitable', which is the word translated 'idle' in Matthew 20. 3, 6 of the unemployed labourers in the market place.—ED.

very real—not from something that no longer exists. Sin is still there, but we are knowing deliverance from its power in increasing measure day by day.

This deliverance is so real that John can boldy write: 'Whosoever is begotten of God doeth no sin . . . he cannot sin' (1 John 3. 9), which is, however, a statement that, wrongly understood, may easily mislead us. By it John is not telling us that sin is now no longer in our history and that we shall not again commit sin. He is saying that to sin is not in the nature of that which is born of God. The life of Christ has been planted in us by new birth and its nature is not to commit sin. But there is a great difference between the nature and the history of a thing, and there is a great difference between the nature of the life within us and *our* history. To illustrate this (though the illustration is an inadequate one) we might say that wood 'cannot' sink, for it is not its nature to do so; but of course in history it will do so if a hand holds it under water. The history is a fact, just as sins in our history are historic facts; but the nature is a fact also, and so is the new nature that we have received in Christ. What is 'in Christ' cannot sin; what is in Adam can sin and will do so whenever Satan is given a chance to exert his power.

So it is a question of our choice of which facts we will count upon and live by: the tangible facts of daily experience or the mightier fact that we are now 'in Christ'. The power of His resurrection is on our side, and the whole might of God is at work in our salvation (Rom. 1. 16), but the matter still rests upon our making real in history what is true in divine fact.

'Now faith is the assurance of things hoped for, the

proving of things not seen' (Heb. 11. 1), and 'the things which are not seen are eternal' (2 Cor. 4. 18). I think we all know that Hebrews 11. 1 is the only definition of faith in the New Testament, or indeed in the Scriptures. It is important that we should really understand that definition. You are familiar with the common English translation of these words, describing faith as 'the substance of things hoped for' (A.V.). However, the word in the Greek has in it the sense of an action and not just of some thing, a 'substance', and I confess I have personally spent a number of years trying to find a correct word to translate this. But the New Translation of J. N. Darby is especially good in regard to this word: 'Faith is the *substantiating* of things hoped for.' That is much better. It implies the making of them real in experience.

How do we 'substantiate' something? We are doing so every day. We cannot live in the world without doing so. Do you know the difference between substance and 'substantiating'? A substance is an object, something before me. 'Substantiating' means that I have a certain power or faculty that makes that substance to be real to me. Let us take a simple illustration. By means of our senses we can take things of the world of nature and transfer them into our consciousness so that we can appreciate them. Sight and hearing, for example, are two of my faculties which substantiate to me the world of light and sound. We have colours: red, yellow, green, blue, violet; and these colours are real things. But if I shut my eyes, then to me the colour is no longer real; it is simply nothing—*to me*. With my faculty of sight, however, I possess the power to 'substantiate', and by that power, yellow becomes yellow *to me*. It is not only that the colour is there, but I have the power to 'substantiate' it. I have the power to make that colour true to me and to give it reality in my consciousness. That is the meaning of 'substantiating'.

If I am blind I cannot distinguish colour, or if I lack the faculty of hearing I cannot enjoy music. Yet music and colour are in fact *real* things, and their reality is unaffected by whether or not I am able to appreciate them. Now we are considering here the things which, though they are not seen, are eternal and therefore real. Of course we cannot substantiate divine things with any of our natural senses; but there is one faculty which can substantiate the 'things hoped for', the things of Christ, and that is faith. Faith makes the *real* things to become real *in my experience*. Faith 'substantiates' *to me* the things of Christ. Hundreds of thousands of people are reading Romans 6. 6; 'Our old man was crucified with him.' To faith it is true; to doubt, or to mere mental assent apart from spiritual illumination, it is not true.

Let us remember again that we are dealing here not with promises but with facts. The promises of God are revealed to us by His Spirit that we may lay hold of them; but facts are facts, and they remain facts whether we believe them or not. If we do not believe the facts of the Cross they still remain as real as ever, but they are valueless to us. It does not need faith to make these things real in themselves, but faith can 'substantiate' them and make them real in our experience.

Whatever contradicts the truth of God's Word we are to regard as the Devil's lie, not because it may not be in itself a very real fact to our senses, but because God has stated a greater fact before which the other must eventually yield. I once had an experience which (though not applicable in detail to the present matter) illustrates this principle. Some years ago I was ill. For six nights I had high fever and could find no sleep. Then at length God gave me from the Scripture a personal word of healing, and because of this I expected all symptoms of sickness to vanish at once. Instead of that, not a wink of sleep could I get, and I was not only sleepless but more restless than ever. My temperature rose higher, my pulse beat faster and my head ached more severely than before. The enemy asked, 'Where is God's promise? Where is your faith? What about all your prayers?' So I was tempted to thrash the whole matter out in prayer again, but was rebuked, and this Scripture came to mind: 'Thy word is truth' (John 17. 17). If God's Word is truth, I thought, then what are these symptoms? They must all be lies? So I declared to the enemy, 'This sleeplessness is a lie, this headache is a lie, this fever is a lie, this high pulse is a lie. In view of what God has said to me, all these symptoms of sickness are just your lies, and God's Word to me is truth.' In five minutes I was asleep, and I awoke the following morning perfectly well.

Now of course in a particular personal matter such as the above it might be quite possible for me to deceive myself as to what God had said, but of the fact of the Cross there can never be any such question. We *must* believe God, no matter how convincing Satan's arguments appear.

A skilful liar lies not only in word but in gesture and deed; he can as easily pass a bad coin as tell an untruth. The Devil is a skilful liar, and we cannot expect him to stop at words in his lying. He will resort to lying signs and feelings

and experiences in his attempts to shake us from our faith
in God's Word. Let me make it clear that I do not deny the
reality of the 'flesh'. Indeed we shall have a good deal more
to say about this further on in our study. But I am speaking
here of our being moved from a revealed position in Christ.
As soon as we have accepted our death with Christ as a fact,
Satan will do his best to demonstrate convincingly by the
evidence of our day-today experience that we are not dead
at all but very much alive. So we must choose. Will we
believe Satan's lie or God's truth? Are we going to be governed by appearances or by what God says?

I am Mr. Nee. I know that I am Mr. Nee. It is a fact upon
which I can confidently count. It is of course possible that I
might lose my memory and forget that I am Mr. Nee, or
I might dream that I am some other person. But whether I
feel like it or not, when I am sleeping I am Mr. Nee and
when I am awake I am Mr. Nee; when I remember it I am
Mr. Nee and when I forget it I am still Mr. Nee.

Now of course, were I to pretend to be someone else,
things would be much more difficult. If I were to try to pose
as Miss K. I should have to keep saying to myself all the
time, 'You are Miss K.; now be sure to remember that you
are Miss K.,' and despite much reckoning the likelihood
would be that when I was off my guard and someone called,
'Mr. Nee!' I should be caught out and should answer to my
own name. Fact would triumph over fiction, and all my
reckoning would break down at that crucial moment. But I
am Mr. Nee and therefore I have no difficulty whatever in
reckoning myself to be Mr. Nee. It is a fact which nothing I
experience or fail to experience can alter.

So also, whether I feel it or not, I am dead with Christ.

How can I be sure? Because Christ has died; and since 'one died for all, therefore all died' (Cor. 5. 14). Whether my experience proves it or seems to disprove it, the fact remains unchanged. While I stand upon that fact, Satan cannot prevail against me. Remember that his attack is always upon our assurance. If he can get us to doubt God's word, then his object is secured and he has us in his power; but if we rest unshaken in the assurance of God's stated fact, assured that He cannot do injustice to His work or His Word, then it does not matter what tactics Satan adopts, we can well afford to laugh at him. If anyone should try to persuade me that I am not Mr. Nee, I could well afford to do the same.

'We walk by faith, not by appearance' (2 Cor. 5. 7, mg.). You probably know the illustration of Fact, Faith and Experience walking along the top of a wall. Fact walked steadily on, turning neither to right nor left and never looking behind. Faith followed, and all went well so long as he kept his eyes focused upon Fact; but as soon as he became concerned about Experience and turned to see how *he* was getting on, he lost his balance and tumbled off the wall, and poor old Experience fell down after him.

All temptation is primarily to look within; to take our eyes off the Lord and to take account of appearances. Faith is always meeting a mountain, a mountain of evidence that seems to contradict God's Word, a mountain of apparent contradiction in the realm of tangible fact—of failures in deed, as well as in the realm of feeling and suggestion—and either faith or the mountain has to go. They cannot both stand. But the trouble is that many a time the mountain stays and faith goes. That must not be. If we resort to our senses to discover the truth, we shall find Satan's lies are often enough true to our experience; but if we refuse to accept as binding anything that contradicts God's Word and maintain an attitude of faith in Him alone, we shall find instead that Satan's lies begin to dissolve and that *our experience is coming progressively to tally with that Word.*

It is our occupation with Christ that has this result, for it means that He becomes progressively real to us on concrete issues. In a given situation we see Him as *real* righteousness, *real* holiness, *real* resurrection life—*for us.* What we see in Him objectively now operates in us subjectively—but *really*—to manifest Him in us in that situation. That is the mark of maturity. That is what Paul means by his words to the Galatians: 'I am again in travail until Christ be formed in you' (4. 19). Faith is 'substantiating' God's facts; and faith is always the 'substantiating' of eternal fact—of something eternally true.

Abiding in Him

Now although we have already spent long on this matter, there is a further thing that may help to make it clearer to us. The Scriptures declare that we are 'dead indeed', but nowhere do they say that we are dead in *ourselves*. We shall look in vain to find death within; that is just the place where it is not to be found. We are dead not in ourselves but *in Christ*. We were crucified with Him because we were in Him.

We are familiar with the words of the Lord Jesus, 'Abide in me, and I in you' (John 15. 4). Let us consider them for a moment. First they remind us once again that we have never to struggle to get into Christ. We are not told to get there, for we are there; but we are told to *stay* where we have been placed. It was God's own act that put us in Christ, and we are to *abide* in Him.

But further, this verse lays down for us a divine principle, which is that God has done the work in Christ and not in us as individuals. The all-inclusive death and the all-inclusive resurrection of God's Son were accomplished fully and finally apart from us in the first place. It is the history of *Christ* which is to become the experience of the Christian, and we have no spiritual experience apart from Him. The Scriptures tell us that we were crucified 'with Him', that we were quickened, raised, and set by God in the heavenlies 'in Him', and that we are complete 'in Him' (Rom. 6. 6; Eph. 2. 5, 6; Col. 2. 10). It is not just something that is still to be effected in us (though it *is* that, of course). It is something that has already been effected, *in association with Him*.

In the Scriptures we find that no Christian experience exists *as such*. What God has done in His gracious purpose is to include us in Christ. In dealing with Christ God has dealt with the Christian; in dealing with the Head He has dealt with all the members. It is altogether wrong for us to think that we can experience anything of the spiritual life in ourselves merely, and apart from Him. God does not intend that we should acquire something exclusively personal in our experience, and He is not willing to effect anything like that for you and me. All the spiritual experience of the Christian is *already true in Christ*. It has already been experienced by Christ. What we call 'our' experience is only our entering into *His* history and *His* experience.

It would be odd if one branch of a vine tried to bear grapes with a reddish skin, and another branch tried to bear grapes with a green skin, and yet another branch grapes with a dark purple skin, each branch trying to produce something of its own without reference to the vine. It is impossible, unthinkable. The character of the branches is determined by the vine. Yet certain Christians are seeking experiences *as experiences*. They think of crucifixion as something, of resurrection as something, of ascension as something, and they never stop to think that the whole is related to a Person. No, only as the Lord opens our eyes to see the Person do we have any true experience. Every true spiritual experience means that we have discovered a certain fact in Christ, and have entered into that; anything that is not from Him in this way is an experience that is going to evaporate very soon. 'I have discovered *that* in Christ; then, Praise the Lord, it is mine! I possess it, Lord, because it is in Thee.' Oh it is a great thing to know the facts of Christ as the foundation for our experience!

So God's basic principle in leading us on experimentally is not to give us something. It is not to bring us through something, and as a result to put something into us which we can call '*our* experience'. It is not that God effects something within *us* so that we can say, 'I died with Christ last March' or 'I was raised from the dead on January 1st, 1937', or even, 'Last Wednesday I asked for a definite experience and I have got it'. No, that is not the way. I do not seek experiences *in themselves* as in this present year of grace. Where spiritual history is concerned, time must not be allowed to dominate my thinking.

Then, some will say, what about the crises so many of us have passed through? True, some of us have passed through real crises in our lives. For instance George Müller could say, bowing himself down to the ground, 'There was a day when George Müller died.' How about that? Well, I am not questioning the reality of the spiritual experiences we go through, nor the importance of crises to which God brings us in our walk with Him; indeed, I have already stressed the need for us to be quite as definite ourselves about such crises in our own lives. But the point is that God does not give individuals individual experiences. All that they have is only an entering into what God has already done. It is the 'realizing' in time of *eternal* things. The history of Christ becomes our experience and our spiritual history; we do not have a separate history from His. The entire work with respect to us is not done in us here but in Christ. He does no separate work in individuals apart from what He has done there. Even eternal life is not given to us as individuals: the life is in the Son, and 'he that hath the Son hath the life'. God has done all in His Son, and He has included us in Him; we are incorporated into Christ.

Now the point of all this is that there is a very real practical value in the stand of faith that says, 'God has put me in Christ, and therefore all that is true of Him is true of me. I will abide in Him.' Satan is always trying to get us out, to keep us out, to convince us that we are out, and by temptations, failures, suffering, trial, to make us feel acutely that we are outside of Christ. Our first thought is that, if we were in Christ, we should not be in this state, and therefore, judging by the feelings we now have, we must be out of Him; and so we begin to pray, 'Lord, put me into Christ.' No! God's injunction is to 'abide' in Christ, and that is the way of deliverance. But how is it so? Because it opens the way for God to take a hand in our lives and to work the thing out in us. It makes room for the operation of His superior power—the power of resurrection (Rom. 6. 4, 9, 10)—so that the facts of Christ do progressively become the facts of our daily experience, and where before 'sin reigned' (Rom. 5. 21) we make now the joyful discovery that we are truly 'no longer . . . in bondage to sin' (Rom. 6. 6).

As we stand steadfastly on the ground of what Christ is, we find all that is true of Him becoming experimentally true in us. If instead we come on to the ground of what we are in ourselves, we will find all that is true of the old nature remaining true of us. If we get *there* in faith we have everything; if we return back *here* we find nothing. So often we go to the wrong place to find the death of self. It is in Christ. We have only to look within to find we are very much alive to sin; but when we look over there to the Lord, God sees to it that death works here but that 'newness of life' is ours also. We are 'alive unto God' (Rom. 6. 4, 11).

'Abide in me, and I in you.' This is a double sentence: a command coupled with a promise. That is to say, there is an objective and a subjective side to God's working, and the subjective side depends upon the objective; the 'I in you' is the outcome of our abiding in Him. We need to guard against being over-anxious about the subjective side of things, and so becoming turned in upon ourselves. We need to dwell upon the objective—'abide in me'—and to let God take care of the subjective. And this He has undertaken to do.

I have illustrated this from the electric light. You are in a room and it is growing dark. You would like to have the light on in order to read. There is a reading-lamp on the table beside you. What do you do? Do you watch it intently to see if the light will come on? Do you take a cloth and polish the bulb? No, you get up and cross over to the other side of the room where the switch is on the wall, and you turn the current on. You turn your attention to the source of power and when you have taken the necessary action there the light comes on here.

So in our walk with the Lord our attention must be fixed on Christ. 'Abide in me, and I in you' is the divine order. Faith in the objective facts makes those facts true subjectively. As the apostle Paul puts it, 'We all . . . beholding . . . the glory of the Lord, are transformed into the same image' (2 Cor. 3. 18 mg.). The same principle holds good in the matter of fruitfulness of life: 'He that abideth in me, and I in him, the same beareth much fruit' (John 15. 5). We do not try to produce fruit or concentrate upon the fruit produced. Our business is to look away to Him. As we do so He undertakes to fulfil His Word in us.

How do we abide? 'Of God are ye in Christ Jesus.' It was the work of God to put you there and He has done it. Now *stay* there! Do not be moved back on to your own ground. Never look at yourself as though you were not in Christ. Look at Christ, and see yourself in Him. *Abide in Him.* Rest in the fact that God has put you in His Son, and live in the expectation that He will complete His work in you. It is for Him to make good the glorious promise that 'sin shall not have dominion over you' (Rom. 6. 14).

5

The Divide of the Cross

THE kingdom of this world is not the kingdom of God. God had His heart set upon a world-system, a universe of His creating, which should be headed up in Christ His Son (Col. 1. 16, 17). But Satan, working through man's flesh, has set up instead a rival system known in Scripture as 'this world'—a system in which we are involved and which he himself dominates. He has in fact become 'the prince of this world' (John 12. 31).

Two creations

Thus, in Satan's hand, the first creation has become the old creation, and God's primary concern is now no longer with that but with a second and new creation. He is bringing in a new creation, a new kingdom and a new world, and nothing of the old creation, the old kingdom or the old world can be transferred to the new. It is a question now of these two rival realms, and of which realm we belong to.

The apostle Paul, of course, leaves us in no doubt as to which of these two realms is now in fact ours. He tells us that God, in redemption, 'delivered us out of the power of darkness, and translated us into the kingdom of the Son of his love' (Col. 1. 12, 13). Our citizenship henceforth is *there*.

But in order to bring us into His new kingdom, God must do something new in us. He must make of us new creatures. Unless we are created anew we can never fit into the new realm. 'That which is born of the flesh is flesh'; and, 'flesh and blood cannot inherit the kingdom of God; neither doth corruption inherit incorruption' (John 3. 6; Cor. 15. 50). However educated, however cultured, however improved it be, flesh is still flesh. Our fitness for the new kingdom is determined by the creation to which we belong. Do we belong to the old creation or the new? Are we born of the flesh or of the Spirit? Our ultimate suitability for the new realm hinges on the question of origin. The question is not 'good or bad?' but 'flesh or Spirit?'. 'That which is born of the flesh *is* flesh', and it will never be anything else. That which is of the old creation can never pass over into the new.

Once we really understand what God is seeking, namely, something altogether new for Himself, then we shall see clearly that we can never bring any contribution from the old realm into that new thing. God wanted to have us for Himself, but He could not bring us *as we were* into that which He had purposed; so He first did away with us by the Cross of Christ, and then by resurrection provided a new life for us. 'If any man is in Christ, he is a new creature [mg. 'there is a new creation']: the old things are passed away; behold, they are become new' (2 Cor. 5. 17). Being now new creatures with a new nature and a new set of faculties, we can enter the new kingdom and the new world.

The Cross was the means God used to bring to an end 'the old things' by setting aside altogether our 'old man', and the resurrection was the means He employed to impart to us all that was necessary for our life in that new world. 'We were buried therefore with him through baptism into death: that like as Christ was raised from the dead through the glory of the Father, so we also might walk in newness of life' (Rom. 6. 4).

The greatest negative in the universe is the Cross, for with it God wiped out everything that was not of Himself: the greatest positive in the universe is the resurrection, for through it God brought into being all He will have in the new sphere. So the resurrection stands at the threshold of the new creation. It is a blessed thing to see that the Cross ends all that belongs to the first regime, and that the resurrection introduces all that pertains to the second. Everything that had its beginning before resurrection must be wiped out. Resurrection is God's new starting-point.

We have now two worlds before us, the old and the new. In the old, Satan has absolute dominion. You may be a good man in the old creation, but as long as you belong to the old you are under sentence of death, because nothing of the old can be carried over to the new. The Cross is God's declaration that all that is of the old creation must die. Nothing of the first Adam can pass beyond the Cross; it all ends there. The sooner we see that, the better, for it is by the Cross that God has made a way of escape for us from that old creation. God gathered up in the Person of His Son all that was of Adam and crucified Him; so in Him all that was of Adam was done away. Then God made, as it were, a proclamation throughout the universe saying: 'Through the Cross I have

set aside all that is not of Me; you who belong to the old creation are all included in that; you too have been crucified
with Christ!' None of us can escape that verdict.

This brings us to the subject of baptism. 'Are ye ignorant
that all we who were baptized into Christ Jesus were baptized into his death? We were buried therefore with him
through baptism into death' (Rom. 6. 3, 4). We must now
ask ourselves what is the significance of these words.

Baptism in Scripture is associated with salvation. 'He that
believeth and is baptized shall be saved' (Mark 16. 16). We
cannot speak scripturally of 'baptismal regeneration' but we
may speak of 'baptismal salvation'. What is salvation? It
relates not to our sins nor to the power of sin, but to the
cosmos or world-system. We are involved in Satan's world-
system. To be saved is to make our exit from his world-
system into God's.

In the Cross of our Lord Jesus Christ, says Paul, 'the world
hath been crucified unto me, and I unto the world' (Gal. 6.
14). This is the figure developed by Peter when he writes of
the eight souls who were 'saved through water' (1 Peter 3.
20). Entering into the ark, Noah and those with him
stepped by faith out of that old corrupt world into a new
one. It was not so much that they were personally not
drowned but that they were *out* of that corrupt system. That
is salvation.

Then Peter goes on: 'Which also after a true likeness [mg.
'in the antitype'] doth now save you, even baptism' (verse
21). In other words, by that aspect of the Cross which is
figured in baptism, you are delivered from this present evil
world, and, by your baptism in water, you confirm this. It is
baptism 'into his death', ending one creation; but it is also

baptism 'into Christ Jesus', having in view a new one (Rom. 6. 3). You go down into the water and your world, in figure, goes down with you. You come up in Christ, but your world is drowned.

'Believe on the Lord Jesus, and thou shalt be saved', said Paul at Philippi, and 'spake the word of the Lord' to the jailer and his household. And he 'was baptized, he and all his, immediately' (Acts 16. 31–34). In doing so, he and those with him testified before God, His people and the spiritual powers that they were indeed saved from a world under judgment. As a result, we read, they rejoiced greatly, 'having believed in God'.

Thus it is clear that baptism is no mere question of a cup of water, nor even of a baptistry of water. It is something far greater, relating as it does to both the death and the resurrection of our Lord, and having in view two worlds. Anyone who has seen men turn to Christ in a pagan country knows what tremendous issues are raised by baptism.

Burial means an end

Peter goes on now to describe baptism in the passage just quoted as 'the answer of a good conscience toward God' (1 Peter 3. 21 A.V.). Now we cannot answer without being spoken to. If God had said nothing, we should have no need to answer. But He has spoken; He has spoken to us by the Cross. By it He has told of His judgment of us, of the world, of the old creation and of the old kingdom. The Cross is not only Christ's personally—an 'individual' Cross. It is an all-inclusive Cross, a 'corporate' Cross, a Cross that includes you and me. God has put us all into His Son, and crucified us in Him. In the last Adam He has wiped out all that was of the first Adam.

What then is my answer to God's verdict on the old creation? I answer by asking for baptism. Why? In Romans 6. 4 Paul explains that baptism means burial: 'We were buried therefore with him through baptism.' Baptism is of course connected with both death and resurrection, though in itself it is neither death nor resurrection: it is burial. But who qualify for burial? Only the dead! So if I ask for baptism I proclaim myself dead and fit only for the grave.

Alas, some have been taught to look on burial as a *means* to death; they try to die by getting themselves buried! Let me say emphatically that, unless our eyes have been opened by God to see that we have died in Christ and been buried with Him, we have no right to be baptized. The reason we step down into the water is that we have recognized that in God's sight we have *already* died. It is to that that we testify. God's question is clear and simple. 'Christ has died, and I have included you there. Now, what are you going to say to that?' What is my answer? 'Lord, I believe You have done the crucifying. I say Yes to the death and to the burial to which You have committed me.' He has consigned me to death and the grave; by my request for baptism I give public assent to that fact.

In China a woman lost her husband, but, becoming deranged by her loss, she flatly refused to have him buried. Day after day for a fortnight he lay in the house. 'No,' she said, 'he is not dead; I talk with him every night.' She was unwilling to have him buried because, poor woman, she did not believe him to be dead. When are we willing to bury our dear ones? Only when we are absolutely sure that they have passed away. While there is the tiniest hope that they are alive, we will never bury them. So when will I ask for baptism? When I see that God's way is perfect and that I deserved to die, and when I truly believe that God has already crucified me. Once I am fully persuaded that, before God, I am quite dead, then I apply for baptism. I say, 'Praise God, I am dead! Lord, You have slain me; now get me buried!'

In China we have two emergency Services, a 'Red Cross' and a 'Blue Cross'. The first deals with those who are wounded in battle but are still alive, to bring them succour and healing; the second deals with those who are already dead in famine, flood or war, to give them burial. God's dealings with us in the Cross of Christ are more drastic than those of the 'Red Cross'. He does not set out to patch up the old creation. By Him even the still living are condemned to death and to burial, that they may be raised again to new life. God has done the work of crucifixion so that now we are counted among the dead; but we must accept this and submit to the work of the 'Blue Cross', by sealing that death with 'burial'.

There is an old world and a new world, and between the two there is a tomb. God has already crucified me, but I must consent to be consigned to the tomb. My baptism confirms God's sentence, passed upon me in the Cross of His Son. It affirms that I am cut off from the old world and belong now to the new. So baptism is no small thing. It means for me a definite conscious break with the old way of life. This is the meaning of Romans 6. 2: 'We who died to sin, how shall we any longer live therein?' Paul asks, in effect, 'If you would continue in the old world, why be baptized? You should never have been baptized if you meant to live on in the old realm.' When once we see the force of this, we are ready enough to clear the ground for the new creation by our assent to the burial of the old.

In Romans 6. 5, still writing to those who 'were baptized' (verse 3), Paul speaks of our being 'united with him by the likeness of his death'. For by baptism we acknowledge in a figure that God has wrought an intimate union between ourselves and Christ in this matter of death and resurrection. One day I was seeking to emphasize to a Christian brother the intimacy of this union. We happened to be drinking tea together, so I took a lump of sugar and stirred it into my tea. A couple of minutes later I asked, 'Can you tell me where the sugar is now, and where the tea?' 'No,' he said, 'you have put them together and the one has become lost in the other; they cannot now be separated.' It was a simple illustration, but it helped him to see the intimacy and the finality of our union with Christ in death. It is God that has put us there, and God's acts cannot be reversed.

What, in fact, does this union imply? The real meaning behind baptism is that in the Cross we were 'baptized' *into the historic death of Christ*, so that His death became ours. Our death and His became then so closely identified that it is impossible to divide between them. It is to this historic 'baptism'—this God-wrought union with Him—that we assent when we go down into the water. Our public testimony in baptism today is our admission that the death of Christ two thousand years ago was a mighty all-inclusive death, mighty enough and all-inclusive enough to carry away in it and bring to an end everything in us that is not of God.

Resurrection unto newness of life

'If we have become united with him by the likeness of his death we shall be also by the likeness of his resurrection' (Rom. 6. 5).

Now with resurrection the figure is different because something new is introduced. I am 'baptized into his death', but I do not enter in quite the same way into His resurrection, for, Praise the Lord! His resurrection enters into me, imparting to me a new life. In the death of the Lord the emphasis is solely upon 'I in Christ'. With the resurrection, while the same thing is true, there is now a new emphasis upon 'Christ in me'. How is it possible for Christ to communicate His resurrection life to me? How do I receive this new life? Paul suggests, I think, a very good illustration with these very same words: 'united with him'. For the word 'united' (A.V. 'planted together') may carry in the Greek the sense of 'grafted'[1] and it gives us a very beautiful picture of the life of Christ which is imparted to us through resurrection.

In Fukien I once visited a man who owned an orchard of *long-ien* trees.[2] He had three or four acres of land and about

---

[1] Greek *sumphutos* 'planted or grown along with', 'united with'. The word is used in the sense of 'grafted in Classical Greek. In the delightful illustration which follows, the analogy of grafting should perhaps not be pressed too closely, for it is not quite safe to imply, without some qualification, that Christ is grafted into the old stock. But what parable can adequately describe the miracle of the new creation?—ED.

[2] *long-ien* (*Euphoria longana*) is a tree native to China. Its fruit resembles an apricot in size and has a round central stone, a dry, light brown, papery skin and a delicious white, grape-like pulp. It is eaten either fresh

three hundred fruit trees. I inquired if his trees had been grafted or if they were of the original native stock. 'Do you think,' he replied, 'that I would waste my land growing ungrafted trees? What value could I ever expect from the old stock?'

So I asked him to explain the process of grafting, which he gladly did. 'When a tree has grown to a certain height,' he said, 'I lop off the top and graft on to it.' Pointing to a special tree he asked, 'Do you see that tree? I call it the father tree, because all the grafts for the other trees are taken from that one. If the other trees were just left to follow the course of nature, their fruit would be only about the size of a raspberry, and would consist mainly of thick skin and seeds. This tree, from which the grafts for all the others are taken, bears a luscious fruit the size of a plum, with very thin skin and a tiny seed; and of course all the grafted trees bear fruit like it.' 'How does it happen?' I asked. 'I simply take a little of the nature of the one tree and transfer it to the other,' he explained. 'I make a cleavage in the poor tree and insert a slip from the good one. Then I bind it up and leave it to grow.' 'But how can it grow?' I asked. 'I don't know,' he said, 'but it does grow.'

Then he showed me a tree bearing miserably poor fruit from the old stock below the graft, and rich juicy fruit from the new stock above the graft. 'I have left the old shoots with their useless fruit on them to show the difference,' he said. 'From it you can understand the value of grafting. You can appreciate, can you not, why I grow only grafted trees?'

---

or dried, and is prized by the Chinese both for its flavour and for its food value.—ED.

How can one tree bear the fruit of another? How can a poor tree bear good fruit? Only by grafting. Only by our implanting into it the life of a good tree. But if a man can graft a branch of one tree into another, cannot God take of the life of His Son and, so to speak, graft it into us?

A Chinese woman burned her arm badly and was taken to hospital. In order to prevent serious contracture due to scarring it was found necessary to graft some new skin over the injured area, but the doctor attempted in vain to graft a piece of the woman's own skin on to the arm. Owing to her age and ill-nourishment the skin-graft was too poor and would not 'take'. Then a foreign nurse offered a piece of skin and the operation was carried out successfully. The new skin knit with the old, and the woman left the hospital with her arm perfectly healed; but there remained a patch of white foreign skin on her yellow arm to tell the tale of the past. You ask how the skin of another grew on that woman's arm? I do not know how it grew, but I know that it did grow.

If an earthly surgeon can take a piece of skin from one human body and graft it on another,[3] cannot the divine Surgeon implant the life of His Son into me? I do not know how it is done. 'The wind bloweth where it listeth, and thou hearest the voice thereof, but knowest not whence it cometh, and whither it goeth; so is every one that is born of the Spirit' (John 3. 8). We cannot tell how God has done His work in us, but it is done. We can do nothing and need do

---

[3] Whatever question medical men may raise as to the account of this unusual incident, the statement which follows is *not* open to challenge.— ED.

nothing to bring it about, for by the resurrection God has already done it.

God has done everything. There is only one fruitful life in the world and that has been grafted into millions of other lives. We call this the 'new birth'. New birth is the reception of a life which I did not possess before. It is not that my natural life has been changed at all; it is that another life, a life altogether new, altogether divine, has become my life.

God has cut off the old creation by the Cross of His Son in order to bring in a new creation in Christ by resurrection. He has shut the door to that old kingdom of darkness and translated me into the kingdom of His dear Son. My glorying is in the fact that it has been done—that, through the Cross of our Lord Jesus Christ, that old world *has* 'been crucified unto me, and I unto the world' (Gal. 6. 14). My baptism is my public testimony to that fact. By it, as by my oral witness, my 'confession is made unto salvation' (Rom. 10. 10).

6

The Path of Progress:
Presenting Ourselves to God

OUR study has now brought us to the point where we are able to consider the true nature of consecration. We have before us the second half of Romans 6 from verse 12 to the end. In Romans 6. 12, 13 we read: 'Let not sin therefore reign in your mortal body, that ye should obey the lusts thereof: neither present your members unto sin as instruments of unrighteousness; but present yourselves unto God, as alive from the dead, and your members as instruments of righteousness unto God.' The operative word here is 'present' and this occurs five times in the chapter, in verses 13, 16 and 19.[1]

---

[1] *Note.*—Two Greek verbs *paristano* and *paristemi* are translated in these verses by 'present' in the R.V. where the A.V. has 'yield'. *Paristemi* occurs frequently with this meaning, e.g. in Rom. 12. 1; 2 Cor. 11. 2; Col. 1. 22, 28, and in Luke 2. 22 where it is used of the presenting of the infant Jesus to God in the Temple. Both words have an active sense for which the R.V. translation 'present' is greatly to be preferred. 'Yield' contains a passive idea of 'surrender' that has coloured much evangelical thought, but which is not in keeping with the context here in Romans.—ED.

Many have taken this word 'present' to imply consecration without looking carefully into its content. Of course that is what it does mean, but not in the sense in which we so often understand it. It is not the consecration of our 'old man' with his instincts and resources, his natural wisdom, strength and other gifts, to the Lord for Him to use.

This will be at once clear from verse 13. Note there the clause 'as alive from the dead'. Paul says, 'Present yourselves unto God, as alive from the dead.' This defines for us the point at which consecration begins. For what is here referred to is not the consecration of anything belonging to the old creation, but only of that which has passed through death to resurrection. The 'presenting' spoken of is the outcome of my knowing my old man to be crucified. Knowing, reckoning, presenting to God: that is the divine order.

When I really know I am crucified with Him, then spontaneously I reckon myself dead (verses 6 and 11); and when I know that I am raised with Him from the dead, then likewise I reckon myself 'alive unto God in Christ Jesus' (verses 9 and 11), for both the death and the resurrection side of the Cross are to be accepted by faith. When this point is reached, giving myself to Him follows. In resurrection He is the source of my life—indeed He *is* my life; so I cannot but present everything to Him, for all is His, not mine. But without passing through death I have nothing to consecrate, nor is there anything God can accept, for He has condemned all that is of the old creation to the Cross. Death has cut off all that *cannot* be consecrated to Him, and resurrection alone has made consecration possible. Presenting myself to God means that henceforth I consider my whole life as belonging to Him.

The third step: 'present yourselves . . .'

Let us observe that this 'presenting' relates to the members of my body—that body which, as we saw earlier, is now unemployed in respect of sin. 'Present yourselves . . . and your members,' says Paul, and again: 'Present your members' (Rom. 6. 13, 19). God requires of me that I now regard all my members, all my faculties, as belonging wholly to Him.

It is a great thing when I discover I am no longer my own but His. If the ten shillings in my pocket belong to me, then I have full authority over them. But if they belong to another who has committed them to me in trust, then I cannot buy what I please with them, and I dare not lose them. Real Christian life begins with knowing this. How many of us know that, because Christ is risen, we are therefore alive 'unto God' *and not unto ourselves*? How many of us dare not use our time or money or talents as we would, because we realize they are the Lord's, not ours? How many of us have such a strong sense that we belong to Another that we dare not squander a shilling of our money, or an hour of our time, or any of our mental or physical powers?

On one occasion a Chinese brother was travelling by train and found himself in a carriage together with three non-Christians who, in order to beguile the time wished to play cards. Lacking a fourth to complete the game, they invited this brother to join them. 'I am sorry to disappoint you,' he said, 'but I cannot join your game for I have not brought my hands with me.' 'Whatever do you mean?' they asked in blank astonishment. 'This pair of hands does not belong to me,' he said, and then there followed the explanation of the transfer of ownership that had taken place in his life. That brother regarded the members of his body as belonging entirely to the Lord. That is true holiness.

Paul says, 'Present your members as servants to righteousness unto sanctification [A.V. 'holiness']' (Rom. 6. 19). Make it a definite act. 'Present yourselves unto God.'

Separated unto the Lord

What is holiness? Many people think we become holy by the eradication of something evil within. No, we become holy by being separated unto God. In Old Testament times, it was when a man was chosen by God to be altogether His that he was publicly anointed with oil and was then said to be 'sanctified'. Thereafter he was regarded as *set apart* to God. In the same manner even animals or material things— a lamb, or the gold of the temple—could be sanctified, not by the eradication of anything evil in them, but by being thus reserved exclusively to the Lord. 'Holiness' in the Hebrew sense meant something thus set apart, and all true holiness is holiness 'to the Lord' (Exod. 28. 36). I give myself over wholly to Christ: that is holiness.

Presenting myself to God implies a recognition that I am altogether His. This giving of myself is a definite thing, just as definite as reckoning. There must be a day in my life when I pass out of my own hands into His, and from that day forward I belong to Him and no longer to myself. That does not mean that I consecrate myself to be a preacher or a missionary. Alas, many people are missionaries not because they have truly consecrated themselves to God but because, in the sense of which we are speaking, they have *not* consecrated themselves to Him. They have 'consecrated' (as they would put it) something altogether different, namely, their own uncrucified natural faculties to the doing of His work; but that is not true consecration. Then to what are we to be consecrated? Not to Christian work, but *to the will of God, to be and to do whatever He requires.*

David had many mighty men. Some were generals and others were gatekeepers, according as the king assigned them their tasks. We must be willing to be either generals or gatekeepers, allotted to our parts just as God wills and not as we choose. If you are a Christian, then God has marked out a pathway for you—a 'course' as Paul calls it in 2 Timothy 4. 7. Not only Paul's path but the path of every Christian has been clearly marked out by God, and it is of supreme importance that each one should know and walk in the God-appointed course. 'Lord, I give myself to Thee with this desire alone, to know and walk in the path Thou hast ordained.' That is true giving. If at the close of a life we can say with Paul: 'I have finished my course', then we are blessed indeed. There is nothing more tragic than to come to the end of life and know we have been on the wrong course. We have only one life to live down here and we are free to do as we please with it, but if we seek our own pleasure our life will never glorify God. A devoted Christian once said in my hearing, 'I want nothing for myself; I want everything for God.' Do you want anything apart from God, or does all your desire centre in his will? Can you truly say that the will of God is 'good and acceptable and perfect' *to you*? (Rom. 12. 2).

For it is our wills that are in question here. That strong self-assertive will of mine must go to the Cross, and I must give myself wholly to the Lord. We cannot expect a tailor to make us a coat if we do not give him any cloth, nor a builder to build us a house if we let him have no building material; and in just the same way we cannot expect the Lord to live out His life in us if we do not give Him our lives in which to live. Without reservations, without controversy, we must give ourselves to Him to do as He pleases with us. 'Present yourselves unto God' (Rom. 6. 13).

Servant or slave?

If we give ourselves unreservedly to God, many adjustments may have to be made: in family, or business, or church relationships, or in the matter of our personal views. God will not let anything of ourselves remain. His finger will touch, point by point, everything that is not of Him, and will say: 'This must go.' Are you willing? It is foolish to resist God, and always wise to submit to Him. We admit that many of us still have controversies with the Lord. He wants something, while we want something else. Many things we dare not look into, dare not pray about, dare not even think about, lest we lose our peace. We can evade the issue in that way, but to do so will bring us out of the will of God. It is always an easy matter to get out of His will, but it is a blessed thing just to hand ourselves over to Him and let Him have His way with us.

How good it is to have the consciousness that we belong to the Lord and are not our own. There is nothing more precious in the world. It is that which brings the awareness of His continual presence, and the reason is obvious. I must first have the sense of God's possession of me before I can have the sense of His presence with me. When once His ownership is established, then I dare do nothing in my own interests, for I am His exclusive property. 'Know ye not, that to whom ye present yourselves as servants unto obedience, his servants ye are whom ye obey?' (Rom. 6. 16). The word here rendered 'servant' really signifies a bondservant, a slave. This word is used several times in the second half of Romans 6. What is the difference between a servant and a slave? A servant may serve another, but the ownership does not pass to that other. If he likes his master he can serve him, but if he does not like him he can give in his notice and seek another master. Not so is it with the slave. He is not only the servant of another but he is the possession of another. How did I become the slave of the Lord? On His part He bought me, and on my part I presented myself to Him. By right of redemption I am God's property, but if I would be His slave I must willingly give myself to Him, for He will never compel me to do so.

The trouble with many Christians today is that they have an insufficient idea of what God is asking of them. How glibly they say: 'Lord, I am willing for anything.' Do you know that God is asking of you your very life? There are cherished ideals, strong wills, precious relationships, much-loved work, that will have to go; so do not give yourself to God unless you mean it. God will take you seriously, even if you did not mean it seriously.

When the Galilean boy brought his bread to the Lord, what did the Lord do with it? He broke it. God will always break what is offered to Him. He breaks what He takes, but after breaking it He blesses and uses it to meet the needs of others. After you give yourself to the Lord, He begins to break what was offered to Him. Everything seems to go wrong, and you protest and find fault with the ways of God. But to stay there is to be no more than just a broken vessel—no good for the world because you have gone too far for the world to use you, and no good for God either because you have not gone far enough for Him to use you. You are out of gear with the world, and you have a controversy with God. This is the tragedy of many a Christian.

My giving of myself to the Lord must be an initial fundamental act. Then, day by day, I must go on giving to Him, not finding fault with His use of me, but accepting with praise even what the flesh finds hard. That way lies true enrichment.

I am the Lord's, and now no longer reckon myself to be my own but acknowledge in everything His ownership and authority. That is the attitude God delights in, and to maintain it is true consecration. I do not consecrate myself to be a missionary or a preacher; I consecrate myself to God to do His will where I am, be it in school, office or kitchen or wherever He may, in His wisdom, send me. Whatever He ordains for me is sure to be the very best, for nothing but good can come to those who are wholly His.

May we always be possessed by the consciousness that we are not our own.

7

The Eternal Purpose

WE have spoken of the need of revelation, of faith and of consecration, if we are to live a normal Christian life. But unless we see the end God has in view, we shall never clearly understand why these steps are necessary to lead us to that end. So before we consider further the question of inward experience, let us first look at the great divine goal before us.

What is God's purpose in creation, and what is His purpose in redemption? It may be summed up in two phrases, one from each of our two sections of Romans. It is: 'the glory of God' (Rom. 3. 23), and: 'the glory of the children of God' (8. 21).

In Romans 3. 23 we read: 'All have sinned, and fall short of the glory of God.' God's purpose for man was glory, but sin thwarted that purpose by causing man to miss God's glory. When we think of sin we instinctively think of the judgment it brings; we invariably associate it with condemnation and hell. Man's thought is always of the punishment that will come to him if he sins, but God's thought is always of the glory man will miss if he sins. The result of sin is that we forfeit God's glory: the result of redemption is that we are qualified again for glory. God's purpose in redemption is glory, glory, glory.

Firstborn among many brethren

This consideration takes us forward into Romans chapter 8, where the topic is developed in verses 16 to 18 and again in verses 29 and 30. Paul says: 'We are children of God: and if children, then heirs; heirs of God, and joint-heirs with Christ; if so be that we suffer with him, that we may be also glorified with him. For I reckon that the sufferings of this present time are not worthy to be compared with the glory which shall be revealed to us-ward' (Rom. 8. 16–18); and again: 'Whom he foreknew, he also foreordained to be conformed to the image of his Son, that he might be the firstborn among many brethren; and whom he foreordained, them he also called: and whom he called, them he also justified: and whom he justified, them he also glorified' (Rom. 8. 29, 30). What was God's objective? It was that His Son Jesus Christ might be the firstborn among many brethren, all of whom should be conformed to His image. How did God realize that objective? 'Whom he justified, them he also glorified.' Thus God's purpose in creation and redemption was to make Christ the firstborn Son among many glorified sons. That may perhaps at first convey very little to many of us, but let us look into it more carefully.

In John 1. 14 we are told that the Lord Jesus was God's only begotten Son: 'The Word became flesh, and dwelt among us (and we beheld his glory, glory as of the only begotten from the Father).' That He was God's only begotten

Son signifies that God had no other Son but this one. He was with the Father from all eternity. But, we are told, God was not satisfied that Christ should remain the only begotten Son; He wanted also to make Him His first begotten. How could an only begotten Son become a first begotten? The answer is simple: by the Father having more children. If you have but one son, then he is the only begotten, but if thereafter you have other children, then the only begotten becomes the first begotten.

The divine purpose in creation and redemption was that God should have many children. He wanted *us*, and could not be satisfied without us. Some time ago I called to see Mr. George Cutting, the writer of the well-known tract *Safety, Certainty and Enjoyment*. When I was ushered into the presence of this old saint of nintey-three years, he took my hand in his and in a quiet, deliberate way he said: 'Brother, do you know, I cannot do without Him? And do you know, He cannot do without me?' Though I was with him for over an hour, his great age and physical frailty made any sustained conversation impossible. But what remains in my memory of that interview was his frequent repetition of these two questions: 'Brother, do you know, I cannot do without Him? And do you know, *He cannot do without me*?'

In reading the story of the prodigal son most people are impressed with all the troubles the prodigal meets; they are occupied in thinking what a bad time he is having. But that is not the point of the parable. 'My son . . . was lost, and is found'—there is the heart of the story. It is not a question of what the son suffers, but of what the Father loses. *He* is the sufferer; *He* is the loser. A sheep is lost: whose is the loss? The shepherd's. A coin is lost: whose is the loss? The woman's. A son is lost: whose is the loss? The Father's. That is the lesson of Luke chapter 15.

The Lord Jesus was the only begotten Son, and as the only begotten He has no brothers. But the Father sent the Son in order that the only begotten might also be the first begotten, and the beloved Son have many brethren. There you have the whole story of the Incarnation and the Cross; and there you have, at the last, the purpose of God fulfilled in His 'bringing many sons unto glory' (Heb. 2. 10).

In Romans 8. 29 we read of 'many brethren'; in Hebrews 2. 10 of 'many sons'. From the point of view of the Lord Jesus they are 'brethren'; from the point of view of God the Father they are 'sons'. Both words in this context convey the idea of maturity. God is seeking full-grown sons; but He does not stop even there. For He does not want His sons to live in a barn or a garage or a field; He wants them in His home; He wants them to share His glory. That is the explanation of Romans 8. 30: 'Whom he justified, them he also glorified.' Sonship—the full expression of His Son—is God's goal in the many sons. How could He bring that about? By justifying them, and then by glorifying them. In His dealings with them God will never stop short of that goal. He set Himself to have sons, and to have those sons, mature and responsible, with Him in glory. He made provision for the whole of heaven to be peopled with glorified sons. That was His purpose in the redemption of mankind.

The grain of wheat

But how could God's only begotten Son become His first begotten? The method is explained in John 12. 24: 'Verily,

verily, I say unto you, Except a grain of wheat fall into the earth and die, it abideth by itself alone; but if it die, it beareth much fruit.' Who was that grain? It was the Lord Jesus. In the whole universe God put His one grain of wheat into the ground and it died, and in resurrection the only begotten grain became the first begotten grain, and from the one grain there have sprung many grains.

In respect of His divinity the Lord Jesus remains uniquely 'the only begotten Son of God'. Yet there is a sense in which, from the resurrection onward through all eternity, He is also the first begotten, and His life from that time is found in many brethren. For we who are born of the Spirit are made thereby 'partakers of the divine nature' (2 Peter 1. 4), though not, mark you, as of ourselves but only, as we shall see in a moment, in dependence upon God and by virtue of our being 'in Christ'. We have 'received the spirit of adoption, whereby we cry, Abba, Father. The Spirit himself beareth witness with our spirit, that we are children of God' (Rom. 8. 15, 16). It was by way of the Incarnation and the Cross that the Lord Jesus made this possible. Therein was the Father-heart of God satisfied, for in the Son's obedience unto death the Father has secured His many sons.

The first and the twentieth chapters of John are in this respect most precious. In the beginning of his Gospel John tell us that Jesus was 'the only begotten from the Father'. At the end of his Gospel he tells us how, after He had died and risen again, Jesus said to Mary Magdalene, 'Go unto my brethren, and say to them, I ascend unto my Father and your Father, and my God and your God' (John 20. 17). Hitherto in this Gospel the Lord had spoken often of 'the Father' or of 'my Father'. Now, in resurrection, He adds,

'. . . and your Father'. It is the eldest Son, the first begotten speaking. By His death and resurrection many brethren have been brought into God's family, and so, in the same verse He uses this very name for them, calling them 'my brethren'. By doing this He affirms that He 'is not ashamed to call them brethren' (Heb. 2. 11.)

The choice that confronted Adam

God planted a great number of trees in the garden of Eden, but 'in the midst of the garden'—that is, in a place of special prominence—He planted two trees, the tree of life and the tree of the knowledge of good and evil. Adam was created innocent; he had no knowledge of good and evil. Think of a grown man, say thirty years old, who has no sense of right or wrong, no power to differentiate between the two! Would you not say such a man was undeveloped? Well, that is exactly what Adam was. And God brings him into the garden and says to him, in effect, 'Now the garden is full of trees, full of fruits, and of the fruit of every tree you may eat freely. But in the very midst of the garden is one tree called "the tree of the knowledge of good and evil"; you must not eat of that, for in the day that you do so you will surely *die*. But remember, the name of the other tree close by is *Life*.' What then, is the meaning of these two trees? Adam was, to so speak, created morally neutral—neither sinful nor holy, but innocent—and God put those two trees there so that he might exercise free choice. He could choose the tree of life, or he could choose the tree of the knowledge of good and evil.

Now the knowledge of good and evil, though forbidden

to Adam, is not wrong in itself. Without it however, Adam is in a sense limited in that he cannot decide *for himself* on moral issues. Judgment of right and wrong resides not in him but in God, and Adam's only course when faced with any question is to refer it to Jehovah God. Thus you have a life in the garden which is totally dependent on God. These two trees, then, typify two deep principles; they represent two planes of life, the divine and the human. The 'tree of life' is God Himself, for God is life. He is the highest form of life, and He is also the source and goal of life. And the fruit: what is that? It is our Lord Jesus Christ. You cannot eat the tree but you can eat the fruit. No one is able to receive God as God, but we can receive the Lord Jesus. The fruit is the edible part, the receivable part of the tree. So—may I say it reverently?—the Lord Jesus is really God in a receivable form. God in Christ we can receive.

If Adam should take of the tree of life, he would partake of the life of God. Thus he would become a 'son' of God, in the sense of having in him a life that derived from God. There you would have God's life in union with man: a race of men having the life of God in them and *living in constant dependence upon God for that life.* But if instead Adam should turn the other way, and take of the tree of the knowledge of good and evil, then he would develop his own manhood along natural lines apart from God. As a self-sufficient being, he would possess in himself the power to form independent judgment, *but he would have no life from God.*

So this was the alternative that lay before him. Choosing the way of the Spirit, the way of obedience, he could become a 'son' of God, living in dependence upon God for his life; or, taking the natural course, he could put the finishing touch to himself, as it were, by becoming a self-dependent being, judging and acting apart from God. The history of humanity is the outcome of the choice he made.

Adam's choice the reason for the Cross

Adam chose the tree of the knowledge of good and evil, and thereby took up independent ground. In doing so he became (as men are now in their own eyes) a 'fully developed' man. He could command a knowledge; he could decide for himself; he could go on, or stop. From then on he was 'wise' (Gen. 3. 6). But the consequence for him was death rather than life, because the choice he had made involved complicity with Satan, and brought him therefore under the judgment of God. That is why access to the tree of life had thereafter to be forbidden to him.

Two planes of life had been set before Adam: that of divine life in dependence upon God, and that of human life with its 'independent' resources. Adam's choice of the latter was sin because thereby he allied himself with Satan to thwart the eternal purpose of God. He did so by choosing to develop his manhood—to become perhaps a very fine man, even by his standards a 'perfect' man—apart from God. But the end was death, because he had not in him the divine life necessary to realize God's purpose in his being, but had chosen to become instead an 'independent' agent of the Enemy. Thus in Adam we all become sinners, equally dominated by Satan, equally subject to the law of sin and death, and equally deserving of the wrath of God.

From this we see the divine reason for the death and resurrection of the Lord Jesus. We see too the divine reason for true consecration—for reckoning ourselves to be dead unto sin but alive unto God in Christ Jesus, and for presenting ourselves unto Him as alive from the dead. We must all go to the Cross, because *what is in us by nature is a self-life*, subject to the law of sin. Adam chose a self-life rather than a divine life; so God had to gather up all that was in Adam and do away with it. Our 'old man' has been crucified. God has put us all in Christ and crucified Him as the last Adam, and thus all that is of Adam has passed away.

Then Christ arose in new form; with a body still, but in the Spirit, no longer in the flesh. 'The last Adam became a life-giving spirit' (1 Cor. 15. 45). The Lord Jesus now has a resurrected body, a spiritual body, a glorious body, and since He is no longer in the flesh, He can now be received by all. 'He that eateth me, he also shall live because of me', said Jesus (John 6. 57). The Jews revolted at the thought of eating His flesh and drinking His blood, but of course they could not receive Him then because He was still literally in the flesh. Now that He is in the Spirit, every one of us can receive Him, and it is by partaking of His resurrection life that we are constituted children of God. 'As many as received him, to them gave he the right to become children of God . . . which were born . . . of God' (John 1. 12, 13).

God is not out to reform our life. It is not His aim to bring that life to a certain stage of refinement, for it is on a totally wrong plane. On that plane He cannot now bring man to glory. He must have a *new* man; one born anew, born of God. Regeneration and justification go together.

He that hath the Son hath the life

There are various planes of life. Human life lies between the life of the lower animals and the life of God. We cannot bridge the gulf that divides us from the plane above or the plane below, and the distance that separates us from the life of God is vastly greater than that which separates us from the life of the lower animals.

One day in China, I called on a Christian leader who was sick in bed, and whom, for the sake of this story, I shall call 'Mr. Wong' (though that was not his real name). He was a very learned man, a Doctor of Philosophy, and one esteemed throughout the whole of China for his high moral principles, and he had long been engaged in Christian work. But he did not believe in the need for generation; he only proclaimed to men a social gospel of love and good works.

When I called on Mr. Wong, his pet dog was by his bed-side, and after speaking with him of the things of God and of the nature of His work in us, I pointed to the dog and inquired his name. He told me he was called Fido. 'Is Fido his Christian name or his surname?' I asked (using the common Chinese terms for 'personal name' and 'family name'). 'Oh, that is just his name,' he said. 'Do you mean that is just his Christian name? Can I call him Fido Wong?' I continued. 'Certainly not!' came the emphatic reply. 'But he lives in your family', I protested. 'Why don't you call him Fido Wong?' Then, indicating his two daughters, I asked, 'Are your daughters not called Miss Wong?' 'Yes!' 'Well then, why cannot I call your dog Master Wong?' The Doctor laughed, and I went on: 'Do you see what I am getting at? Your daughters were born into your family and they bear your name because you have communicated your life to them. Your dog may be an intelligent dog, a well-behaved dog, and altogether a most remarkable dog; but the question is not, Is he a good or a bad dog? It is merely, Is he a dog? He does not need to be bad to be disqualified from being a member of your family; he only needs to be a dog. The same principle applies to you in your relationship to God. The question is not whether you are a bad man or a good man, more or less, but simply, Are you a man? If your life is on a lower plane than that of God's life, then you cannot belong to the divine family. Throughout your life your aim in preaching has been to turn bad men into good men; but *men as such*, whether good or bad, can have no vital relationship with God. Our only hope as men is to receive the Son of God, and when we do so, His life in us will constitute us sons of God.' The Doctor saw the truth, and that day he became a member of God's family by receiving the Son of God into his heart.

What we today possess in Christ is more than Adam lost. Adam was only a developed *man*. He remained on that plane, and never possessed the life of God. But when we receive the Son of God, not only do we receive the forgiveness of sins; we receive also the divine life which was represented in the garden by the tree of life. By the new birth we possess what Adam missed, for we receive a life he never had.

They are all of one

God's desire is for sons who shall be joint-heirs with Christ in glory. That is His goal; but how can He bring that about? Turn now to Hebrews 2. 10 and 11: 'It became him, for whom are all things, and through whom are all things, in bringing many sons unto glory, to make the author of their salvation perfect through sufferings. For both he that sanctifieth and they that are sanctified are all of one: for which cause he is not ashamed to call them brethren.'

There are two parties mentioned here, namely, 'many sons' and 'the author of their salvation', or, in different terms, 'he that sanctifieth' and 'they that are sanctified'. But these two parties are said to be 'all of one'. The Lord Jesus as Man derived His life from God, and (in another sense, but just as truly) we derive our new life from God. He was 'begotten . . . of the Holy Ghost' (Matt. 1. 20 mg.), and we were 'born of . . . the Spirit', 'born . . . of God' (John 3. 5; 1. 13). So, God says, we are all of One. 'Of' in the Greek means 'out of'. The first begotten Son and the many sons are all (though in different senses) 'out of' the one Source of life. Do you realize that we have the same life today that God has? The life which He possesses in heaven is the life which He has imparted to us here on the earth. That is the precious 'gift of God' (Rom. 6. 23). It is for this reason that we can live a life of holiness, for it is not our own life that has been changed, but the life of God that has been imparted to us.

Do you notice that, in this consideration of the eternal purpose, the whole question of sin ultimately goes out? It no longer has a place. Sin came in with Adam, and even when it has been dealt with, as it has to be, we are only brought back to the point where Adam was. But in relating us again to the divine purpose—in, as it were, restoring to us access to the tree of life—redemption has given us far more than Adam ever had. It has made us partakers of the very life of God Himself.

8

The Holy Spirit

WE have spoken of the eternal purpose of God as the motive and explanation of all His dealings with us. Now, before we return to our study of the phases of Christian experience as set forth in Romans, we must digress yet again in order to consider something which lies at the heart of all our experience as the vitalizing power of effective life and service. I refer to the personal presence and ministry of the Holy Spirit of God.

And here, too, let us take as our starting-point two verses from Romans, one from each of our sections. 'The love of God hath been shed abroad in our hearts through the Holy Ghost which was given unto us' (Rom. 5. 5). 'If any man hath not the Spirit of Christ, he is none of his' (Rom. 8. 9).

God does not give His gifts at random, nor dispense them in an arbitrary fashion. They are given freely to all, but they are given on a definite basis. God has truly 'blessed us with every spiritual blessing in the heavenly places in Christ' (Eph. 1. 3), but if those blessings which are ours in Christ are to become ours in experience, we must know on what ground we can appropriate them.

In considering the gift of the Holy Spirit it is helpful to think of this in two aspects, as the Spirit outpoured and the Spirit indwelling, and our purpose now is to understand on what basis this twofold gift of the Holy Spirit becomes ours. I have no doubt that we are right in distinguishing thus between the outward and the inward manifestations of His working, and that as we go on we shall find the distinction helpful. Moreover, when we compare them, we cannot but come to the conclusion that the inward activity of the Holy Spirit is the more precious. But to say this is not for one moment to imply that His outward activity is not also precious, for God only gives good gifts to His children.

Unfortunately we are apt to esteem our privileges lightly by reason of their sheer abundance. The Old Testament saints, who were not as favoured as we are, could appreciate more readily than we do the preciousness of this gift of the outpoured Spirit. In their day it was a gift given only to the few—chiefly to priests, judges, kings and prophets—whereas now it is the portion of every child of God. Think! we who are mere nonentities can have the same Spirit resting upon us as rested upon Moses the friend of God, upon David the beloved king, and upon Elijah the mighty prophet. By receiving the gift of the outpoured Holy Spirit we join the ranks of God's chosen servants of the Old Testament dispensation. Once we see the value of this gift of God, and realize too our deep need of it, we shall immediately ask, How can I receive the Holy Spirit in this way, to equip me with spiritual gifts and to empower me for God's service? Upon what basis has the Spirit been given to His children?

The Spirit outpoured

Let us turn first to the Book of the Acts chapter 2 verses 32 to 36 and consider this passage briefly:

'(32) This Jesus did God raise up, whereof we all are witnesses. (33) Being therefore by the right hand of God exalted, and having received of the Father the promise of the Holy Ghost, he hath poured forth this, which ye see and hear. (34) For David ascended not into the heavens; but he saith himself, The Lord said unto my Lord, Sit thou on my right hand, (35) Till I make thine enemies the footstool of thy feet. (36) Let all the house of Israel therefore know assuredly, that God hath made him both Lord and Christ, this Jesus whom ye crucified.'

We will set aside for the moment verses 34 and 35, and consider verses 33 and 36 together. The former are a quotation from the 110th Psalm and are really a parenthesis, so we shall get the force of Peter's argument better if we ignore them for the time being. In verse 33 Peter states that the Lord Jesus was exalted 'at the right hand of God' (mg.). What was the result? He 'received of the Father the promise of the Holy Ghost'. And what followed? The miracle of Pentecost! The result of His exaltation was—'this, which ye see and hear'.

Upon what basis, then, was the Spirit first given to the Lord Jesus to be poured out upon His people? It was upon the fact of His exaltation to heaven. This passage makes it quite clear that the Holy Spirit was poured out because Jesus was exalted. The outpouring of the Spirit has no relation to your merits or mine, but only to the merits of the Lord Jesus. The question of what *we* are does not come into consideration at all here, but only what *He* is. He is glorified; therefore the Spirit is poured out.

Because the Lord Jesus died on the Cross, I have received forgiveness of sins; because the Lord Jesus rose from the dead, I have received new life; because the Lord Jesus has been exalted to the right hand of the Father, I have received the outpoured Spirit. All is because of Him; nothing is because of me. Remission of sins is not based on human merit, but on the Lord's crucifixion; regeneration is not based on human merit, but on the Lord's resurrection; and the enduement with the Holy Spirit is not based on human merit, but on the Lord's exaltation. The Holy Spirit has not been poured out on you or me to prove how great we are, but to prove the greatness of the Son of God.

Now look at verse 36. There is a word here which demands our careful attention: the word 'therefore'. How is this word generally used? Not to introduce a statement, but to follow a statement that has already been made. Its use always implies that something has been mentioned before. Now what has preceded this particular 'therefore'? With which is it connected? It cannot reasonably be connected with either verse 34 or verse 35, but it quite obviously relates back to verse 33. Peter has just referred to the out-pouring of the Spirit upon the disciples 'which ye see and hear', and he says: 'Let all the house of Israel *therefore* know assuredly, that God hath made him both Lord and Christ, this Jesus whom ye crucified.' Peter says, in effect, to his audience: 'This outpouring of the Spirit, which you have witnessed with your own eyes and ears, proves that Jesus of Nazareth whom ye crucified is now both Lord and Christ.' The Holy Spirit was poured out on earth to prove what had taken place in heaven—the exaltation of Jesus of Nazareth to the right hand of God. The purpose of Pentecost is to prove the Lordship of Jesus Christ.

There was a young man named Joseph, who was dearly loved of his father. One day news reached the father of the death of his son, and for years Jacob lamented Joseph's loss. But Joseph was not in the grave; he was in a place of glory and power. After Jacob had been mourning the death of his son for years, it was suddenly reported to him that Joseph was alive and in a high position in Egypt. At first Jacob could not take it in. It was too good to be true. But ultimately he was persuaded that the story of Joseph's exaltation was really a fact. How did he come to believe in it? He went out, and saw the chariots that Joseph had sent from Egypt.

What do those chariots represent? They surely typify here the Holy Spirit, sent both to be the evidence that God's Son is in glory, and to convey us there. How do we know that Jesus of Nazareth, who was crucified by wicked men nearly two thousand years ago, did not just die a martyr's death but is at the Father's right hand in glory? How can we know for a surety that He is Lord of lords and King of kings? We can know it beyond dispute because He has poured out His Spirit upon us. Hallelujah! Jesus *is* Lord! Jesus *is* Christ! Jesus of *Nazareth is* both Lord and Christ!

If the gift of the Spirit depends thus upon the exaltation of the Lord Jesus alone, is it possible that *He* has been glorified and *you* have not received the Spirit? On what basis did you receive forgiveness of sins? Was it because you prayed so earnestly, or because you read your Bible from cover to cover, or because of your regular attendance at church? Was it because of your merits at all? No! A thousand times, No! On what ground then were your sins forgiven? 'Apart from shedding of blood there is no remission' (Heb. 9. 22). The sole ground of forgiveness is the shedding of blood; and since the precious Blood has been shed, your sins have been forgiven.

Now the principle on which we receive the enduement of the Holy Spirit is the very same as that on which we receive forgiveness of sins. The Lord has been crucified, therefore our sins have been forgiven; the Lord has been glorified, therefore the Spirit has been poured out upon us. Is it possible that the Son of God shed His Blood and that your sins, dear child of God, have not been forgiven? Never! Then is it possible that the Son of God has been glorified and you have not received the Spirit? Never!

Some of you may say: I agree with all this, but I have no experience of it. Am I to sit down smugly and say I have everything, when I know perfectly well I have nothing? No, we must never rest content with objective facts alone. We need subjective experience also; but that experience will only come as we rest upon divine facts. God's facts are the basis of our experience.

Go back again to the question of justification. How were you justified? Not by doing anything at all, but by accepting the fact that the Lord had done everything. And enduement with the Holy Spirit becomes yours in exactly the same way, not by your doing anything yourself, but by your putting your faith in what the Lord has already done.

If we lack the experience, we must ask God only for a revelation of this eternal fact, that the baptism of the Holy Spirit is the gift of the exalted Lord to His Church. Once we see that, effort will cease, and prayer will give place to praise. It was a revelation of what the Lord had done for the world that brought to an end our efforts to secure forgiveness of sins, and it is a revelation of what the Lord has done for His Church that will bring to an end our efforts to secure the baptism of the Holy Spirit. We work because we have not seen the work of Christ. But when once we have seen that, faith will spring up in our hearts, and as we believe, experience will follow.

Some time ago a young man, who had only been a Christian for five weeks and who had formerly been violently opposed to the Gospel, attend a series of meetings which I was addressing in Shanghai. At the close of one in which I was speaking on the above lines, he went home and began to pray earnestly, 'Lord, I do want the power of the Holy Spirit. Seeing Thou hast now been glorified, wilt Thou not now pour out Thy Spirit upon me?' Then he corrected himself: 'Oh no, Lord, that's all wrong!' and began to pray again: 'Lord Jesus, we are in a life-partnership, Thou and I, and the Father has promised us two things—glory for Thee, and the Spirit for me. Thou, Lord, hast received the glory; therefore it is unthinkable that I have not received the Spirit. Lord, I praise Thee! Thou hast already received the glory, and I have already received the Spirit.' From that day the power of the Spirit was consciously upon him.

Faith is again the key

As with forgiveness, so equally with the coming upon us of the Holy Spirit, the whole question is one of faith. As soon as we see the Lord Jesus on the Cross, we know our sins are forgiven; and as soon as we see the Lord Jesus on the Throne, we know the Holy Spirit has been poured out upon us. The basis upon which we receive the enduement of the Holy Spirit is not our praying and fasting and waiting, but the exaltation of Christ. Those who emphasize tarrying and hold 'tarrying meetings' only mislead us, for the gift is not for the 'favoured few' but for all, because it is not given on the ground of what we are at all, but of what Christ is. The Spirit has been poured out to prove *His* goodness and greatness, not ours. Christ has been crucified, therefore we have been forgiven: Christ has been glorified, therefore we have been endued with power from on high. It is all because of Him.

Suppose an unbeliever expresses the desire to be saved, and you explain to him the way of salvation and pray with him. Suppose he then prays after this fashion: 'Lord Jesus, I believe Thou hast died for me, and that Thou canst blot out all my sins. I truly believe Thou wilt forgive me.' Have you any confidence that that man is saved? When will you rest assured that he has really been born again? Not when he prays: 'Lord, I believe Thou *wilt* forgive my sins', but when he says: 'Lord, I thank Thee that Thou *hast* forgiven my sins. Thou *hast* died for me; therefore my sins *are* blotted out.' You believe a person is saved when his prayer yields to praise, and from asking the Lord to forgive him, he turns to praising Him that He has already done so because the Blood of the Lamb has already been shed.

In the same way, you can pray and wait for years and never experience the Spirit's power; but when you cease to plead with the Lord to pour out His Spirit upon you, and when instead you trustfully praise Him that the Spirit *has been* poured out because the Lord Jesus *has been* glorified, you will find that your problem is solved. Praise God! no single child of His need agonize, nor even wait, for the Spirit to be given. Jesus is not *going to be made* Lord, He *is* Lord. Therefore I am not *going to receive* the Spirit; I *have received* the Spirit. It is all a question of the faith which comes by revelation. When our eyes are opened to see that the Spirit has already been poured out because Jesus has already been glorified, then prayer turns to praise in our hearts.

All spiritual blessings come to us on a definite basis. God's gifts are freely given, but there are conditions to be fulfilled on our part before their reception is possible. There is a passage in God's Word which states the conditions of receiving the outpoured Spirit: 'Repent ye, and be baptized every one of you in the name of Jesus Christ unto the remission of your sins; and ye shall receive the gift of the Holy Ghost. For to you is the promise, and to your children, and to all that are far off, even as many as the Lord our God shall call unto him' (Acts 2. 38, 39).

Four things are mentioned here: Repentance, Baptism, Forgiveness and the Holy Spirit. The first two are conditions, the second two are gifts. What are the conditions to be fulfilled if we are to have forgiveness of sins? According to this scripture they are two: repentance and baptism.

First is repentance, which means a change of mind! Formerly I thought sin a pleasant thing, but now I have changed my mind about it; formerly I thought the world an attractive place, but now I know better; formerly I regarded it a miserable business to be a Christian, but now I think differently. Once I thought certain things delightful, now I think them vile; once I thought other things utterly worthless, now I think them most precious. That is a change of mind, and that is repentance. No life can be truly changed apart from such a change of mind.

The second condition is baptism. Baptism is an outward expression of an inward faith. When in my heart I truly believe that I have died, have been buried and have risen with Christ, then I ask for baptism. Thereby I declare publicly what I believe privately. Baptism is faith in action.

Here then are two divinely appointed conditions of forgiveness—repentance, and faith publicly expressed. Have you repented? Have you testified publicly to your union with your Lord? Then have you received remission of sins and the gift of the Holy Ghost? You say you have only received the first gift, not the second. But, my friend, God offered you two things if you fulfilled two conditions! Why have you only taken one? What are you doing about the second?

Suppose I went into a book-shop, selected a two-volume book, priced at ten shillings, and, having put down a ten-shilling note, walked out of the shop, carelessly leaving one volume on the counter. When I reached home and discovered the oversight, what do you think I should do? I should go straight back to the shop to get the forgotten book, but I should not dream of paying anything for it. I should simply remind the shopkeeper that both volumes were duly paid for, and ask him if he would therefore kindly let me have the second one; and without any further payment I should march happily out of the shop with my possession under my arm. Would you not do the same under the same circumstances?

But you *are* under the same circumstances. If you have

fulfilled the conditions, you are entitled to two gifts, not just to one. You have already taken the one; why not just come and take the other now? Say to the Lord, 'Lord, I have complied with the conditions for receiving remission of sins and the gift of the Holy Ghost, but I have foolishly taken only the former. Now at length I have come back to Thee to take the gift of the Holy Ghost, and to praise Thee for it.'

The diversity of the experience

But you ask: 'How shall I know that the Holy Spirit is come upon me?' I cannot tell *how* you will know, but you will know. No description has been given us of the personal sensations and emotions of the disciples at Pentecost. We do not know exactly how they felt, but we do know that their feelings and behaviour were somewhat abnormal, because people seeing them said they were intoxicated. When the Holy Spirit falls upon God's people there will be some things which the world cannot account for. There will be supernatural accompaniments of some kind, though it be no more than an overwhelming sense of the divine Presence. We cannot and we must not stipulate what particular form such outward expressions will take in any given case, but one thing is sure, that each one upon whom the Spirit of God falls *will unfailingly know it.*

When the Holy Spirit came upon the disciples at Pentecost there was something quite extraordinary about their behaviour, and Peter offered an explanation from God's Word to all who witnessed it. This, in substance, is what he said: 'When the Holy Spirit falls upon believers, some will prophesy, some will dream dreams, and others will see visions. This is what God has stated through the prophet Joel.' But did Peter prophesy? Well, hardly in the sense in which Joel meant it. Did the hundred and twenty prophesy or see visions? We are not told that they did. Did they dream dreams? How could they, for were they not all wide awake? Well then, what did Peter mean by using a quotation that seems scarcely to fit the case at all? In the passage quoted (Joel 2. 28, 29), prophecy, dreams, and visions are said to accompany the outpouring of the Spirit, yet these evidences were apparently lacking at Pentecost.

On the other hand, Joel's prophecy said not a word about 'a sound as of the rushing of a mighty wind', nor about 'tongues parting asunder like as of fire' as accompaniments of the Spirit's outpouring; yet these were manifest in that upper room. And where in Joel do we find mention of speaking in other tongues? And yet the disciples at Pentecost did so.

What did Peter mean? Imagine him quoting God's Word to show that the experience of Pentecost was the outpouring of the Spirit spoken of by Joel, without a single one of the evidences mentioned by Joel being found at Pentecost. What the Book mentioned the disciples lacked, and what the disciples had the Book did not mention! It looks as though Peter's quotation of the Book disproves his point rather than proving it. What is the explanation of this mystery?

Let us recall that Peter was himself speaking under the control of the Holy Spirit. The Book of the Acts was written by the Spirit's inspiration, and not one word was spoken at random. There is no misfit, but a perfect harmony. Note carefully that Peter did not say: 'What you see and hear fulfils what was spoken by the prophet Joel.' What he said was: 'This is that which hath been spoken by the prophet Joel' (Acts 2. 16). It was not a case of fulfilment, but of an experience *of the same order*. 'This is that' means that 'this which you see and hear is of the same order as that which is foretold'. When it is a case of fulfilment, each experience is reduplicated, and prophecy is prophecy, dreams are dreams, and visions are visions; but when Peter says 'This is that', it is not a question of the one being a replica of the other, but of the one belonging to the same category as the other. 'This' amounts to the same thing as 'that'; 'this' is the equivalent of 'that'; 'this *is* that'. What is being emphasized by the Holy Spirit through Peter is the diversity of the experience. The outward evidences may be many and varied, and we have to admit that occasionally they are strange; but the Spirit is one, and He is Lord. (See 1 Cor. 12. 4–6.)

What happened to R. A. Torrey when the Holy Spirit came upon him after he had been a minister for years? We will let him tell the story in his own words:

'I recall the exact spot where I was kneeling in prayer in my study. . . . It was a very quiet moment, one of the most quiet moments I ever knew. . . . Then God simply said to me, not in any audible voice, but in my heart, "It's yours. Now go and preach." He had already said it to me in His Word in 1 John 5. 14, 15; but I did not then know my Bible as I know it now, and God had pity on my ignorance and said it directly to my soul. . . . I went and preached, and I have been a new minister from that day to this. . . . Some time after this experience (I do not recall just how long after), while sitting in my room one day . . . suddenly . . . I found myself shouting (I was not brought up to shout and I am not of a shouting temperament, but I shouted like the loudest shouting Methodist), "Glory to God, glory to God, glory to God", and I could not stop. . . . But that was not when I was baptized with the Holy Spirit. I was baptized with the Holy Spirit when I took Him by simple faith in the Word of God.'[1]

The outward manifestations in Torrey's case were not the same as those described by Joel or by Peter, but 'this is that'. It is not a facsimile, yet it is the same thing.

And how did D. L. Moody feel and act when the Spirit of God cam upon him to transform his life and ministry?

'I was crying all the time that God would fill me with His Spirit. Well, one day, in the city of New York—oh, what a day!—I cannot describe it, I seldom refer to it; it is almost too sacred an experience to name. Paul had an experience of which he never spoke for fourteen years. I can only say that God revealed Himself to me, and I had such an experience of His love that I had to ask Him to stay His hand. I went preaching again. The sermons were not different; I did not present any new truths; and yet hundreds were converted. I would not now be placed back where I was before that blessed experience if you should give me all the world—it would be as the small dust of the balance.'[2]

The outward manifestations that accompanied Moody's experience did not tally exactly with Joel's description, or Peter's, or Torrey's, but who could doubt that 'this' which Moody experienced was 'that' experienced by the disciples

---

[1] *The Holy Spirit, who He is and what He does*, by R. A. Torrey, D.D., pp. 198–9.

[2] *The Life of Dwight L. Moody*, by his son, W. R. Moody, p. 149.

at Pentecost? It was not the same in manifestation, but it was the very same in essence.

And what was the experience of the great Charles Finney when the power of the Holy Ghost came upon him?

> 'I received a mighty baptism of the Holy Ghost without any expectation of it, without ever having the thought in my mind that there was any such thing for me, without any recollection that I had ever heard the thing mentioned by any person in the world, the Holy Spirit descended upon me in a manner that seemed to go through me body and soul. No words can express the wonderful love that was shed abroad in my heart. I wept aloud with joy and love.'[3]

Finney's experience was not a duplicate of Pentecost, nor of Torrey's experience, nor yet of Moody's; but 'this' certainly was 'that'.

When the Holy Spirit is poured out upon God's people their experiences will differ widely. Some will receive new vision, others will know a new liberty in soul-winning, others will proclaim the Word of God with fresh power, and yet others will be filled with heavenly joy or overflowing praise. 'This . . . and this . . . and this . . . is that!' Let us praise the Lord for every new experience that relates to the exaltation of Christ, and of which it can truly be said that 'this' is an evidence of 'that'. There is nothing stereotyped about God's dealings with His children. Therefore we must not, by our prejudices and preconceptions, make water-tight compartments for the working of His Spirit, either in our own lives or in the lives of others. This applies equally

---

[3] *Autobiography of Charles E. Finney*, chapter 2.

to those who require some particular manifestation (such as 'speaking with tongues') as evidence that the Spirit has come upon them, and to those who deny that any manifestation is given at all. We must leave God free to work as He wills, and to give what evidence He pleases of the work He does. He is Lord, and it is not for us to legislate for Him.

Let us rejoice that Jesus is on the throne, and let us praise Him that, since He has been glorified, the Spirit has been poured out upon us all. As we behold Him there, and accept the divine fact in all the simplicity of faith, we shall know it with such assurance in our own hearts that we shall dare to proclaim once again with confidence—'This is that!'

The Spirit indwelling

We move on now to the second aspect of the gift of the Holy Spirit, which, as we shall see in our next chapter, is more particularly the subject of Romans 8. It is that which we have spoken of as the Spirit indwelling. 'If so be that the Spirit of God dwelleth in you . . .' (Rom. 8. 9). 'If the Spirit of him that raised up Jesus from the dead dwelleth in you . . .' (Rom. 8. 11).

As with the Spirit outpoured, so with the Spirit indwelling, if we are to know in experience that which is ours in fact, our first need is of divine revelation. When we see Christ as Lord objectively—that is, exalted to the throne in heaven—then we shall experience the power of the Spirit upon us. When we see Christ as Lord subjectively—that is, as effective Ruler within our lives—then we shall know the power of the Spirit within us.

A revelation of the indwelling Spirit was the remedy Paul

offered the Corinthian Christians for their unspirituality. It
is important to note that the Christians in Corinth had
become pre-occupied with the visible signs of the Holy
Spirit's outpouring and were making much of 'tongues' and
miracles, while at the same time their lives were full of con-
tradictions and were a reproach to the Lord's Name. Quite
evidently they had received the Holy Spirit, and yet they
remained spiritually immature; and the remedy God
offered them for this is the remedy He offers His Church
today for the same complaint.

In his letter to them Paul wrote: '*Know ye not* that ye are
a temple of God, and that the Spirit of God dwelleth in
you?' (1 Cor. 3. 16). For others he prayed for enlighten-
ment of heart, '. . . that ye may *know*' (Eph. 1. 18). A
knowledge of divine facts was the need of the Christians
then, and it is no less the need of Christians today. We need
the eyes of our understanding opened to know that God
Himself, through the Holy Spirit, has taken up His abode in
our hearts. In the person of the Spirit, God is present, and
Christ is no less truly present too. Thus if the Holy Spirit
dwells in our hearts we have the Father and the Son abiding in us. That is no mere theory or doctrine, but a blessed
reality. We may perhaps have realized that the Spirit is actually within our hearts, but have we realized that He is a Person? Have we understood that to have the Spirit with us is
to have the living God within?

To many Christians the Holy Spirit is quite unreal. They
regard Him as a mere influence—an influence for good, no
doubt, but just an influence for all that. In their thinking,
conscience and the Spirit are more or less identified as some
'thing' within them, that brings them to book when they

are bad and tries to show them how to be good. The trouble with the Corinthian Christians was not that they lacked the indwelling Spirit but that they lacked the knowledge of His presence. They failed to realize the greatness of the One who had come to make His abode in their hearts; so Paul wrote to them: 'Know ye not that ye are a temple of God, and that the Spirit of God dwelleth in you?' Yes, that was the remedy for their unspirituality—just to know who He really was who dwelt within.

The treasure in the vessel

Do you know, my friends, that the Spirit within you is very God? Oh that our eyes were opened to see the greatness of God's gift! Oh that we might realize the vastness of the resources secreted in our own hearts! I could shout with joy as I think, 'The Spirit who dwells within me is no mere influence, but a living Person; He is very God. The infinite God is within my heart!' I am at a loss to convey to you the blessedness of this discovery, that the Holy Spirit dwelling within my heart is a Person. I can only repeat: 'He is a Person!' and repeat it again: 'He is a Person!' and repeat it yet again: 'He is a Person!' Oh, my friends, I would fain repeat it to you a hundred times—*The Spirit of God within me is a Person!* I am only an earthen vessel, but in that earthen vessel I carry a treasure of unspeakable worth, even the Lord of glory.

All the worry and fret of God's children would end if their eyes were opened to see the greatness of the treasure hid in their hearts. Do you know, there are resources enough in your own heart to meet the demand of every circumstance in which you will ever find yourself? Do you know there is power enough there to move the city in which you live? Do you know there is power enough to shake the universe? Let me tell you once more—I say it with the utmost reverence: You who have been born again of the Spirit of God—you carry God in your heart!

All the flippancy of the children of God would cease too if they realized the greatness of the treasure deposited within them. If you have only ten shillings in your pocket you can march gaily along the street, talking lightly as you go, and swinging your stick in the air. It matters little if you lose your money, for there is not much at stake. But if you carry a thousand pounds in your pocket, the position is vastly different, and your whole demeanour will be different too. There will be great gladness in your heart, but no careless jaunting along the road; and once in a while you will slacken your pace and slipping your hand into you pocket, you will quietly finger your treasure again, and then with joyful solemnity continue on your way.

In Old Testament times there were hundreds of tents in the camp of Israel, but there was one tent quite different from all the rest. In the common tents you could do just as you pleased—eat or fast, work or rest, be joyful or sober, noisy or silent. But that other tent was a tent that commanded reverence and awe. You might move in and out of the common tents talking noisily and laughing gaily, but as soon as you neared that special tent you instinctively walked more quietly, and when you stood right before it you bowed your head in solemn silence. No one could touch it with impunity. If man or beast dared to do so, death was the sure penalty. What was so very special about it? *It was the temple of the living God.* There was little unusual about the tent itself, for it was outwardly of very ordinary material, but the great God had chosen to make it His abode.

Do you realize what happened at your conversion? God came into your heart and made it His temple. In Solomon's days God dwelt in a temple made of stone; today He dwells in a temple composed of living believers. When we really see that God has made our hearts His dwelling-place, what a deep reverence will come over our lives! All lightness, all frivolity will end, and all self-pleasing too, when we *know* that we are the temple of God and that the Spirit of God dwells within us. Has it really come home to you that wherever you go you carry with you the Holy Spirit of God? You do not just carry your Bible with you, or even much good teaching about God, but God Himself.

The reason why many Christians do not experience the power of the Spirit, though He actually dwells in their hearts, is that they lack reverence. And they lack reverence because they have not had their eyes opened of the fact of His presence. The fact is there, but they have not seen it. Why is it that some of God's children live victorious lives while others are in a state of constant defeat? The difference is not accounted for by the presence or absence of the Spirit (for He dwells in the heart of every child of God) but by this, that some recognize His indwelling and others do not. True revelation of the fact of the Spirit's indwelling will revolutionize the life of any Christian.

The absolute Lordship of Christ

'Know ye not that your body is a temple of the Holy Ghost which is in you, which ye have from God? and ye are not your own; for ye were bought with a price: glorify God therefore in your body' (1 Cor. 6. 19, 20).

This verse now takes us a stage further, for, when once we have made the discovery of the fact that we are the dwelling-place of God, then a full surrender of ourselves to God must follow. When we see that we are the temple of God, we shall immediately acknowledge that we are not our own. Consecration will follow revelation. The difference between victorious Christians and defeated ones is not that some have the Spirit while others have not, but that some *know* His indwelling and others do not, and that consequently some recognize the divine ownership of their lives while others are still their own masters.

Revelation is the first step to holiness, and consecration is the second. A day must come in our lives, as definite as the day of our conversion, when we give up all right to ourselves and submit to the absolute Lordship of Jesus Christ. There may be a practical issue raised by God to test the reality of our consecration, but whether that be so or not, there must be a day when, without reservation, we surrender everything to Him—ourselves, our families, our possessions, our business and our time. All we are and have becomes His, to be held henceforth entirely at His disposal. From that day we are no longer our own masters, but only stewards. Not until the Lordship of Christ in our hearts is a settled thing can the Spirit really operate effectively in us. He cannot direct our lives until all control of them is committed to Him. If we do not give Him absolute authority there, He can be present, but He cannot be powerful. The power of the Spirit is stayed.

Are you living for the Lord or for yourself? Perhaps that

is too general a question, so let me be more specific. Is there anything God is asking of you that you are withholding from Him? Is there any point of contention between you and Him? Not till every controversy is settled and the Holy Spirit is given His full place can He reproduce the life of Christ in any believer.

An American friend, now with the Lord, whose name we will call Paul, cherished the hope from his early youth that one day he would be called 'Dr. Paul'. When he was quite a little chap he began to dream of the day when he would enter the university, and he imagined himself first studying for his M.A. degree and then for his Ph.D. Then at length the glad day would arrive when all would greet him as 'Dr. Paul'.

The Lord saved him and called him to preach, and before long he became pastor of a large congregation. By that time he had his degree and was studying for his doctorate, but, despite splendid progress in his studies and a good measure of success as a pastor, he was a very dissatisfied man. He was a Christian minister, but his life was not Christ-like; he had the Spirit of God within him, but he did not enjoy the Spirit's presence or experience His power. He thought to himself, 'I am a preacher of the Gospel and the pastor of a church. I tell my people they should love the Word of God, but I do not really love it myself. I exhort them to pray, but I myself have little inclination to pray. I tell them to live a holy life, but my own life is not holy. I warn them not to love the world, and, though outwardly I shun it, yet in my heart I myself still love it dearly.' In his distress he cried to the Lord to cause him to know the power of the indwelling Spirit, but though he prayed and prayed for months, no answer came. Then he fasted, and besought the Lord to show him any hindrance there might be in his life. That answer was not long in coming, and it was this: 'I long that you should know the power of My Spirit, but your heart is set on something that I do not wish you to have. You have yielded to me all but one thing, and that one thing you are holding to yourself—your Ph.D.' Well, to you or me it might be of little consequence whether we were addressed as plain 'Mr. Paul' or as 'Dr. Paul', but to him it was his very life. He had dreamed of it from childhood, and laboured for it all through his youth, and now the thing he prized above all else was almost within his grasp. In two short months it would be his.

So he reasoned with the Lord in this wise: 'Is there any harm for me to be a Doctor of Philosophy? Will it not bring much more glory to Thy Name to have a Dr. Paul preaching the Gospel than a plain Mr. Paul?' But God does not change His mind, and all Mr. Paul's sound reasoning did not alter the Lord's word to him. Every time he prayed about the matter he got the same answer. Then, reasoning having failed, he resorted to bargaining with the Lord. He promised to go here or there, to do this or that, if only the Lord would allow him to have his doctor's degree; but still the Lord did not change. And all the while Mr. Paul was becoming more and more hungry to know the fulness of the Spirit. This state of affairs continued to within two days of his final examination.

It was Saturday, and Mr. Paul settled down to prepare his sermon for the following day, but, study as he would, he could get no message. The ambition of a lifetime was just within reach of realization, but God made it clear that he must choose between the power he could sway through a doctor's degree and the power of God's Spirit swaying his life. That evening he yielded. 'Lord,' he said, 'I am willing to be plain Mr. Paul all my days, but I want to know the power of the Holy Ghost in my life.'

He rose from his knees, and wrote a letter to his examiners asking to be excused from the examination on the Monday, and giving his reason. Then he retired, very happy, but not conscious of any unusual experience. Next morning he told his congregation that for the first time in six years he had no sermon to preach, and explained how it came about. The Lord blessed that testimony more abundantly than any of his well-prepared sermons, and from that time God owned him in an altogether new way. For from that day he knew separation from the world, no longer merely as an outward thing but as a deep inward reality, and as a result, the blessedness of the Spirit's presence and power became his daily experience.

God is waiting for a settlement of all our controversies with Him. With Mr. Paul it was question of his doctor's degree, but with us it may be something quite different. Our complete surrender of ourselves to the Lord generally hinges upon some one particular thing, and God waits for that one thing. He must have it, for He must have our all. I was greatly impressed by something a great national leader wrote in his autobiography: 'I want nothing for myself; I want everything for my country.' If a man can be willing that his country should have everything and he himself nothing, cannot we say to our God: 'Lord, I want nothing for myself; I want all for Thee. *I* will what *Thou* willest, and I want to have nothing outside Thy will.' Not until we take the place of a servant can He take His place as Lord. He is not calling us to devote ourselves to His cause: He is asking us to yield ourselves unconditionally to His will. Are you prepared for that?

Another friend of mine, like Mr. Paul, had a controversy with the Lord. Before his conversion he fell in love, and as soon as he was saved he sought to win the one he loved to Christ, but she would have nothing to do with spiritual things. The Lord made it clear to him that his relations with that girl must be broken off, but he was deeply devoted to her, so he evaded the issue, while continuing as before to serve the Lord and to win souls for Him. But he became conscious of his need for holiness, and that consciousness marked for him the beginning of dark days. He asked for the Spirit's fulness, that he might have power to live a holy life, but God seemed continually to ignore his request.

One morning he had to preach in another city and he spoke from Psalm 73. 25: 'Whom have I in heaven but thee? And there is none upon earth that I desire beside thee.' On his return home he went to a prayer-meeting where, to his surprise, a sister got up and read the very same verse from which, unknown to her, he had just preached, following it with the question: 'Can we truly say: "There is none upon earth that I desire beside thee"?' There was power in that word. It struck right home to his heart and he had to admit to himself that he could not truthfully say he desired no one in heaven or earth apart from his Lord. There and then he saw that, for him, everything hinged upon his willingness to give up the girl he loved.

For some perhaps, it might not have involved so much, but for him it was everything. So he began to reason with the Lord: 'Lord I will go to Tibet and work for Thee there if I may marry that girl.' But the Lord seemed to care a great deal more about his relationship with that girl than about his going to Tibet, and no amount of reasoning on his part availed to effect any change of emphasis on the part of the Lord. The controversy went on for several months, and whenever the young man pleaded for the fulness of the Spirit, God still pointed to the same thing. But a day came when His grace triumphed, and that young man looked up to him and acknowledged: 'Lord, I can truly say now, "There is none upon earth that I desire beside thee".' It was the dawn of a new day for him.

A forgiven sinner is quite different from an ordinary sinner, and a consecrated Christian is quite different from an ordinary Christian. May the Lord bring each of us to a definite issue regarding the question of His Lordship. If we yield wholly to Him and claim the power of His indwelling Spirit, we need wait for no special feelings or supernatural manifestations, but can simply look up and praise Him that something has already happened. We can confidently thank Him that the glory of God has already filled His temple. 'Know ye not that your body is a temple of the Holy Ghost which is in you, *which ye have from God*?'

9

The Meaning and Value of Romans Seven

WE must return now to Romans. We broke off at the end of chapter 6 in order to consider two related subjects, namely, God's eternal purpose, which is the motive and goal of our walk with Him, and the Holy Spirit, who supplies the power and resource to bring us to that goal. We come now to Romans 7, a chapter which many have felt to be almost superfluous. Perhaps indeed it would be so if Christians really saw that the old creation has been ruled out by the Cross of Christ, and an entirely new creation brought in by His resurrection. If we have come to the point where we really 'know' that, and 'reckon' on that, and 'present ourselves' on the basis of that, then *perhaps* we have no need of Romans 7.

Others have felt that the chapter is in the wrong place. They would have put it between the fifth and sixth chapters After chapter 6 all is so perfect, so straightforward; and then comes this astonishing breakdown and the cry, 'O wretched man that I am!' Could anything be more of an anticlimax? And so some have argued that Paul is speaking here of his unregenerate experience and of his failure, as a Jew, to keep the Law. Well, we must admit that some of what he describes here is not a *Christian* experience, but none the less many Christians do experience it. When then is the teaching of this chapter?

Romans 6 deals with freedom from sin. Romans 7 deals with freedom from the Law. In chapter 6 Paul has told us how we could be delivered from sin, and we concluded that this was all that was required. Chapter 7 now teaches that deliverance from sin is not enough, but that we also need to know deliverance from the Law. If we are not fully emancipated from the Law, we can never know full emancipation from sin. But what is the difference between deliverance from sin and deliverance from the Law? We all see the value of the former, but where, we wonder, is the need for the latter? For answer, we must first of all ask ourselves what the Law is, and what is its special value for us.

The flesh and man's breakdown

Romans 7 has a new lesson to teach us. It is found in the discovery that I am 'in the flesh' (Rom. 7. 5), that 'I am carnal' (7. 14), and that 'in me, that is, in my flesh, dwelleth no good thing' (7. 18). This goes beyond the question of sin, for it relates also to the matter of pleasing God. We are dealing here not with sin in its forms but with man in his carnal state. The latter includes the former, but it takes us a stage further, for it leads to the discovery that in this realm too we are totally impotent, and that 'they that are in the flesh cannot please God' (Rom. 8. 8). How then is this discovery made? It is made with the help of the Law.

Let us retrace our steps for a minute and attempt to describe what is probably the experience of many. Many a Christian is truly saved and yet bound by sin. It is not that he is necessarily living under the power of sin all the time, but that there are certain particular sins hampering him continually so that he commits them over and over again. One day he hears the full message of the Gospel, that the Lord Jesus not only died to cleanse away our sins, but that when He died He included us sinners in His death; so that not only were our sins dealt with, but we ourselves were dealt with too. The man's eyes are opened and he *knows* he has been crucified with Christ. Two things follow that revelation. In the first place he *reckons* that he has died and risen with his Lord. In the second place, recognizing God's claim upon him, and that he has no more right over himself, he *presents himself* to God as alive from the dead. This is the commencement of a beautiful Christian life, full of praise to the Lord.

But then he begins to reason as follows: 'I have died with Christ and am raised with Him, and I have given myself over to Him for ever; now I must do something for Him, since He has done so much for me. I want to please Him and do His will.' So, after the step of consecration, he seeks to discover the will of God, and sets himself to carry it out. Then he makes a strange discovery. He thought he could do the will of God, because he thought he loved it, but gradually he finds he does not always like it at all. At times he even feels a distinct reluctance to pursue it, and often when he tries to put it into practice, he finds he cannot. Then he begins to question his experience. He asks himself: 'Did I really know? Yes! Did I really reckon? Yes! Did I really give

myself to Him? Yes! Have I withdrawn my consecration?
No! Then whatever is the matter now?' For the more this
man tries to do the will of God the more he fails. Ultimately
he comes to the conclusion that he never really loved God's
will at all, so he prays for the desire as well as the power to
do it. He confesses his disobedience and promises never to
disobey again. But scarcely has he got up from his knees
when he falls once more; before he reaches the point of victory he is conscious of defeat. Then he says to himself: 'Perhaps my last decision was not definite enough. This time I
will be absolutely definite.' So he brings all his will-power
to bear on the situation, only to find greater defeat than
ever awaiting him the next time a choice has to be made.
Then at last he echoes the words of Paul: 'For I know that
in me, that is, in my flesh, dwelleth no good thing: for to
will is present with me, but to do that which is good is not.
For the good which I would I do not: but the evil which I
would not, that I practise' (Rom. 7. 18, 19). He has reached
the point of desperation.

What the law teaches

Many Christians find themselves suddenly launched into
the experience of Romans 7 and they do not understand
why. They fancy Romans 6 is quite enough. Having grasped
that, they think there can be no more question of failure,
and then to their utmost surprise they find themselves right
in the midst of Romans 7. What is the explanation?

First let us be quite clear that the death with Christ described in Romans 6 is fully adequate to cover all our need.
It is the explanation of that death, with all that follows from

it in chapter 6, that is as yet incomplete. We are still in ignorance of the truth set forth in chapter 7. For Romans 7 is
given to us to explain and make real the statement in
Romans 6. 14, that: 'Sin shall not have dominion over you:
for ye are not under law, but under grace.' The trouble is
that we do not yet know deliverance from law. What, then,
is the meaning of Law?

Grace means that God does something for me; law means
that I do something for God. God has certain holy and righteous demands which He places upon me: that is law. Now
if law means that God requires something of me for their
fulfilment, then deliverance from law means that He no
longer requires that from me, but Himself provides it. Law
implies that God requires me to do something for Him;
deliverance from law implies that He exempts me from
doing it, and that in grace He does it Himself. *I* (where 'I' is
the 'carnal' man of chapter 7. 14) *need do nothing for God:*
that is deliverance from law. The trouble in Romans 7 is that
man in the flesh tried to do something for God. As soon as
you try to please God in that way, then you place yourself
under law, and the experience of Romans 7 begins to be
yours.

As we seek to understand this, let it be settled at the outset that the fault does not lie with the Law. Paul says, 'the
law is holy, and the commandment holy, and righteous, and
good' (Rom. 7. 12). No, there is nothing wrong with the
Law, but there is something decidedly wrong with me. The
demands of the Law are righteous, but the person upon
whom the demands are made is unrighteous. The trouble is
not that the Law's demands are unjust, but that I am unable
to meet them. It may be all right for the Government to

require payment of £100, but it will be all wrong if I have only ten shillings with which to meet the payment!

I am a man 'sold under sin' (Rom. 7. 14). Sin has dominion over me. True, as long as you leave me alone I seem to be rather a fine type of man. It is when you ask me to *do* something that my sinfulness comes to light.

If you have a very clumsy servant and he just sits still and does nothing, then his clumsiness does not appear. If he does nothing all day he will be of little use to you, it is true, but at least he will do no damage that way. But if you say to him: 'Now come along, don't idle away your time: get up and do something', then immediately the trouble begins. He knocks the chair over as he gets up, stumbles over a footstool a few paces further on, then smashes some precious dish as soon as he handles it. If you make no demands upon him his clumsiness is never noticed, but as soon as you ask him to do anything his awkwardness is apparent at once. The demands were all right, but the man was all wrong. He was as clumsy a man when he was sitting still as when he was working, but it was your demands that made manifest the clumsiness which, whether he was active or inactive, was all the time in his make-up.

We are all sinners by nature. If God asks nothing of us, all seems to go well, but as soon as He demands something of us, the occasion is provided for a grand display of our sinfulness. The Law makes our weakness manifest. While you let me sit still I appear to be all right, but when you ask me to do anything I am sure to spoil it, and if you trust me with a second thing I will as surely spoil that also. When a holy law is applied to a sinful man, then it is that his sinfulness comes out in full display.

God knows who I am; He knows that from head to foot I am full of sin; He knows that I am weakness incarnate; that I can do nothing. The trouble is that *I* do not know it. I admit that all men are sinners, and that therefore I am a sinner; but I imagine that I am not such a hopeless sinner as some. God must bring us all to the place where we see that we are utterly weak and helpless. While we say so, we do not wholly believe it, and God has to do something to convince us of the fact. Had it not been for the Law, we should never have known how weak we are. Paul had reached that point. He makes this clear when he says in Romans 7. 7: 'I had not known sin, except through the law: for I had not known coveting, except the law had said, Thou shalt not covet.' Whatever might be his experience with the rest of the Law, it was the tenth commandment, which literally translated is, 'Thou shalt not desire . . .', that found him out. There his total incapacity stared him in the face!

The more we try to keep the Law the more our weakness is manifest and the deeper we get into Romans 7, until it is clearly demonstrated to us that we are hopelessly weak. God knew it all along, but we did not, and so God had to bring us through painful experiences to a recognition of the fact. We need to have our weakness proved to ourselves beyond dispute. That is why God gave us the Law.

So we can say, reverently, that God never gave us the Law to keep: He gave us the Law to break! He well knew that we could not keep it. We are so bad that He asks no favour and makes no demands. Never has any man succeeded in making himself acceptable to God by means of the Law. Nowhere in the New Testament are men of faith told that they are to keep the Law; but it does say that the

Law was given so that there should be transgression. 'The law came in . . . that the trespass might abound' (Rom. 5. 20). The Law was given to make us law-breakers! No doubt I *am* a sinner in Adam; 'Howbeit, I had not known sin, except through the law: . . . for apart from the law sin is dead . . . but when the commandment came, sin revived, and I died' (Rom. 7. 7–9). The Law is that which exposes our true nature. Alas, we are so conceited, and think ourselves so strong, that God has to give us something to test us and prove how weak we are. At last we see it, and confess, 'I am a sinner through and through, and of myself I can do nothing whatever to please a holy God.'

No, the law was not given in the expectation that we would keep it. It was given in the full knowledge that we would break it; and when we have broken it so completely as to be convinced of our utter need, then the Law has served its purpose. It has been our schoolmaster to bring us to Christ, that in us He may Himself fulfil it (Gal. 3. 24).

Christ the end of the Law

In Romans 6 we saw how God delivered us from sin: in Romans 7 we see how He delivers us from the Law. Chapter 6 shows us the way of deliverance from sin in the picture of a master and his slave; chapter 7 shows us the way of deliverance from the Law in the picture of two husbands and a wife. The relation between sin and the sinner is that of master to slave; the relation between the Law and the sinner is that of husband to wife.

Notice first that in the picture by which, in Romans 7. 1–4, Paul illustrates our deliverance from the Law, there is only one woman, while there are two husbands. The woman is in a very difficult position, for she can only be wife of one of the two, and unfortunately she is married to the less desirable one. Let us make no mistake, the man to whom she is married is a good man; but the trouble lies here, that the husband and wife are totally unsuited to one another. He is a most particular man, accurate to a degree; she on the other hand is decidedly easy-going. With him all is definite and precise; with her all is casual and haphazard. He wants everything just so, while she takes things as they come. How could there be happiness in such a home?

And then that husband is so exacting! He is always making demands upon her. And yet one cannot find fault with him, for as a husband he has a right to expect something of his wife; and besides, all his demands are perfectly legitimate. There is nothing wrong with the man and nothing wrong with his demands; the trouble is that he has the wrong kind of wife to carry them out. The two cannot get on at all; theirs are utterly incompatible natures. Thus the poor woman is in great distress. She is fully aware that she often makes mistakes, but living with such a husband it seems as though *everything* she says and does is wrong! What hope is there for her? If only she were married to that other Man all would be well. He is no less exacting than her husband, but He also helps much. She would fain marry Him, but her husband is still alive. What can she do? She is 'bound by law to the husband' and unless he dies she cannot legitimately marry that other Man.

This picture is not drawn by me but by the apostle Paul. The first husband is the Law; the second husband is Christ; and you are the woman. The law requires much, but offers no help in the carrying out of its requirements. The Lord Jesus requires just as much, yea more (Matt. 5. 21–48), but what He requires from us He Himself carries out in us. The law makes demands and leaves us helpless to fulfil them; Christ makes demands, but He Himself fulfils in us the very demands He makes. Little wonder that the woman desires to be freed from the first husband that she may marry that other Man! But her only hope of release is through the death of her first husband, and he holds on to life most tenaciously. Indeed there is not the least prospect of his passing away. 'Till heaven and earth pass away, one jot or one tittle shall in no wise pass away from the law, till all things be accomplished' (Matt. 5. 18).

The Law is going to continue for all eternity. If the Law will never pass away, then how can I ever be united to Christ? How can I marry a second husband if my first husband resolutely refuses to die? There is one way out. If *he* will not die, *I* can die, and if I die the marriage relationship is dissolved. And that is exactly God's way of deliverance from the Law. The most important point to note in this section of Romans 7 is the transition from verse 3 to verse 4. Verses 1 to 3 show that the husband should die, but in verse 4 we see that in fact it is the woman who dies. The Law does not pass away, but I pass away, and by death I am freed from the Law. Let us realize clearly that the Law can never pass away. *God's righteous demands remain for ever*, and if I live I must meet those demands; but if I die the Law has lost its claim upon me. It cannot follow me beyond the grave.

Thus exactly the same principle operates in our deliverance from the Law as in our deliverance from sin. When I have died my old master, Sin, still continues to live, but his power over his slave extends as far as the grave and no further. He could ask me to do a hundred and one things when I was alive, but when I am dead he calls on me in vain. I am for ever freed from his tyranny. So it is with regard to the Law. While the woman lives she is bound to her husband, but with her death the marriage bond is dissolved and she is 'discharged from the law of her husband'. The Law may still make demands, but for me its power to enforce them is ended.

Now the vital question arises: 'How do I die?' And the preciousness of our Lord's work comes in just here: 'Ye also were made dead to the law through the body of Christ' (Rom. 7. 4). When Christ died His body was broken, and since God placed me in Him (1 Cor. 1. 30), I have been broken too. When He was crucified, I was crucified with Him. In the sight of God, His death included mine. On the hill of Calvary it was for ever done.

'Wherefore, my brethren, ye also were made dead to the law.' That woman's husband may be very well and strong, but if she dies, he may make as many demands upon her as he likes; it will not affect her in the slightest. Death has released her from all his claims. The all-inclusive death of Jesus Christ has for ever freed us from the Law.

But that is not all. Remember, our Lord did not remain in the grave. On the third day He rose again; and since we are still in Him we too are risen. The body of the Lord Jesus speaks not only of His death but of His resurrection, for His resurrection was a bodily resurrection. Thus 'through the body of Christ' we are not only 'dead to the law' but alive unto God.

God's purpose in uniting us to Christ was not merely

negative; it was gloriously positive—'that ye should be joined to another' (Rom. 7. 4). Death has dissolved the old marriage relationship, so that the woman, driven to despair by the constant demands of her former husband, who never lifted a little finger to help her carry them out, is now set free to marry the other Man, who with every demand He makes becomes in her the power for its fulfilment.

And what is the issue of this new union? 'That we might bring forth fruit unto God' (Rom. 7. 4). By the body of Christ, that foolish, sinful woman has died, but being united to Him in death she is united to Him also in resurrection, and in power of that resurrection, hers becomes a fruitful life. The life of the risen Lord within her empowers her for all the claims God's holiness makes upon her. The Law of God is not annulled; it is perfectly fulfilled, for the risen Lord Jesus now lives out His life in her, and His life is always well-pleasing to the Father.

What is the most obvious thing that happens when a woman marries? She changes her name. She no longer bears her own name but that of her husband; and she shares not his name only but his possessions also. Everything that belongs to him belongs now equally to her. All of a sudden she is amazingly enriched. And so it is when we are joined to Christ. All that is His becomes ours, and with His infinite resources at our disposal, we need never again fear that we shall be unable to meet all His demands.

Our end is God's beginning

Now that we have settled the doctrinal side of the question we must come down to practical issues, staying a little longer with the negative aspect and keeping the positive for our next chapter. What does it mean in everyday life to be delivered from the Law? At risk of a little overstatement I reply: It means that from henceforth I am going to do nothing whatever for God; I am never again going to try to please Him. 'What a doctrine!' you exclaim. 'What awful heresy! You cannot possibly mean that!'

But remember, if I try to please God 'in the flesh', then immediately I place myself under the Law. I broke the Law; the Law pronounced the death sentence; the sentence was executed, and now by death I—the carnal 'I' (Rom. 7. 14)— have been set free from all its claims. There is still a Law of God, and now there is in fact a 'new commandment' that is infinitely more exacting than the old, but, praise God, its demands are being met, for it is Christ who now fulfils them; it is Christ who works in me what is well-pleasing to God. '*I* came . . . to fulfil (the law)' were His words (Matt. 5. 17). Thus it is that Paul, from the ground of resurrection, can say: 'Work out your own salvation with fear and trembling; for it is God which worketh in you both to will and to work, for his good pleasure' (Phil. 2. 12, 13).

It is God which worketh in you. Deliverance from law does not mean that we are free from doing the will of God. It certainly does not mean that we are going to be lawless. Very much the reverse! What it does mean however is that we are free from doing that will *as of ourselves.* Being fully persuaded that we cannot do it, we cease trying to please God *from the ground of the old man.* Having at last reached the point of utter despair in ourselves so that we cease even to try, we put our trust in the Lord to manifest His resurrection life in us.

Let me illustrate by what I have seen in my own country. In China, most bearers can carry a load of salt weighing 120 kilos, a few even as much as 250 kilos. Now along comes a man who can carry only 120 kilos, and here is a load of 250 kilos. He knows perfectly well he cannot carry it, and if he is wise he will say: 'I won't touch it!' But the temptation to try is ingrained in human nature, so although he cannot possibly carry it, nevertheless he has a go. As a youngster I used to amuse myself watching ten or twenty of these fellows come along and try, though every one of them knew he could not possibly manage it. In the end he must give up and make way for the man who could.

The sooner we too give up trying the better, for if we monopolize the task, there is left no room for the Holy Spirit. But if we say: 'I'll not do it; I'll trust Thee to do it for me', then we shall find that a Power stronger than ourselves is carrying us through.

In 1923 I met a famous Canadian evangelist. I had said in an address something along the above lines, and as we walked back to his home afterwards he remarked: 'The note of Romans 7 is seldom sounded nowadays; it is good to hear it again. The day I was delivered from the Law was a day of heaven on earth. After being a Christian for years I was still trying my best to please God, but the more I tried the more I failed. I regarded God as the greatest Demander in the universe, but I found myself impotent to fulfil the least of His demands. Suddenly one day, as I read Romans 7, light dawned and I saw that I had not only been delivered from sin but from the Law as well. In my amazement I jumped up and said: "Lord, are you really making no demands on me? Then I need do nothing more for You!"'

God's requirements have not altered, but we are not the ones to meet them. Praise God, He is the Lawgiver on the Throne, and He is the Lawkeeper in my heart. He who gave the Law, Himself keeps it. He makes the demands, but He also meets them. My friend could well jump up and shout when he found he had nothing to do, and all who make a like discovery can do the same. As long as we are trying to do anything, He can do nothing. It is because of our trying that we fail and fail and fail. God wants to demonstrate to us that we can do nothing at all, and until that is fully recognized our despair and disillusion will never cease.

A brother who was trying to struggle into victory remarked to me one day, 'I do not know why I am so weak.' 'The trouble with you', I said, 'is that you are weak enough not to do the will of God, but you are not weak enough to keep out of things altogether. You are still not weak enough. When you are reduced to utter weakness and are persuaded that you can do nothing whatever, then God will do everything.' We all need to come to the point where we say: 'Lord. I am unable to do anything for Thee, but I trust Thee to do everything in me.'

I was once staying in a place in China with some twenty other brothers. There was inadequate provision for bathing in the home where we stayed, so we went for a daily plunge in the river. On one occasion a brother got cramp in his leg, and I suddenly saw he was sinking fast, so I motioned to another brother, who was an expert swimmer, to hasten to his rescue. But to my astonishment he made no move. Growing desperate I cried out: 'Don't you see the man is drowning?' and the other brothers, about as agitated as I was, shouted vigorously too. But our good swimmer still did not move. Calm and collected, he remained just where he was, apparently postponing the unwelcome task. Meantime the voice of the poor drowning brother grew fainter and his efforts feebler. In my heart I said: 'I hate that man! Think of his letting a brother drown before his very eyes and not going to the rescue!'

But when the man was actually sinking, with a few swift strokes the swimmer was at his side, and both were soon safely ashore. Nevertheless, when I got an opportunity, I aired my views. 'I have never seen any Christian who loved his life quite as much as you do,' I said. 'Think of the distress you would have saved that brother if you had considered yourself a little less and him a little more.' But the swimmer, I soon discovered, knew his business better than I did. 'Had I gone earlier,' he said, 'he would have clutched me so fast that both of us would have gone under. A drowning man cannot be saved until he is utterly exhausted and ceases to make the slightest effort to save himself.'

Do you see the point? When we give up the case, then God will take it up. He is waiting until we are at an end of our resources and can do nothing more for ourselves. God has condemned all that is of the old creation and consigned it to the Cross. The flesh profiteth *nothing*! God has declared it to be fit only for death. If we truly believe that, then we shall confirm God's verdict by abandoning all fleshly efforts to please him. For our every attempt to do His will is a denial of His declaration in the Cross that we are utterly powerless to do so. It is a misunderstanding on the one hand of God's demands and on the other hand of the source of supply.

We see the Law, and we think that we must meet its

claims, but we need to remember that, though the Law in itself is all right, it will be all wrong if it is applied to the wrong person. The 'wretched man' of Romans 7 tried to meet the claims of God's law *himself*, and that was the cause of his trouble. The repeated use of the little word 'I' in this chapter gives the clue to the failure. 'The good which I would I do not: but the evil which I would not, that I practise' (Rom. 7. 19). There was a fundamental misconception in this man's mind. He thought God was asking *him* to keep the Law, so of course he was trying to do so, whereas God was requiring no such thing of him. What was the result? Far from doing what pleased God, he found himself doing what displeased Him. In his very efforts to do the will of God, he did exactly the opposite of what he knew to be His will.

I thank God!

Romans 6 deals with 'the body of sin', Romans 7 with 'the body of this death' (6. 6; 7, 24). In chapter 6 the whole question before us is sin; in chapter 7 the whole question before us is death. What is the difference between the body of sin and the body of death? In regard to sin (that is, to whatever displeases God) I have a body of sin—a body, that is to say, which is actively engaged in sin. But in regard to the Law of God (that is, to that which expresses the will of God) I have a body of death. My activity in regard to sin makes my body a body of sin; my failure in regard to God's will makes my body a body of death. In regard to all that is wicked, worldly and Satanic I am, in my nature, wholly positive; but in regard to all that pertains to holiness and heaven and God I am wholly negative.

Have you discovered the truth of that in your life? It is no good merely to discover it in Romans 6 and 7. Have you discovered that you carry the encumbrance of a lifeless body in regard to God's will? You have no difficulty in speaking about worldly matters, but when you try to speak for the Lord you are tongue-tied; when you try to pray you feel sleepy; when you try to do something for the Lord you feel unwell. You can do anything but that which relates to God's will. There is something in this body that does not harmonize with the will of God.

What does death mean? We may illustrate from a well-known verse in the first letter to the Corinthians: 'For this cause many among you are weak and sickly, and not a few sleep' (1 Cor. 11. 30). Death is weakness produced to its extremity—weakness, sickness, death. Death means utter weakness; it means you are weak to such a point that you can become no weaker. That I have a body of death in relation to God's will means that I am so weak when it comes to serving God, so utterly weak, that I am reduced to a point of dire helplessness. 'O wretched man that I am!' cried Paul, 'who shall deliver me out of the body of this death?' and it is good when anyone cries out as he did. There is nothing more musical in the ears of the Lord. This cry is the most spiritual and the most scriptural cry a man can utter. He only utters it when he knows he can do nothing, and gives up making any further resolutions. Up to this point, every time he failed, he made a new resolution and doubled and redoubled his will-power. At last he discovers there is no use in his making up his mind any more, and he cries out in desperation: 'O wretched man that I am!' Like someone who awakes suddenly to find himself in a burning building, his cry is now for help, for he has come to the point where he despairs of himself.

Have you despaired of yourself, or do you hope that if you read and pray more you will be a better Christian? Bible-reading and prayer are not wrong, and God forbid that we should suggest that they are, but *it is wrong to trust even in them for victory.* Our help is in Him who is the object of that reading and prayer. Our trust must be in Christ alone. Happily the 'wretched man' does not merely deplore his wretchedness; he asks a fine question, namely: 'Who shall deliver me?' '*Who?*' Hitherto he has looked for some *thing*; now his hope is in a Person. Hitherto he has looked within for a solution to his problem; now he looks beyond himself for a Saviour. He no longer puts forth self-effort; all his expectation is now in Another.

How did we obtain forgiveness of sins? Was it by reading, praying, almsgiving, and so on? No, we looked to the Cross, believing in what the Lord Jesus had done; and deliverance from sin becomes ours on exactly the same principle, nor is it otherwise with the question of pleasing God. In the matter of forgiveness we look to Christ on the Cross; in the matter of deliverance from sin and of doing the will of God we look to Christ in our hearts. For the one we depend on what He has done; for the other we depend on what He will do in us; but in regard to both, our dependence is on Him alone. From start to finish, He is the One who does it all.

At the time when the Epistle to the Romans was written a murderer was punished in a peculiar and terrible manner. The dead body of the one murdered was tied to the living body of the murderer, head to head, hand to hand, foot to foot, and the living one was bound to the dead one till death. The murderer could go where he pleased, but wherever he went he had to drag the corpse of that murdered man with him. Could punishment be more appalling? Yet this is the illustration Paul now uses. It is as though he were bound to a dead body—his own 'body of death'—and unable to get free. Wherever he goes he is hampered by this terrible burden. At last he can bear it no longer and cries: 'O wretched man that I am! who shall deliver me . . .?' And then, in a flash of illumination, his cry of despair changes to a song of praise. He has found the answer to his question. 'I thank God through Jesus Christ our Lord' (Rom. 7. 25).

We know that justification is ours through the Lord Jesus and requires no work on our part, but we think sanctification is dependent on our own efforts. We know we can receive forgiveness only by entire reliance on the Lord; yet we believe we can obtain deliverance by doing something ourselves. We fear that if we do nothing, nothing will happen. After salvation the old habit of 'doing' reasserts itself and we begin our old self-efforts again. Then God's word comes afresh to us: 'It is finished' (John 19. 30). He has done everything on the Cross for our forgiveness and He will do everything in us for our deliverance. In both cases *He* is the doer. 'It is *God* that worketh in you.'

The first words of the delivered man are very precious— 'I thank God'. If someone gives you a cup of water you thank the person who gave it, not someone else. Why did Paul say 'Thank God'? Because God was the One who did everything. Had it been Paul who did it, he would have said, 'Thank Paul'. But he saw that Paul was a 'wretched man' and that God alone could meet his need; so he said, 'Thank God'. God wants to do all the work, for He must have all the glory. If we did some of it, then we could claim some of the glory ourselves. But God must have it all. He does all the work from beginning to end.

What we have said in this chapter might seem negative and unpractical if we were to stop at this point, as though the Christian life were a matter of sitting still and waiting for something to happen. Of course it is very far from being so. All who truly live it know it to be a matter of very positive and active faith in Christ and in an altogether new principle of life—the law of the Spirit of life. We are now going to look at the efforts in us of this new life principle.

10

The Path of Progress:
Walking in the Spirit

COMING now to Romans 8 we may first summarize the argument of our second section of the letter from chapter 5. 12 to chapter 8. 39 in two phrases, each containing a contrast and each marking an aspect of Christian experience. They are:

Romans 5. 12 to 6. 23: 'In Adam' and 'in Christ'.
Romans 7. 1 to 8. 39: 'In the flesh' and 'in the spirit'.

We need to understand the relationship of these four things. The former two are 'objective' and set forth our *position*, firstly as we were by nature and secondly, as we now are by faith in the redemptive work of Christ. The latter two are 'subjective' and relate to our *walk* as a matter of practical experience. Scripture makes it clear that the first two give us only a part of the picture and that the second two are required to complete it. We think it enough to be 'in Christ', but we learn now that we must also walk 'in the spirit' (Rom. 8. 9). The frequent occurrence of 'the Spirit' in the early part of Romans 8 serves to emphasize this further important lesson of the Christian life.

The flesh and the Spirit

The flesh is linked with Adam; the Spirit with Christ. Leaving aside now as settled the question of whether we are in Adam or in Christ, the time has come to ask ourselves: Am I living in the flesh or in the Spirit?

To live in the flesh is to do something 'out from'[1] myself as in Adam. It is to derive strength from the old natural source of life that I inherited from him, so that I enjoy in experience all Adam's very complete provision for sinning which all of us have found so effective. Now the same is true of what is in Christ. To enjoy in experience what is true of me as in Him, I must learn what it is to walk in the Spirit. It is a historic fact that in Christ my old man was crucified, and it is a present fact that I am blessed 'with every spiritual blessing in the heavenly places in Christ' (Eph. 1. 3); but if I do not live in the Spirit, then my life may be quite a contradiction of the fact that I am in Christ, for what is true of me in Him is not expressed in me. I may recognize that I am in Christ, but I may also have to face the fact that, for example, my old temper is very much in evidence.

What is the trouble? It is that I am holding the truth merely objectively, whereas what is true objectively must be made true subjectively; and that is brought about as I live in the Spirit.

---

[1] The author has in mind the Greek preposition *ek*, the sense of which is not easily conveyed by any single English word.—Ed.

Not only am I in Christ, but Christ is in me. And just as, physically, a man cannot live and work in water but only in air, so, spiritually, Christ dwells and manifests Himself not in terms of 'flesh' but of 'spirit'. Therefore, if I live 'after the flesh', I find that what is mine in Christ is, so to say, held in suspense in me. Though *in fact* I am in Christ, yet if I live in the flesh—that is, in my own strength and under my own direction—then *in experience* I find to my dismay that it is what is in Adam that manifests itself in me. If I would know in experience all that is in Christ, then I must learn to live in the Spirit.

Living in the Spirit means that I trust the Holy Spirit to do in me what I cannot do myself. This life is completely different from the life I would naturally live of myself. Each time I am faced with a new demand from the Lord, I look to Him to do in me what He requires of me. It is not a case of trying but of trusting; not of struggling but of resting in Him. If I have a hasty temper, impure thoughts, a quick tongue or a critical spirit, I shall not set out with a determined effort to change myself, but instead, reckoning myself dead in Christ to these things, I shall look to the Spirit of God to produce in me the needed purity of humility or meekness, confident that He will do so. This is what it means to 'stand still, and see the salvation of the Lord, which he will work for you' (Exod. 14. 13).

Some of you have no doubt had an experience something like the following. You have been asked to go and see a friend, and you knew the friend was not very friendly, but you trusted the Lord to see you through. You told Him before you set out that in yourself you could not but fail, and you asked Him for all that was needed. Then, to your surprise, you did not feel at all irritated, though your friend was far from gracious. On your return you thought over the experience and marvelled that you had kept so calm, and you wondered if you would be just as calm next time. You were amazed at yourself and sought an explanation. This is the explanation: *the Holy Spirit carried you through.*

Unfortunately we only have this kind of experience once in a while, but it should be ours constantly. When the Holy Spirit takes things in hand, there is no need for strain on our part. It is not a case of clenching our teeth and taking a grip on ourselves, and thinking that thus we have controlled ourselves beautifully and have had a glorious victory. No, where there is real victory, it is not fleshly effort that carries us through, but the Lord.

The object of temptation is always to get us to do something. During the first three months of the Japanese war in China we lost a great many tanks, and so were unable to deal with the Japanese armour, until the following scheme was devised. A single shot would be fired at a Japanese tank by one of our snipers in ambush. After a considerable lapse of time the first shot would be followed by a second; then, after a further silence, by another shot; until the tank driver, eager to locate the source of the disturbance, would pop his head out to look around. The next shot, carefully aimed, would put an end to him.

As long as he remained under cover he was perfectly safe. The whole scheme was devised to bring him out into the open. In just the same way, Satan's temptations are not designed primarily to make us do something particularly sinful, but merely to cause us to act in our energy; and as soon as we step out of our hiding-place to do something on that basis, he has gained the victory over us. But if we do not move, if we do not come out of the cover of Christ into the realm of the flesh, then he cannot get us.

The divine way of victory does not therefore permit of our doing anything at all—anything, that is to say, outside of Christ. This is because as soon as we move we run into danger, for our natural inclinations carry us in the wrong direction. Where, then, are we to look for help? Turn now to Galatians 5. 17: 'The flesh lusteth against the Spirit, and the Spirit against the flesh.' This tells us where the real tussle takes place. The fight with the flesh is not ours but the Holy Spirit's, 'for these are contrary the one to the other', and it is He, not we, who meets and deals with it. What is the result? 'That ye may not do the things that ye would.'

I think we have often failed to grasp the full import of that last clause. Let us consider if for a moment. What 'would we do' naturally? We would move off on some course of action dictated by our own instincts and apart from the will of God. The effect, therefore, of our refusal to come out of cover and act out from ourselves is that the Holy Spirit is free to do His work—free, that is, to meet and deal with the flesh in us, so that in fact we do not do what we naturally would do. Instead of going off on a plan and course of our own, we find our satisfaction in *His* perfect plan. Hence the command is a positive one: 'Walk by the Spirit, and ye shall not fulfil the lust of the flesh' (Gal. 5. 16). If we live in the Spirit, if we walk by faith in the risen Christ, we can truly 'stand aside' while the Spirit gains new victories over the flesh every day. He has been given to us to take charge of this business. Our victory lies in hiding in Christ, and in counting in simple trust upon His Holy Spirit within us to overcome our fleshly lusts with His own new desires. The Cross has been given to procure salvation for us; the Spirit has been given to produce salvation in us. Christ risen and ascended is the basis of our salvation; Christ in our hearts by the Spirit is its power.

Christ our life

'I thank God through Jesus Christ'! That exclamation of Paul's is fundamentally the same in its import as his other words in Galatians 2. 20 which we have taken as the key to our study: 'I live; and yet no longer I, *but Christ*'. We saw how prominent is the word 'I' throughout Romans 7, culminating in the agonized cry: 'O wretched man that *I* am!' Then follows the shout of deliverance: 'Thank God . . . *Jesus Christ*'! and it is clear that the discovery Paul has made is this, that *the life we live is the life of Christ alone*. We think of the Christian life as a 'changed life' but it is not that. What God offers us is an 'exchanged life', a 'substituted life', and Christ is our Substitute within. 'I live; and yet no longer I, but Christ liveth in me.' This life is not something which we ourselves have to produce. It is Christ's own life reproduced in us.

How many Christians believe in 'reproduction' in this sense, as something more than regeneration? Regeneration means that the life of Christ is planted in us by the Holy Spirit at our new birth. 'Reproduction' goes further: it means that that new life grows and becomes manifest progressively in us, until the very likeness of Christ begins to be reproduced in our lives. That is what Paul means when he speaks of his travail for the Galatians 'until Christ be formed in you' (Gal. 4. 19).

Let me illustrate with another story. I once stayed in America in the home of a saved couple who, soon after my arrival, requested me to pray for them. I inquired the cause of their trouble. 'Oh, Mr. Nee, we have been in a bad way lately,' they confessed. 'We are so easily irritated by the children, and during the past few weeks we have both lost our tempers several times a day. We are really dishonouring the Lord. Will you ask Him to give us patience?' 'That is the one thing I cannot do,' I said. 'What do you mean?' they asked. 'I mean that one thing is certain,' I answered, 'and that is that God is not going to answer your prayer.' At that they said in amazement, 'Do you mean to tell us we have gone so far that God is not willing to hear us when we ask Him to make us patient?' 'No, I do not mean quite that, but I would like to ask you if *you* have ever prayed in this respect. You have. But did God answer? No! Do you know why? Because you have no need of patience.' Then the wife's eyes flashed. 'What are you saying?' she burst out. 'We do not need patience, and yet we get irritated the whole day long! It doesn't make sense. What *do* you mean?' Quietly I replied, 'It is not patience you have need of. It is Christ.'

And this is the truth. God will not give me humility or patience or holiness or love as separate gifts of His grace. He is not a retailer dispensing grace to us in packets, measuring out some patience to the impatient, some love to the unloving, some meekness to the proud, in quantities that we take and work on as a kind of capital. He has given only one gift to meet all our need: His Son Christ Jesus. As I look to Him to live out His life in me, He will be humble and patient and loving and everything else I need—in my stead. Remember the word in the first Epistle of John: 'God gave unto us eternal life, and this life is in his Son. He that hath the Son hath the life; and he that hath not the Son of God hath not the life' (1 John 5. 11, 12). The life of God is not given us as a separate item; the life of God is given us in the Son. It is 'eternal life in Christ Jesus our Lord' (Rom. 6. 23). Our relationship to the Son is our relationship to the life.

It is a blessed thing to discover the difference between Christian graces and Christ: to know the difference between meekness and Christ, between patience and Christ, between love and Christ. Remember again what is said in 1 Corinthians 1. 30: 'Christ Jesus . . . was made unto us wisdom from God, and righteousness and sanctification, and redemption.' The common conception of sanctification is that every item of the life should be holy; but that is not holiness, it is the fruit of holiness. Holiness is Christ. It is the Lord Jesus being made over to us to *be* that. So you can put in anything there; love, humility, power, self-control. Today there is a call for patience: He is our patience! Tomorrow the call may be for purity: He is our purity! He is the answer to every need. That is why Paul speaks of 'the fruit of the Spirit' as one (Gal. 5. 22) and not of 'fruits' as separate items. God has given us His Holy Spirit, and when love is needed the fruit of the Spirit is love; when joy is needed the fruit of the Spirit is joy. It is always true. It does not matter what your personal deficiency, or whether it be a hundred and one different things, God has always one sufficient answer, His Son Jesus Christ, and He is the answer to every human need.

How can we know more of Christ in this way? Only by way of an increasing awareness of need. Some are afraid to discover deficiency in themselves, and so they never grow.

Growth *in grace* is the only sense in which we can grow, and grace, we have said, is God doing something for us. We all have the same Christ dwelling within, but revelation of some new need will lead us spontaneously to trust Him to live out His life in us in that particular. Greater capacity means greater enjoyment of God's supply. Another letting go, a fresh trusting in Christ, and another stretch of land is conquered. 'Christ my life' is the secret of enlargement.

We have spoken of trying and trusting, and the difference between the two. Believe me, it is the difference between heaven and hell. It is not something just to be talked over as a satisfying thought; it is stark reality. 'Lord, I cannot do it, therefore I will no longer try to do it.' This is the point most of us fall short of. 'Lord, I cannot; therefore I will take my hands off; from now on I trust *Thee* for that.' We refuse to act; we depend on Him to do so, and then we enter fully and joyfully into the action He initiates. It is not passivity; it is a most active life, trusting the Lord like that; drawing life from Him, taking Him to be our very life, letting Him live His life in us as we go forth in His Name.

The law of the Spirit of life

'There is therefore now no condemnation to them that are in Christ Jesus, who walk not after the flesh, but after the Spirit. For the law of the Spirit of life in Christ Jesus hath made me free from the law of sin and death' (Rom. 8. 1, 2, A.V.).

It is in chapter 8 that Paul presents to us in detail the positive side of life in the Spirit. 'There is therefore now no condemnation', he begins, and this statement may at first seem out of place here. Surely condemnation was met by the

Blood, through which we found peace with God and salvation from wrath (Rom. 5. 1, 9). But there are two kinds of condemnation, namely, that before God and that before myself (just as earlier we saw there are two kinds of peace) and the second may at times seem to us even more awful than the first. When I see that the Blood of Christ has satisfied God, then I know my sins are forgiven, and there is for me no more condemnation before God. Yet I may still be knowing defeat, and the sense of inward condemnation on this account may be very real, as Romans 7 shows. But if I have learned to live by Christ as my life, than I have discovered the secret of victory, and, praise God, in this inward sense also, 'there is therefore now no condemnation.' 'The mind of the spirit is life and peace' (Rom. 8. 6), and this becomes my experience as I learn to walk in the Spirit. With peace in my heart I have no time to feel condemned, but only to praise Him who leads me on from one fresh victory to another.

But what lay behind my sense of condemnation? Was it not the experience of defeat and the sense of helplessness to do anything about it? Before I saw that Christ is my life, I laboured under a constant sense of handicap. Limitation dogged my steps; I felt disabled at every turn; I was always crying out, 'I cannot do this! I cannot do that!' Try as I would, I had to acknowledge that I 'cannot please God' (Rom. 8. 8). But there is no 'I cannot' in Christ. Now it is: 'I can do all things in him that strengtheneth me' (Phil. 4. 13).

How can Paul be so daring? On what ground does he declare that he is now free from limitation and 'can do all things'? Here is his answer: 'For the law of the Spirit of life in Christ Jesus made me free from the law of sin and of death' (Rom. 8. 2). Why is there no more condemnation? For . . .' says Paul. There is a reason for it; there is something definite to account for it. And the reason is that a law called 'the law of the Spirit of life' has proved stronger than another law called 'the law of sin and of death'. What are these laws? How do they operate? And what is the difference between sin and the law of sin, and between death and the law of death?

First let us ask ourselves, What is a law? Strictly speaking, a law is a generalization examined until it is proved that there is no exception. We might define it more simply as something which happens over and over again. Each time the thing happens it happens in the same way. We can illustrate this both from statutory and from natural law. For example, in Britain, if I drive a car on the right hand side of the road, the traffic police will stop me. Why? Because it is against the law of the land. If *you* do it you will be stopped too. Why? For the same reason that I would be stopped: it is against the law, and the law makes no exceptions. It is something which happens repeatedly and unfailingly. Or again, we all know what is meant by gravity. If I drop my handkerchief in London it falls to the ground. That is the effect of gravity. But the same is true if I drop it in New York or Hong Kong. No matter where I let it go, gravity operates, and it always produces the same results. Whenever the same conditions prevail the same effects are seen. There is thus a 'law' of gravity.

Now what of the law of sin and death? If someone passes an unkind remark about me, at once something goes wrong inside me. That is not law; that is sin. But if, when different people pass unkind remarks, the same 'something' goes wrong inside, then I discern a law within—a law of sin. Like the law of gravity, it is something constant. It always works the same way. And so too with the law of death. Death, we have said, is weakness produced to its limit. Weakness is 'I cannot'. Now if when I try to please God in this particular matter I find I cannot, and if when I try to please Him in that other thing I again find I cannot, then I discern a law at work. There is not only sin in me but a *law* of sin; there is not only death in me but a *law* of death.

Then again, not only is gravity a law in the sense that it is constant, admitting of no exception, but, unlike the rule of the road, it is a 'natural' law and not the subject of discussion and decision but of discovery. The law is there, and the handkerchief 'naturally' drops of itself without any help from me. And the 'law' discovered by the man in Romans 7. 23 is just like that. It is a law of sin and of death, opposed to that which is good, and crippling the man's will to do good. He 'naturally' sins according to the 'law of sin' in his members. He wills to be different, but that law in him is relentless, and no human will can resist it. So this brings me to the question: How can I be set free from the law of sin and death? I need deliverance from sin, and still more do I need deliverance from death, but most of all I need deliverance from the *law* of sin and of death. How can I be delivered from the constant repetition of weakness and failure? In order to answer this question, let us follow out our two illustrations further.

One of our great burdens in China used to be the *likin* tax, a law which none could escape, originating in the Ch'in Dynasty and operating right down to our own day. It was an inland tax on the transit of goods, applied throughout the empire and having numerous barriers for collection, and officers enjoying very large powers. The result was that the charge on goods passing through several provinces might become very heavy indeed. But a few years ago a second law came into operation which set aside the *likin* law. Can you imagine the feelings of relief in those who had suffered under the old law? Now there was no need to think or hope or pray; the new law was already there and had delivered us from the old law. No longer was there need to think before-hand what one would say if one met a *likin* officer tomorrow!

And as with the law of the land, so it is with natural law. How can the law of gravity be annulled? With regard to my handkerchief that law is at work clearly enough, pulling it down, but I have only to place my hand under the handkerchief and it does not drop. Why? The law is still there. I do not deal with the law of gravity; in fact I *cannot* deal with the law of gravity. Then why does my handkerchief not fall to the ground? Because there is a power keeping it from doing so. The law is there, but another law superior to it is operating to overcome it, namely the law of life. Gravity can do its utmost, but the handkerchief will not drop, because another law is working against the law of gravity to maintain it there. We have all seen the tree which was once a small seed fallen between the slabs of a paving, and which has grown until heavy stone blocks have been lifted by the power of the life within it. That is what we mean by the triumph of one law over another.

In just such a manner God delivers us from one law by introducing another law. The law of sin and death is there all the time, but God has put another law into operation—

the law of the Spirit of life in Christ Jesus, and that law is strong enough to deliver us from the law of sin and death. It is, you see, a law of *life in Christ*—the resurrection life that in Him has met death in all its forms and triumphed over it (Eph. 1. 19, 20). The Lord Jesus dwells in our hearts in the person of His Holy Spirit, and if, committing ourselves to Him, we let Him have a clear way, we shall find His new law of life superseding that old law. We shall learn what it is to be kept, not by our own unsufficient strength, but 'by the power of God' (1 Peter 1. 5).

The manifestation of the law of life

Let us seek to make this practical. We touched earlier on the matter of our will in relation to the things of God. Even older Christians do not realize how great a part will-power plays in their lives. That was part of Paul's trouble in Romans 7. His will was good, but all his actions contradicted it, and however much he made up his mind and set himself to please God, it led him only into worse darkness. 'I *would* do good', but 'I *am* carnal, sold under sin'. That is the point. Like a car without petrol, that has to be pushed and that comes to a standstill as soon as it is left alone, many Christians endeavour to drive themselves by will-power, and then think the Christian life a most exhausting and bitter one. Some even force themselves to do Christian things because others do them, while admitting they have no meaning to them. They force themselves to be what they are not, and it is worse than trying to make water run up-hill. For after all, the very highest point the will can reach is that of willingness (Matt. 26. 41).

If we have to exert so much effort in our Christian living, it simply says that we are not really like that at all. We don't need to force ourselves to speak our native language. In fact we only have to exert will-power in order to do things we do *not* do naturally. We may do them for a time, but the law of sin and death wins in the end. We may be able to say. 'To will is present with me, and I perform that which is good for two weeks', but eventually we shall have to confess, 'How to perform it I know not'. No, what I already am I do not long to be. If I 'would' it is because I am not.

You ask, Why do men use will-power to try to please God? There may be two reasons. They may of course never have experienced the new birth, in which case they have no new life to draw upon; or they may have been born again and the life be there, but they have not learned to trust in that life. It is this lack of understanding that results in habitual failure and sinning, bringing them to the place where they almost cease to believe in the possibility of anything better.

But because we have not believed fully, that does not mean that the feeble life we intermittently experience is all God has given us. Romans 6. 23 states that 'the free gift of God is eternal life in Christ Jesus our Lord', and now in Romans 8. 2 we read that 'the law of the Spirit of life in Christ Jesus' has come to our aid. So Romans 8. 2 speaks not of a new gift but of the life already referred to in Romans 6. 23. In other words, it is a *a new revelation of what we already have*. I feel I cannot emphasize this too much. It is not something fresh from God's hand, but a new unveiling of what He has already given. It is a new discovery of a work already done in Christ, for the words 'made me free' are in the past tense. If I really see this and put my faith in Him, there is no absolute necessity for the experience of Romans 7—either the unhappy struggle and failure or the fruitless display of will-power—to be repeated in me.

If we will let go our own wills and trust Him, we shall not fall to the ground and break, but we shall fall into a *different law*, the law of the Spirit of life. For God has given us not only life but a law of life. And just as the law of gravity is a natural law and not the result of human legislation, so the law of life is a 'natural' law, similar in principle to the law that keeps our heart beating or that controls the movements of our eyelids. There is no need for us to think about our eyes, or to decide that we must blink every so often to keep them cleansed; and still less do we bring our will to bear upon our heart-beat. Indeed to do so might rather harm than help it. No, so long as it has life it works spontaneously. Our wills only interfere with the law of life. I discovered that fact once in the following way.

I used to suffer from sleeplessness. Once after several sleepless nights, when I had prayed much about it and exhausted all my resources, I confessed at length to God that the fault must lie with me and asked to be shown where. I said to God: 'I demand an explanation.' His answer was: 'Believe in nature's laws.' Sleep is as much a law as hunger is, and I realized that though I had never thought of worrying whether I would get hungry or not, I had been worrying about sleeping. I had been trying to help nature, and that is the chief trouble with most sufferers from sleeplessness. But now I trusted not only God but God's law of nature, and very soon slept well.

Should we not read the Bible? Of course we should or

our spiritual life will suffer. But that should not mean forcing ourselves to read. There is a new law in us which gives
us a hunger for God's Word. *Then* half an hour can be more
profitable than five hours of forced reading. And it is the
same with giving, with preaching, with testimony. Forced
preaching is apt to result in preaching a warm gospel with
a cold heart, and we all know what men mean by 'cold
charity'.

If we will let ourselves live in the new law, we shall be
less conscious of the old. It is still there, but it is no longer
governing and we are no longer in its grip. That is why the
Lord says in Matthew 6: 'Behold the birds . . . Consider the
lilies.' If we could ask the birds whether they were not
afraid of the law of gravity, how would they reply? They
would say: 'We never heard the name of Newton. We know
nothing about his law. We fly because it is the law of our life
to fly.' Not only is there in them a life with the power of
flight, but that life has a law which enables these living
creatures, quite spontaneously and consistently, to overcome the law of gravity. Yet gravity remains. If you get up
early one morning when the cold is intense and the snow
thick on the ground, and there is a dead sparrow in the
courtyard, you are reminded at once of the persistence of
that law. But while birds live they overcome it, and the life
within them is what dominates their consciousness.

God has been truly gracious to us. He has given us this
new law of the Spirit, and for us to 'fly' is no longer a question of our will but of His life. Have you noticed what a trial
it is to make an impatient Christian patient? To require
patience of him is enough to make him ill with depression.
But God has never told us to force ourselves to be what we

are not naturally; to try, by taking thought, to add to our spiritual stature. Worrying may possibly decrease a man's height, but it certainly never added anything to it. 'Be not anxious', are His words. 'Consider the lilies, . . . they *grow*.' He is directing our attention to the new law of life in us. Oh, for a new appreciation of the life that is ours!

What a precious discovery this is! It can make altogether new men of us, for it operates in the smallest things as well as in the bigger ones. It checks us when, for example, we put out a hand to look at a book in someone else's room, reminding us that we have not asked permission and have no right to do so. We cannot, the Holy Spirit tells us, encroach thus upon the rights of others.

Once I was talking to a Christian friend and he turned to me and said: 'Do you know, I believe that if anyone is willing to live by the law of the Spirit of life, such a man will become truly refined.' 'What do you mean?' I asked. He replied: 'That law has the power to make a man a perfect gentleman. Some scornfully say: "You can't blame those people for the way they act; they are just country folk and have no educational advantages." But the real question is, Have they the life of the Lord within? For I tell you, *that* life can say to them: "Your voice is too loud", or, "That laughter was not right", or, "Your motive in passing that remark was wrong." In a thousand details the Spirit of life can tell them how to act, so producing in them a true refinement. There is no such inherent power in education.' And yet my friend was himself an educationist!

But it is true. Take, for example, talkativeness. Are you a person of too many words? When you stay with people, do you say to yourself: 'What shall I do? I am a Christian; but if I am to glorify the name of the Lord, I simply *must not* talk so much. So today let me be extra careful to hold myself in check'? And for an hour or two you succeed—until on some pretext you lose control and, before you know where you are, find yourself once again in difficulty with your garrulous tongue. Yes, let us be fully assured that the will is useless here. For me to exhort you to exercise your will in this matter would be but to offer you the vain religion of the world, not the life in Christ Jesus. For consider again: a talkative person remains just that, though he keep silent all day, for there is a 'natural' law of talkativeness governing him (or her!), just as a peach tree is a peach tree whether or not it bears peaches. But as Christians we discover a new law in us, the law of the Spirit of life, which transcends all else and which has already delivered us from the 'law' of our talkativeness. If, believing the Lord's Word, we yield ourselves to that new law, *it* will tell us when we should stop talking— or not start!—and *it* will empower us to do so. On that basis you can go to your friend's house for two or three hours, or stay for two or three days, and experience no difficulty. On your return you will just thank God for His new law of life.

It is this spontaneous life that is the Christian life. It manifests itself in love for the unlovely—for the brother whom on natural grounds we would not like and certainly could not love. It works on the basis of what the Lord sees of possibility in that brother. 'Lord, *You* see he is lovable and *You* love him. Love him, now, through me!' And it manifests itself in reality of life—in a true genuineness of moral character. There is too much hypocrisy in the lives of Christians, too much play-acting. Nothing takes away from the effectiveness of Christian witness as does a pretence of something that is not really there, for the man in the street unfailingly penetrates such a disguise in the end, and finds us out for what we are. Yes, pretence gives way to reality when we trust the law of life.

The fourth step: 'walk . . . after the Spirit'

'For what the law could not do, in that it was weak through the flesh, God, sending his own Son in the likeness of sinful flesh and as an offering for sin, condemned sin in the flesh: that the ordinance of the law might be fulfilled in us, who walk not after the flesh, but the Spirit' (Rom. 8. 3, 4).

Every careful reader of these two verses will see that there are two things presented here. They are, firstly, what the Lord Jesus has done *for* us, and secondly, what the Holy Spirit will do *in* us. The flesh is 'weak': consequently the ordinance of the law cannot be fulfilled in us 'after the flesh'. (Remember, it is again here a question not of salvation but of pleasing God.) Now, because of our inability, God took two steps. In the first place He intervened to deal with the heart of our problem. He sent His Son in the flesh, who died for sin and in doing so 'condemned sin in the flesh'. That is to say, He took to death representatively all that belonged to the old creation in us, whether we speak of it as 'our old man', 'the flesh', or the carnal 'I'. Thus God struck at the very root of our trouble by removing the fundamental ground of our weakness. This was the first step.

But still 'the ordinance of the law' remained to be fulfilled 'in us'. How could this be done? It required God's further provision of the indwelling Holy Spirit. It is He who is sent to take care of the inward side of this thing, and He is able to do so, we are told, as we 'walk . . . after the Spirit'.

What does it mean to walk after the Spirit? It means two things. Firstly, it is not a work; it is a walk. Praise God, the burdensome and fruitless effort I involved myself in when I sought 'in the flesh' to please God gives place to a quiet and restful dependence on 'his working, which worketh in me mightily' (Col. 1. 29). That is why Paul contrasts the 'works' of the flesh with the 'fruit' of the Spirit (Gal. 5. 19, 22).

Then secondly, to 'walk after' implies subjection. Walking after the flesh means that I yield to the dictates of the flesh, and the following verses in Romans 8. 5–8 make clear where that leads me. It only brings me into conflict with God. To walk after the Spirit is to be subject to the Spirit. There is one thing that the man who walks after the Spirit cannot do, and that is be independent of Him. I *must* be subject to the Holy Spirit. The initiative of my life must be with Him. Only as I yield myself to obey Him shall I find the 'law of the Spirit of life' in full operation and the 'ordinance of the law' (all that I have been trying to do to please God) being fulfilled—no longer *by* me but *in* me. 'As many as are led by the Spirit of God, these are sons of God' (Rom. 8. 14).

We are all familiar with the words of the benediction in 2 Corinthians 13. 14; 'The grace of the Lord Jesus Christ, and the love of God, and the communion of the Holy Ghost, be with you all.' The love of God is the source of all spiritual blessing; the grace of the Lord Jesus has made it possible for that spiritual wealth to become ours; and the communion of the Holy Ghost is the means whereby it is imparted to us. Love is something hidden in the heart of God; grace is that love expressed and made available in the Son; communion is the impartation of that grace by the Spirit. What the Father has devised concerning us the Son has accomplished for us, and now the Holy Spirit communicates it to us. When therefore we discover something fresh that the Lord Jesus has procured for us in His Cross, let us look, for its realization, in the direction that God has indicated, and, by our steadfast obedience to the Holy Spirit, keep wide open the way for Him to impart it to us. That is His ministry. He has come for that very purpose—that He may make real in us all that is ours through the finished work of Christ.

We have learned in China that, when leading a soul to Christ, we must be very thorough, for there is no certainty when he will again have the help of other Christians. We always seek to make it clear to a new believer that, when he has asked the Lord to forgive his sins and to come into his life, his heart has become the residence of a living Person. The Holy Spirit of God is now within him, to open to him the scriptures that he may find Christ there, to direct his prayer, to govern his life, and to reproduce in him the character of his Lord.

I remember, late one summer, I went for a prolonged period of rest to a hill-resort where accommodation was difficult to obtain, and while there it was necessary for me to sleep in one house and take my meals in another, the latter being the home of a mechanic and his wife. For the first two weeks of my visit, apart from asking a blessing at each meal, I said nothing to my hosts about the Gospel; and then one day my opportunity came to tell them about the Lord Jesus. They were ready to listen and to come to Him in simple faith for the forgiveness of their sins. They were born again, and a new light and joy came into their lives, for theirs was a real conversion. I took care to make clear to them what had happened, and then, as the weather turned colder, the time came for me to leave them and return to Shanghai.

During the cold winter months the man was in the habit of drinking wine with his meals, and he was apt to do so to excess. After my departure, with the return of the cold weather, the wine appeared on the table again, and that day, as he had become accustomed to do, the husband bowed his head to return thanks for the meal—but no words would come. After one or two vain attempts he turned to his wife. 'What is wrong?' he asked. 'Why cannot we pray today? Fetch the Bible and see what it has to say about wine-drinking.' I had left a copy of the Scriptures with them, but though the wife could read she was ignorant of the Word, and she turned the pages in vain seeking for light on the subject. They did not know how to consult God's Book and it was impossible to consult God's messenger, for I was many miles away and it might be months before they could see me. 'Just drink your wine,' said his wife. 'We'll refer the matter to brother Nee at the first opportunity.' But still the man found he just could not return thanks to the Lord for that wine. 'Take it away!' he said at length; and when she had done so, together they asked a blessing on their meal.

When eventually the man was able to visit Shanghai he told me the story. Using an expression familiar in Chinese: 'Brother Nee' he said, 'Resident Boss[2] wouldn't let me have

---

[2] 'Resident Boss'—The author's own rendering of *li-mien tang-cia tih.*—
ED.

that drink!' 'Very good, brother,' I said. 'You always listen to Resident Boss!'

Many of us know that Christ is our life. We believe that the Spirit of God is resident in us, but this fact has little effect upon our behaviour. The question is, do we know Him as a living Person, and do we know Him as 'Boss'?

11

One Body in Christ

B EFORE we pass on to our last important subject we will review some of the ground we have covered and summarize the steps taken. We have sought to make things simple, and to explain clearly some of the experiences which Christians commonly pass through. But it is clear that the new discoveries that we make as we walk with the Lord are many, and we must be careful to avoid the temptation to over-simplify the work of God. To do so may lead us into serious confusion.

There are children of God who believe that all our salvation, in which they would include the matter of leading a holy life, lies in an appreciation of the value of the precious Blood. They rightly emphasize the importance of keeping short accounts with God over known specific sins, and the continual efficacy of the Blood to deal with sins committed, but they think of the Blood as doing everything. They believe in a holiness which in fact means only separation of the man from his past; that, through the up-to-date blotting out of what he has done on the ground of the shed Blood, God separates a man out of the world to be His, and that is holiness; and they stop there. Thus they stop short of God's basic demands, and so of the full provision He has made. I think we have by now seen clearly the inadequacy of this.

Then there are those who go further and see that God has included them in the death of His Son on the Cross, in order to deliver them from sin and the Law by dealing with the old man. These are they who really exercise faith in the Lord, for they glory in Christ Jesus and have ceased to put confidence in the flesh (Phil. 3. 3). In them God has a clear foundation on which to build. And from this as starting-point, many have gone further still and recognized that consecration (using that word in the truest sense) means giving themselves without reserve into His hands and following Him in all things. All these are first steps. Starting from them we have already touched upon yet other phases of experience set before us by God and enjoyed by many. It is always essential for us to remember that, while each of them is a precious fragment of truth, no single one of them is by itself the whole of truth. All come to us as the fruit of the work of Christ on the Cross, and we cannot afford to ignore any,

A gate and a path

Recognizing a number of such phases in the life and experience of a believer, we note now a further fact, namely that, though these phases do not necessarily occur always in a fixed and precise order, they seem to be marked by certain recurring steps or features. What are these steps? First there is revelation. As we have seen, this always precedes faith and experience. Through His Word God opens our eyes to the truth of some fact concerning His Son, and then only, as in faith we accept that fact for ourselves, does it become actual as experience in our lives. Thus we have:

1. Revelation (Objective).
2. Experience (Subjective)

Then further, we note that such experience usually takes the two-fold form of a crisis leading to a continuous process. It is most helpful to think of this in terms of John Bunyan's 'wicket gate' through which Christian entered upon a 'narrow path'. Our Lord Jesus spoke of such a gate and a path leading unto life (Matt. 7. 14), and experience accords with this. So now we have:

1. Revelation.
2. Experience: (*a*) A wicket gate (Crisis).
                (*b*) A narrow path (Process).

Now let us take some of the subjects we have been dealing with and see how this helps us to understand them. We will take first our *justification* and *new birth*. This begins with a revelation of the Lord Jesus in His atoning work for our sins on the Cross; there follows the crisis of repentance and faith (the wicket gate), whereby we are initially 'made nigh' to God (Eph. 2. 13); and this leads us into a walk of maintained fellowship with Him (the narrow path), for which the ground of our day-to-day access is still the precious Blood (Heb. 10. 19, 22). When we come to *deliverance from sin*, we again have three steps: the Holy Spirit's work of revelation, or 'knowing' (Rom. 6.6); the crisis of faith, or 'reckoning' (Rom. 6. 11); and the continuing process of consecration, or 'presenting ourselves' to God (Rom. 6. 13) on the basis of a walk in newness of life. Consider next *the gift of the Holy Spirit*. This too begins with a new 'seeing' of the Lord Jesus as exalted to the throne, which issues in the dual experience of the Spirit outpoured and the Spirit indwelling. Going a stage further, to the matter of *pleasing God*, we find again the need for spiritual illumination, that we may see the values of the Cross in regard to 'the flesh'— the entire self-life of man. Our acceptance of this by faith leads at once to a 'wicket gate' experience (Rom. 7. 25), in which we initially cease from 'doing' and accept by faith the mighty working of the life of Christ to satisfy God's practical demands in us. This in turn leads us into the 'narrow path' of a walk in obedience to the Spirit (Rom. 8. 4).

The picture is not identical in each case, and we must beware of forcing any rigid pattern upon the Holy Spirit's working; but perhaps any new experience will come to us more or less on these lines. There will certainly always be first an opening of our eyes to some new aspect of Christ and His finished work, and then faith will open a gate into a pathway. Remember, too, that our division of Christian experience into various subjects: justification, new birth, the gift of the Spirit, deliverance, sanctification, etc., is for our clearer understanding only. It does not mean that these stages must or will always follow one another in a certain prescribed order. In fact, if a full presentation of Christ and His Cross is made to us at the very outset, we may well step into a great deal of experience from the first day of our Christian life, even though the full explanation of much of it may only follow later. Would that all Gospel preaching were of such a kind!

One thing is certain, that revelation will always precede faith. Seeing and believing are two principles which govern Christian living. When we see something that God has *done* in Christ our natural response is: 'Thank you, Lord!' and faith follows spontaneously. Revelation is always the work of the Holy Spirit, who is given in order that by coming alongside and opening to us the Scriptures He may guide us into all the truth (John 16. 13). Count upon Him, for He is here for that very thing; and when such difficulties as lack of understanding or lack of faith confront you, address those difficulties directly to the Lord: 'Lord, open my eyes. Lord, make this new thing clear to me. Lord, help Thou my unbelief!' He will not let such prayers go unheeded.

The fourfold work of Christ in his Cross

We are now in a position to go a step further still and to consider how great a range is compassed by the Cross of the Lord Jesus Christ. In the light of Christian experience and for the purpose of analysis, it may help us if we recognize four aspects of God's redemptive work. But in doing so it is essential to keep in mind that the Cross of Christ is *one divine work*, and not many. Once in Judæa two thousand years ago the Lord Jesus died and rose again, and He is now 'by the right hand of God exalted' (Acts 2. 33). The work is finished and need never be repeated, nor can it be added to.

Of the four aspects of the Cross which we shall now mention, we have already dealt with three in some detail. The last will be considered in the two succeeding chapters of our study. They may be briefly summarized as follows:

1. *The Blood of Christ* to deal with sins and guilt.
2. *The Cross of Christ* to deal with sin, the flesh and the natural man.
3. *The Life of Christ* made available to indwell, re-create and empower man.
4. *The Working of Death* in the natural man that that indwelling Life may be progressively manifest.

The first two of these aspects are remedial. They relate to the undoing of the work of the Devil and the undoing of the sin of man. The last two are not remedial but positive, and relate more directly to the securing of the purpose of God. The first two are concerned with recovering what Adam lost by the Fall; the last two are concerned with bringing us into, and bringing into us, something that Adam never had. Thus we see that the achievement of the Lord Jesus in His death and resurrection comprises both a work which provided for the redemption of man and a work which made possible the realization of the purpose of God.

We have dealt at some length in earlier chapters with the two aspects of His death represented by the Blood for sins and guilt and the Cross for sin and the flesh. In our discussion of the eternal purpose we have also looked briefly at the third aspect—that represented by Christ as the grain of wheat—and we have just seen something of its practical outworking in our last chapter, when considering Christ as our life. Before, however, we pass on to the fourth aspect, which I shall call 'bearing the cross', we must say a little more about this third side, namely, the release of the risen life in Christ to indwell man and empower him for service.

We have spoken already of the purpose of God in creation

and have said that it embraced far more than Adam ever came to enjoy. What was that purpose? God wanted to have a race of men whose members were gifted with a spirit whereby communion would be possible with Himself, who is Spirit. That race, possessing God's own life, was to co-operate in securing His purposed end by defeating every possible uprising of the enemy and undoing his evil works. That was the great plan. How will it now be effected? The answer is again to be found in the death of the Lord Jesus. It is a mighty death. It is something positive and purposive, going far beyond the recovery of a lost position; for by it, not only are sin and the old man dealt with and their effects annulled, but something more, something infinitely greater and more far-reaching, is introduced.

The love of Christ

We must have before us now two passages of the Word, one from Genesis 2 and one from Ephesians 5, which, considered together, are of great importance at this point.

'And the Lord God caused a deep sleep to fall upon the man, and he slept; and he took one of his ribs, and closed up the flesh instead thereof: and the rib, which the Lord God had taken from the man, made he a woman, and brought her unto the man. And the man said, This is now bone of my bones, and flesh of my flesh: she shall be called Woman, because she was taken out of Man' (Gen. 2. 21–23).

'Husbands, love your wives, even as Christ also loved the church, and gave himself up for it; that he might sanctify it, having cleansed it by the washing of water with the word, that he might present the church to himself a glorious church, not having spot or wrinkle or any such thing; but that it should be holy and without blemish' (Eph. 5. 25–27).

In Ephesians 5 we have the only chapter in the Bible which explains the passage in Genesis 2. What we have presented to us in Ephesians is indeed very remarkable, if we reflect upon it. I refer to what is contained in those words: 'Christ . . . loved the church.' There is something most precious here.

We have been taught to think of ourselves as sinners needing redemption. For generations that has been instilled into us, and we praise the Lord for that as our beginning; but it is not what God has in view as *His end*. God speaks here rather of 'a glorious church, not having spot or wrinkle or any such thing; but . . . holy and without blemish'. All too often we have thought of the Church as being merely so many 'saved sinners'. It *is* that; but we have made the terms almost equal to one another, as though it were *only* that, which is not the case. Saved sinners—with that thought you have the whole background of sin and the Fall; but in God's sight the Church is *a divine creation in His Son*. The one is largely individual, the other corporate. With the one the view is negative, belonging to the past; with the other it is positive, looking forward. The 'eternal purpose' is something in the mind of God from eternity concerning His Son, and it has as its objective that the Son should have a Body to express His life. Viewed from that standpoint— from the standpoint of the heart of God—the Church is something which is beyond sin and has never been touched by sin.

So we have an aspect of the death of the Lord Jesus in

Ephesians which we do not have so clearly in other places. In Romans things are viewed from the standpoint of fallen man, and beginning with 'Christ died for sinners, enemies, the ungodly' (Rom. 5) we are led progressively to 'the love of Christ' (Rom. 8. 35). In Ephesians, on the other hand, the standpoint is that of God 'before the foundation of the world' (Eph. 1. 4), and the heart of the gospel is: 'Christ . . . loved the church, and gave himself up for it' (Eph. 5. 25). Thus, in Romans it is 'we sinned', and the message is of God's love for sinners (Rom. 5. 8); whereas in Ephesians it is 'Christ loved', and the love here is the love of husband for wife. That kind of love has fundamentally nothing to do with sin as such. What is in view in this passage is not atonement for sin but the creation of the Church, for which end it is said that He 'gave himself'.

There is thus an aspect of the death of the Lord Jesus which is altogether positive and a matter particularly of love to His Church, where the question of sin and sinners does not directly appear. To bring this fact home Paul takes that incident in Genesis 2 as illustration. Now this is one of the marvellous things in the Word, and if our eyes have been opened to see it, it will certainly call forth from us worship.

From Genesis 3 onwards, from the 'coats of skins' to Abel's sacrifice, and on from there through the whole Old Testament, there are numerous types which set forth the death of the Lord Jesus as an atonement for sin; yet the apostle does not appeal here to any of those types of His death, but to this one in Genesis 2. Note that; and then recall that it was not until Genesis 3 that sin came in. There is one type of the death of Christ in the Old Testament which has nothing to do with sin, for it is not subsequent to the Fall but prior to it, and that type is here in Genesis 2. Let us look at it for a moment.

Could we say that Adam was put to sleep because Eve had committed a serious sin? Is that what we have here? Certainly not, for Eve was not yet even created. There were as yet no moral issues involved and no problems at all. No, Adam was put to sleep for the express purpose that something might be taken out of him to be formed into someone else. His sleep was not for her sin but for her *existence*. That is what is taught in these verses. This experience of Adam had as its object the creation of Eve, as something determined in the divine counsels. God wanted a woman. He put the man to sleep, took a rib from his side and made it into a woman, and brought her to the man. That is the picture which God is giving us. It foreshadows an aspect of the death of the Lord Jesus that is not primarily for atonement, but answerable to the sleep of Adam in this chapter.

God forbid that I should suggest that the Lord Jesus did not die for purposes of atonement. Praise God, He did. We must remember that today we are in fact in Ephesians 5 and not in Genesis 2. Ephesians was written *after* the Fall, to men who had suffered from its effects, and in it we have not only the purpose in Creation but also the stars of the Fall— or there would need to be no mention of 'spot or wrinkle'. Because we are still on the earth and the Fall is a historic fact, redemption is needed (Eph. 1. 7).

But we must always view redemption as an interruption, an 'emergency' measure, made necessary by a catastrophic break in the straight line of the purpose of God. Redemption is big enough, wonderful enough, to occupy a very large place in our vision, but God is saying that we should not make redemption to be everything, *as though man were created to be redeemed*. The Fall is indeed a tragic dip downwards in that line of purpose, and the atonement a blessed recovery whereby our sins are blotted out and we are restored; but when it is accomplished there yet remains a work to be done to bring us into possession of that which Adam never possessed, and to give God what His heart most desires. For God has never forsaken the purpose which is represented by that straight line. Adam was never in possession of the life of God as presented in the tree of life. But because of the one work of the Lord Jesus in His death and resurrection (and we must emphasize again that it is all one work) His life was released to become ours by faith, and we have received more than Adam ever possessed. The very purpose of God is brought within reach of fulfilment in us by our receiving Christ as our life.

Adam was put to sleep. We remember that it is said of believers that they fall asleep, rather than that they die. Why? Because whenever death is mentioned sin is there in the background. In Genesis 3 sin entered into the world and death through sin, but Adam's sleep preceded that. So the type of the Lord Jesus here is not like other types in the Old Testament. In relation to sin and atonement there is a lamb or a bullock slain; but here Adam was not slain, but only put to sleep *to awake again*. Thus he prefigures a death that is not on account of sin, but that has in view increase in resurrection. Then too we must note that Eve was not created as a separate entity by a separate creation, parallel to that of Adam. Adam slept, and Eve was created out of Adam. That is God's method with the Church. God's 'second Man' has awakened from His 'sleep' and His Church is created in Him and of Him, to draw her life from Him and to display that resurrection life.

God has a Son, His only begotten, and He seeks that that Son should have brethren. From the position of only begotten He will become the first begotten, and instead of the Son alone, God will have many sons. One grain of wheat has died and many grains will spring up. The first grain was once the only grain; now it has become the first of many. The Lord Jesus laid down His life, and that life emerged in many lives. These are the Biblical figures we have used hitherto in our study to express this truth. Now, in the figure of Eve, the singular takes the place of the plural. The outcome of the Cross is shown to be a single person: a Bride for the Son. Christ loved the Church and gave Himself up for it.

One living sacrifice

We have said that there is an aspect of the death of Christ presented to us in Ephesians 5 which differs in some degree from that which we have been studying in Romans. Yet in fact this aspect is the very end to which our study of Romans has been moving, and it is into this that the letter is leading us as we shall now see, for redemption leads us back into God's original line of purpose.

In chapter 8 Paul speaks to us of Christ as the first-born Son among many Spirit-led 'sons of God' (Rom. 8. 14). 'For whom he foreknew, he also foreordained to be conformed to the image of his Son, that he might be the firstborn among many brethren: and whom he foreordained, them he also called: and whom he called, them he also justified:

and whom he justified, them he also glorified' (Rom. 8. 29, 30). Here justification is seen to lead on to glory, a glory that is expressed not in one or more individuals but in a plurality: in many who manifest the image of One. And this object of our redemption is further set forth, as we have seen, in 'the love of Christ' for His own, which is the subject of the last verses of the chapter (8. 35–39). But what is implicit here in chapter 8 becomes explicit as we move over into chapter 12, the subject of which is the Body of Christ.

After the first eight chapters of Romans, which we have been studying, there follows a parenthesis in which God's sovereign dealings with Israel are taken up and dealt with, before the theme of the first chapters is resumed. Thus, for our present purpose, the argument of chapter 12 follows that of chapter 8 and not of chapter 11. We might very simply summarize these chapters thus: Our sins are forgiven (ch. 5), we are dead with Christ (ch. 6), we are by nature utterly helpless (ch. 7), therefore we rely upon the indwelling Spirit (ch. 8). After this, and as a consequence of it: 'We . . . are one body in Christ' (ch. 12). It is as though this were the logical outcome of all that has gone before, and the thing to which it has all been leading.

Romans 12 and the following chapters contain some very practical instructions for our life and walk. These are introduced with an emphasis once again on consecration. In chapter 6. 13 Paul has said: 'Present yourselves unto God, as alive from the dead, and your members as instruments of righteousness unto God.' But now in chapter 12. 1 the emphasis is a little different: 'I beseech you therefore, brethren, by the mercies of God, to present your bodies a living sacrifice, holy, acceptable to God, which is your reasonable service.' This new appeal for consecration is made to us as 'brethren', linking us in thought to the 'many brethren' of chapter 8. 29. It is a call to us for a united step of faith, expressed in terms of the presenting of our bodies as one 'living sacrifice' unto God.

This is something that goes beyond the merely individual, for it implies contribution to a whole. The 'presenting' is personal but the sacrifice is corporate; it is one sacrifice. Intelligent service to God is one service. We need never feel our contribution is not needed, for if it contributes to *the* service, God is satisfied. And it is through this kind of service that we prove 'what is the good and acceptable and perfect will of God' (ch. 12. 2), or in other words, realize our part in God's eternal purpose in Christ Jesus. So Paul's appeal 'to every man that is among you' (12. 3) is in the light of this new divine fact, that 'we, who are many, are one body in Christ, and severally members one of another' (12. 5), and it is on this basis that the practical instructions follow.

The vessel through which the Lord Jesus can reveal Himself in this generation is not the individual but the Body. True, 'God hath dealt to each man a measure of faith' (12. 3), but alone in isolation man can never fulfil God's purpose. It requires a complete Body to attain to the stature of Christ and to display His glory. Oh that we might really see this!

So Romans 12. 3–6 draws from the figure of the human body the lesson of our inter-dependence. Individual Christians are not the Body. They are its members, and in a human body 'all the members have not the same office'. The ear must not imagine itself to be an eye. No amount of prayer will give sight to the ear—but the whole body can see through the eye. So (speaking figuratively) I may have only the gift of hearing, but I can see through others who have the gift of sight; or, perhaps I can walk but cannot work, so I receive help from the hands. An all-too-common attitude to the things of the Lord is that, 'What I know, I know; and what I don't know, I don't know, and can do quite well without.' But in Christ, the things we do not know others do, and we may know them and enter into the enjoyment of them through others.

Let me stress that this is not just a comfortable thought. It is a vital factor in the life of God's people. We cannot get along without one another. That is why fellowship in prayer is so important. Prayer together brings in the help of the Body, as must be clear from Matthew 18. 19, 20. Trusting the Lord by myself may not be enough. I must trust Him with others. I must learn to pray '*Our* Father . . .' on the basis of oneness with the Body, for without the help of the Body I cannot get through. In the sphere of service this is even more apparent. Alone I cannot serve the Lord effectively, and He will spare no pains to teach me this. He will bring things to an end, allowing doors to close and leaving me ineffectively knocking my head against a blank wall until I realize that I need the help of the Body as well as of the Lord. For the life of Christ is the life of the Body, and His gifts are given to us for work that builds up the Body.

The Body is not an illustration but a fact. The Bible does not just say that the Church is *like* a body, but that it *is* the Body of Christ. 'We, who are many, are one body in Christ, and severally members one of another.' All the members together *are* one Body, for all share His life—as though He were Himself distributed among His members. I was once with a group of Chinese believers who found it very hard to understand how the Body could be one when they were all separate individuals who made it up. One Sunday I was about to break the bread at the Lord's table and I asked them to look very carefully at the loaf before I broke it. Then, after it had been distributed and eaten, I pointed out that though it was inside all of them it was still one loaf— not many. The loaf was divided, but Christ is not divided even in the sense in which that loaf was. He is still one Spirit in us, and we are all one in Him.

This is the very opposite of man's condition by nature. In Adam I have the life of Adam, but that is essentially individual. There is no union, no fellowship in sin, but only self-interest and distrust of others. As I go on with the Lord I soon discover, not only that the problem of sin and of my natural strength has to be dealt with, but that there is also a further problem created by my 'individual' life, the life that is sufficient in itself and does not recognize its need for and union in the Body. I may have got over the problems of sin and the flesh, and yet still be a confirmed individualist. I want holiness and victory and fruitfulness for myself personally and apart, albeit from the purest motives. But such an attitude ignores the Body, and so cannot provide God with satisfaction. He must deal with me therefore in this matter also, or I shall remain in conflict with His ends. God does not blame me for being an individual, but for my individual*ism*. His greatest problem is not the outward divisions and denominations that divide His Church but our own individualistic hearts.

Yes, the Cross must do its work here, reminding me that

in Christ I have died to that old life of independence which I inherited from Adam, and that in resurrection I have become not just an individual believer in Christ but a member of His Body. There is a vast difference between the two. When I see this, I shall at once have done with independence and shall seek fellowship. The life of Christ in me will gravitate to the life of Christ in others. I can no longer take an individual line. Jealousy will go. Competition will go. Private work will go. My interests, my ambitions, my preferences, all will go. It will no longer matter which of us does the work. All that will matter will be that the Body grows.

I said: 'When I *see* this . . .' That is the great need: to *see* the Body of Christ as another great divine fact; to have it break in upon our spirits by heavenly revelation that 'we, who are many, *are* one body in Christ.' Only the Holy Spirit can bring this home to us in all its meaning, but when He does it will revolutionize our life and work.

More than conquerors through Him

We only see history back to the Fall. God sees it from the beginning. There was something in God's mind *before* the Fall, and in the ages to come that thing is to be fully realized. God knew all about sin and redemption; yet in His great purpose for the Church set forth in Genesis 2 there is no view of sin. It is as though (to speak in finite terms) He leaps in thought right over the whole story of redemption and sees the Church in future eternity, having a ministry and a (future) history which is altogether apart from sin and wholly of God. It is the Body of Christ in glory, expressing nothing of fallen man, but only that which is the image of the glorified Son of man. *This* is the Church that has satisfied God's heart and has attained dominion.

In Ephesians 5 we stand within the history of redemption, and yet through grace we still have this eternal purpose of God in view as expressed in the statement that He will 'present unto himself a glorious Church'. But now we note that the water of life and the cleansing Word are needed to prepare the Church (now marred by the Fall) for presentation to Christ in glory. For now there are defects to be remedied and wounds to be healed. And yet how precious is the promise and how gracious are the words used of her: 'not having spot'—the scars of sin, whose very history is now forgotten; 'or wrinkle'—the marks of age and of time lost, for all is now made up and all is new; and 'without blemish'—so that Satan or demons or men can find no ground for blame in her.

This is where we are now. The age is closing, and Satan's power is greater than ever. Our warfare is with angels and principalities and powers (Rom. 8. 38; Eph. 6. 12) who are set to withstand and destroy the work of God in us by laying many things to the charge of God's elect. Alone we could never be their match, but what we alone cannot do the Church can. Sin, self-reliance and individualism were Satan's master-strokes at the heart of God's purpose in man, and in the Cross God has undone them. As we put our faith in what He has done—in 'God that justifieth' and in 'Christ Jesus that died' (Rom. 8. 33, 34)—we present a front against which the very gates of Hades shall not prevail. We, His Church, are 'more than conquerors through him that loved us' (Rom. 8. 37).

12

The Cross and the Soul Life

GOD has made full provision for our redemption in the Cross of Christ, but He has not stopped there. In that Cross He has also made secure beyond possibility of failure that eternal plan which Paul speaks of as having been from all the ages 'hid in God who created all things'. That plan He has now proclaimed 'to the intent that now unto the principalities and the powers in the heavenly places might be made known through the church the manifold wisdom of God, according to the eternal purpose which he purposed in Christ Jesus our Lord' (Eph. 3. 9–11).

We have said that the work of the Cross has two results which bear directly upon the realizing of that purpose in us. On the one hand it has issued in the release of His life that it may find expression in us through the indwelling Spirit. On the other hand it has made possible what we speak of as 'bearing the cross'; that is, our co-operation in the daily inworking of His death whereby way is made in us for the manifestation of that new life, through the bringing of the 'natural man' progressively into his right place of subjection to the Holy Spirit. Clearly these are the positive and the negatives sides of one thing. Equally clearly we are now touching more particularly on the matter of progress in a life lived for God. Hitherto in dealing with the Christian life we have placed our main emphasis upon the crisis by which it is entered. Now our concern is more definitely with the walk of the disciple, having especially in view his training as a servant of God. It is of him that the Lord Jesus said: 'Whosoever doth not bear his own cross, and come after me, cannot be my disciple' (Luke 14. 27).

So we come to a consideration of the natural man and the 'bearing of the cross'. To understand this we must, at the risk of being tedious, go back once more to Genesis and consider what it was that God sought to have in man at the beginning, and how His purpose was frustrated. In this way we shall be able to grasp more clearly the principles by which we can come again to live in harmony with that purpose.

The true nature of the Fall

If we have even a little revelation of the plan of God we shall always think much of the word 'man'. We shall say with the Psalmist, 'What is man, that thou art mindful of him?' The Bible makes it clear that what God desires above all things is a man—a man who will be after His own heart.

So God created a man. In Genesis 2. 7 we learn that Adam was created *a living soul*, with a *spirit* inside to commune with God and with a *body* outside to have contact with the material world. (Such New Testament verses as 1 Thessalonians 5. 23 and Hebrews 4. 12 confirm this three-fold character of man's being.) With his spirit Adam was in touch with the spiritual world of God; with his body he was in touch with the physical world of material things. He gathered up these two sides of God's creative act into himself to become a personality, an entity living in the world, moving by itself and *having powers of free choice*. Viewed thus as a whole, he was found to be a self-conscious and self-expressing being, 'a living soul'.

We saw earlier that Adam was created perfect—by which we mean that he was without imperfections because created by God—but that he was not yet perfected. He needed a finishing touch somewhere. God had not yet done all that He intended to do in Adam. There was more in view, but it was as yet in abeyance. God was moving towards the fulfilment of His purpose in creating man, a purpose which went beyond man himself, for it had in view the securing to God of all His rights in the universe through man's instrumentality. But how could man be instrumental in this? Only by a co-operation that sprang from living union with God. God was seeking to have not merely a race of men of one blood upon the earth, but a race which had, in addition, His life resident within its members. Such a race will eventually compass Satan's downfall and bring to fulfilment all that God has set His heart upon. It is this that was in view with the creation of man.

Then again, we saw that Adam was created neutral. He had a spirit which enabled him to hold communion with God, but as man he was not yet, so to speak, finally orientated; he had powers of choice and he could, if he liked, turn the opposite way. God's goal in man was 'sonship', or, in other words, the expression of His life in human sons. That divine life was represented in the garden, as we saw, by the tree of life, bearing a fruit that could be accepted,

received, taken in. If Adam, created neutral, were voluntarily to turn that way and, choosing dependence upon
God, were to receive of the tree of life (representing God's
own life), God would then have that life in union with men;
He would have secured His spiritual sons. But if instead
Adam should turn to the tree of the knowledge of good and
evil, he would as a result be 'free', in the sense of being able
to develop himself on his own lines apart from God.
Because, however, this latter choice involved complicity
with Satan, Adam would thereby put beyond his reach the
attaining of his God-appointed goal.

The human soul

Now we know the course that Adam chose. Standing
between the two trees, he yielded to Satan and took of the
fruit of the tree of knowledge. This determined the lines of
his development. From then on he could command a
knowledge; he 'knew'. But—and here we come to the
point—the fruit of the tree of knowledge made the first man
over-developed in his soul. The emotion was touched, because
the fruit was pleasant to the eyes, making him 'desire'; the
mind with its reasoning power was developed, for he was
'made wise'; and the will was strengthened, so that in
future he could always decide which way he would go. The
whole fruit ministered to the expansion and full development of the soul, so that not only was the man a living soul,
but from henceforth man will *live by the soul*. It is not merely
that man has a soul, but that from that day on, the soul,
with its independent powers of free choice, usurps the place
of the spirit as the animating power of man.

We have to distinguish here between two things, for the difference is most important. God does not mind—in fact He of course intends—that we should have a soul such as He gave to Adam. But what God has set himself to do is to reverse something. There is something in man today which is not just the fact of having and exercising a soul, but which constitutes a living by the soul. It was this that Satan brought about in the Fall. He trapped man into taking a course by which he could develop his soul so as to derive from it his very spring of life.

We must, however, be careful. To remedy this does not mean that we are going to cross out the soul altogether. You cannot do that. When today the Cross is really working in us, we do not become inert, insensate, characterless. No, we still possess a soul, and whenever we receive something from God the soul will still be used in relation to it, as an instrument, a faculty, in a true subjection to Him. But the point is: Are we keeping within God's appointed limit, that is to say, within the bounds set by Him in the Garden at the beginning, with regard to the soul, or are we getting outside those bounds?

What God is now doing is the pruning work of the vine-dresser. In our souls there is an uncontrolled development, an untimely growth, that has to be checked and dealt with. God must cut that off. So now there are two things before us to which our eyes must be opened. On the one hand God is seeking to bring us to the place where we live by the life of His Son. On the other hand He is doing a direct work in our hearts to undo that other natural resource that is the result of the fruit of knowledge. Every day we are learning these two lessons: a rising up of the life of this One, and a checking and a handing over to death of that other soul-life. These two processes go on all the time, for God is seeking the fully developed life of His Son in us in order to manifest Himself, and to that end He is bringing us back, as to our soul, to Adam's starting-point. So Paul says: 'We which live are alway delivered unto death for Jesus' sake, that the life also of Jesus may be manifested in our mortal flesh' (2 Cor. 4. 11).

What does this mean? It simply means that I will not take any action without relying on God. I will find no sufficiency in myself. I will not take any step just because I have the power to do so. Even though I have that inherited power within me, I will not go ahead solely upon it as basis; I will put no reliance on myself. By taking the fruit, Adam became possessed of an inherent power to act, but a power which, by its independence of God, played right into Satan's hands. You lose that power to act when you come to know the Lord. The Lord cuts it off and you find you can no longer act on your own initiative. You have to live by the life of Another; you have to draw everything from Him.

Oh, friends, I think we all know ourselves in measure, but many a time we do not truly tremble at ourselves. We may, in a manner of courtesy to God, say: 'If the Lord does not want it, I cannot do it,' but in reality our subconscious thought is that really we can do it quite well ourselves, even if God does not ask us to do it nor empower us for it. Too often we have been caused to act, to think, to decide, to have power, regardless of Him. Many of us Christians to-day are men with over-developed souls. We have grown too big in ourselves. When we are in that condition, it is possible for the life of the Son of God in us to be confined and crowded almost out of action.

Natural energy in the work of God

The power, the energy of the soul is present with us all. Those who have been taught by the Lord repudiate that principle as a life principle; they refuse to live by it; they will not let it reign, nor allow it to be the power-spring of the work of God. But those who have not been taught of God rely upon it; they utilize it; they think it is *the* power.

Let us take first an obvious illustration of this. Far too many of us in the past have reasoned as follows. Here is a delightfully good-natured man, with a clear brain, splendid managing powers and sound judgment. In our hearts we say, 'If that man could be a Christian, what an asset he would be to the Church! If only he were the Lord's, what a lot it would mean to His cause!'

But think for a moment. Where did that man's good nature come from? Whence are those splendid managing powers and that good judgment? Not from new birth, for he is not yet born again. We know we have all been born of the flesh; therefore we need a new birth. But the Lord Jesus had something to say about this in John 3. 6: 'That which is born of the flesh is flesh.' Everything which comes not by new birth but by natural birth is flesh and will only bring glory to man, not God. That statement is not very palatable, but it is true.

We have spoken of soul-power or natural energy. What is this natural energy? It is simply what *I* can do, what *I* am of myself, what *I* have inherited of natural gifts and resources. We are none of us without the power of the soul, and our first need is to recognize it for what it is.

Take for example the human mind. I may have by nature

a keen mind. Before my new birth I had it naturally, as something developed from my natural birth. But the trouble arises here. I become converted, I am born anew, a deep work is affected in my spirit, an essential union has been wrought with the Father of our spirits. Thereafter there are in me two things: I have now a union with God that has been set up in my spirit, but at the same time I carry over with me something which I derive from my natural birth. Now what am I going to do about it?

The natural tendency is this. Formerly I used to use my mind to pore over history, over business, over chemistry, over questions of the world, or literature, or poetry. I used my keen mind to get the best out of those studies. But now my desire has been changed, so henceforth I employ the same mind in just the same way in the things of God. *I have therefore changed my subject of interest, but I have not changed my method of working.* That is the whole point. My interests have been utterly changed (praise God for that!), but now I utilize the same power to study Corinthians and Ephesians that I used before to pursue history and geography. But that power is not of the new creation; and God will not be satisfied with this simple exchange of interests. The trouble with so many of us is that we have changed the channel into which our energies are directed, but we have not changed the source of those energies.

You will find there are many such things which we carry over into the service of God. Consider the matter of eloquence. There are some men who are born orators; they can present a case very convincingly indeed. Then they become converted, and, without asking ourselves where they really stand in relation to spiritual things, we put them on the platform and make preachers of them. We encourage them to use their natural powers for preaching, and again it is a change of subject but the same power. We forget that, in the matter of our resource for handling the things of God, it is a question not of comparative value but of *origin*—of where the resource springs from. It is not so much a matter of what we are doing, but of what powers we are employing to do it, and who is controlling those powers. The man God can use may well be eloquent, but there is the mark of the Cross upon that eloquence, and the controlling hand of the Spirit of God is apparent in its use. We think too little of the source of our energy and too much of the end to which it is directed, forgetting that with God the end never justifies the means.

To test the truth of this, let us take a hypothetical case. Mr. A. is a very good speaker: he can talk fluently and most convincingly on any subject, but in practical things he is a very bad manager. Mr. B., on the other hand, is a poor speaker: he cannot express himself clearly but wanders all round his subject, never coming to a point; yet on the other hand he is a splendid manager, most competent in all matters of business. Both these men get converted, and both become earnest Christians. Let us suppose now that I call on them both and ask them to speak at a convention, and that both accept.

Now what will happen? I have asked the self-same thing of both men, but who do you think will pray the harder! Almost certainly Mr. B. Why? Because he is no speaker. In the matter of eloquence he has no resources of his own to depend upon. He will pray: 'Lord, if you do not give me power for this, I cannot do it.' Of course Mr. A. will pray too, but maybe not in the same way as Mr. B. because he has something of natural aptitude upon which to rely.

Now let us suppose that, instead of asking them to speak, I ask them both to take charge of the practical side of affairs at the convention. What will happen? The position will be exactly reversed. Now it will be Mr. A.'s turn to pray hard, for he knows full well that he has no organizing ability. Mr. B. of course will pray too, but perhaps without quite the same urgency, for though he knows his need of the Lord, he is not nearly so conscious of his need in business matters as is Mr. A.

Do you see the difference between natural and spiritual gifts? Anything we can do without prayer and without an utter dependence upon God must come from the spring of *natural* life that is tainted with the flesh. We must see this clearly. Of course it is not true that those only are suited for a particular work who lack the natural gift for it. The point is that, whether naturally gifted or not—and we should praise God for all His gifts—they must know the touch of the Cross in death upon all that is of nature, and their complete dependence upon the God of resurrection. All too readily do we envy our neighbour who has some outstanding natural gift, and fail to realize that our own possession of it, apart from such a working of the Cross, could prove a barrier to the very thing that God is seeking to manifest in us.

Shortly after my conversion I went out preaching in the villages. I had had a good education and was well-versed in the Scriptures, so I considered myself thoroughly capable of instructing the village folk, among whom were quite a number of illiterate women. But after several visits I discovered that, despite their illiteracy, those women had an

intimate knowledge of the Lord. I knew the Book they halt-
ingly read; they knew the One of whom the Book spoke. I
had much in myself; they had much in the Spirit. How
many Christian teachers today are teaching others as I was
then, very largely in the strength of their carnal equipment!

Once I met a young brother—young, that is to say, in
years, but who had learned a good deal of the Lord. God
had brought him through much tribulation to gain that
knowledge of Himself. As I was talking with him I said,
'Brother, what has the Lord really been teaching you these
days?' He replied, 'Only one thing: that I can do nothing
apart from Him.' 'Do you really *mean*', I asked, 'that you can
do nothing?' 'Well, no', he said. 'Of course I *can* do many
things! In fact that has been just my trouble. Oh, you know,
I have always been so confident in myself. I know I am well
able to do lots of things.' So I asked, 'What then do you
mean when you say you can do nothing apart from Him?'
He answered, 'The Lord has shown me that I *can* do anything, but that *He* has said, "Apart from me ye can do nothing." So it comes to this, that everything I have done and
can still do apart from Him *is nothing*!'

We have to come to that valuation. I do not mean to say
we cannot do a lot of things, for we can. We can take meetings and build churches, we can go to the ends of the earth
and found missions, and we can seem to bear fruit; but
remember that the Lord's word is: 'Every plant which my
heavenly Father planted not, shall be rooted up' (Matt. 15.
13). God is the only legitimate Originator in the universe
(Gen. 1. 1), and His Holy Spirit is the only legitimate initi-
ator in our hearts. Anything that you or I plan and set on
foot without Him has the taint of the flesh upon it, and it

will never reach the realm of the Spirit however earnestly we seek God's blessing on it. It may last for years, and then we may think we will adjust here and improve there and maybe bring it on a better plane, but it cannot be done.

Origin determines destination, and what was 'of the flesh' originally will never be made spiritual by any amount of 'improvement'. That which is born of the flesh is flesh, and it will never be otherwise. So anything for which we are sufficient in ourselves is 'nothing' in God's estimate, and we have to accept His estimate and write it down as nothing. 'The flesh profiteth nothing.' It is only what comes from above that will abide.

We cannot see this simply by being told it. God must teach us what is meant, by putting His finger on something which He sees and saying: 'This is natural; this has its source in the old creation, and did not originate with Me; this cannot abide.' Until He does so, we may agree in principle, but we can never really *see* it. We may assent to, and even enjoy, the teaching, but we shall never truly loathe ourselves.

But there will come a day when God opens our eyes. Facing a particular issue we shall have to say, as by revelation: 'it is unclean, it is impure; Lord, I see it!' The word 'purity' is a blessed word. I always associate it with the Spirit. Purity means something altogether of the Spirit. Impurity means mixture. When God opens our eyes to see that the natural life is something that, in itself, He can never use in His work, then we find we do not *enjoy* the doctrine any longer. Rather we loathe ourselves for the impurity that is in us: but when that point is reached, God begins His work of deliverance. We are going on shortly to look at the provision

He has made for that deliverance, but we must stay for a little longer with this matter of revelation.

The light of God and knowledge

Of course, if one does not set out to serve the Lord wholeheartedly, one does not feel the necessity for light. It is only when one has been apprehended by God, and seeks to go forward with Him, that one finds how necessary light is. There is a fundamental need of light in order for us to know the mind of God; to know what is of the spirit and what is of the soul; to know what is divine and what is merely of man; to discern what is truly heavenly and what is only earthly; to understand the difference between things which are spiritual and things which are carnal; to know whether God is really leading us or whether we are just being moved by our feelings, senses of imaginations. It is when we have reached a position where we would like to follow God fully that we find light to be the most necessary thing in the Christian life.

In my conversations with younger brothers and sisters, one question comes up again and again. It is: How can I know that I am walking in the Spirit? How do I distinguish which prompting within me is from the Holy Spirit and which is from myself? It seems that all are alike in this; but some have gone further. They are trying to look within, to differentiate, to discriminate, to analyse, and in doing so are bringing themselves into deeper bondage. Now this is a situation which is really dangerous to Christian life, for inward knowledge will never be reached along the barren path of self-analysis.

We are never told in the Word of God to examine our inward condition.[1] That way leads only to uncertainty, vacillation and despair. Of course we have to have self-knowledge. We have to know what is going on within. We do not want to live in a fool's paradise; to have gone altogether wrong and yet not know we have gone wrong; to have a spartan will and yet think we are pursuing the will of God. But such self-knowledge does not come by our turning within; by our analysing our feelings and motives and everything that is going on inside, and then trying to pronounce whether we are walking in the flesh or in the Spirit.

There are several passages in the Psalms which illumine this subject. The first is in Psalm 36. 9: 'In thy light shall we see light.' I think that is one of the best verses in the Old Testament. There are two lights there. There is 'thy light', and then, when we have come into that light, we shall 'see light'.

Now those two lights are different. We might say that the first is objective and the second subjective. The first light is the light which belongs to God but is shed upon us; the second is the knowledge imparted by that light. 'In thy light shall we see light': we shall know something; we shall be clear about something; we shall *see*. No turning within, no

---

[1] The two apparent exceptions to this are found in 1 Corinthians 11. 28, 31 and 2 Corinthians 13. 5. But the former passage calls upon us to discern ourselves as to whether we recognize the Lord's body or not, and this is in particular connection with the Lord's table. It is not concerned with self-knowledge as such. The strong command of Paul in the latter passage is to examine ourselves as to whether or not we are 'in the faith'. It is a question of the existence or otherwise in us of a fundamental faith; of whether, in fact, we are Christians. This is in no way related to our daily walk in the Spirit, or to self-knowledge.—W. N.

introspective self-examination will ever bring us to that clear place. No, it is when there is light coming from God that we see.

I think it is so simple. If we want to satisfy ourselves that our face is clean, what do we do? Do we feel it carefully all over with our hands? No, of course not. We find a mirror and we bring it to the light. In that light everything becomes clear. No sight ever came by feeling or analysing. Sight only comes by the light of God coming in; and when once it has come, there is no longer need to ask if a thing is right or wrong. We know.

You remember again how in Psalm 139. 23 the writer says: 'Search me, O God, and know my heart.' You realize, do you not, what it means to say 'Search me'? It certainly does not mean that I search myself. 'Search me' means '*You* search me!' That is the way of illumination. It is for God to come in and search; it is not for me to search. Of course that will never mean that I may go blindly on, careless of my true condition. That is not the point. The point is that however much my self-examination may reveal in me that needs putting right, such searching never really gets below the surface. My true knowledge of self comes not from my searching myself but from God searching me.

But, you ask, what does it mean in practice for us to come into the light? How does it work? *How* do we see light in His light? Here again the Psalmist comes to our help. 'The entrance of thy words giveth light; it giveth understanding unto the simple' (Psalm 119. 130 A.V.). In spiritual things we are all 'simple'. We are dependent upon God to give us understanding, and especially is this so in the matter of our own true nature. And it is here that the Word of God operates. In the New Testament the passage which states this most clearly is in the Epistle to the Hebrews: 'The word of God is living, and active, and sharper than any two-edged sword, and piercing even to the dividing of soul and spirit, of both joints and marrow, and quick to discern the thoughts and intents of the heart. And there is no creature that is not manifest in his sight: but all things are naked and laid open before the eyes of him with whom we have to do' (Heb. 4. 12, 13). Yes, it is the Word of God, the penetrating Scripture of truth, that settles our questions. It is that which discerns our motives and defines for us their true source in soul or spirit.

With this I think we can pass on from the doctrinal to the practical side of things. Many of us, I am sure, are living quite honestly before God. We have been making progress, and we do not know of anything much wrong with us. Then one day, as we go on, we meet with a fulfilment of that word: 'The entrance of thy words giveth light.' Some servant of God has been used by Him to confront us with His living Word, and that Word has made an entrance into us. Or perhaps we ourselves have been waiting before God and, whether from our memory of Scripture or from the page itself, His Word has come to us in power. Then it is we see something which we have never seen before. We are convicted. We know where we are wrong, and we look up and confess: 'Lord, I see it. There is impurity there. There is mixture. How blind I was! Just fancy that for so many years I have been wrong there and have never known it!' Light comes in and we see light. The light of God brings us to see the light concerning ourselves, and it is an abiding principle that every knowledge of self comes to us in that way.

It may not always be the Scriptures. Some of us have known saints who really knew the Lord, and through praying with them or talking with them, in the light of God radiating from them, we have seen something which we never saw before. I have met one such, who is now with the Lord, and I always think of her as a 'lighted' Christian. If I did but walk into her room, I was brought immediately to a sense of God. In those days I was very young and had been converted about two years, and I had lots of plans, lots of beautiful thoughts, lots of schemes for the Lord to sanction, a hundred and one things which I thought would be marvellous if they were all brought to fruition. With all these things I came to her to try to persuade her; to tell her that this or that was the thing to do.

Before I could open my mouth, she would just say a few words in quite an ordinary way. Light dawned! It simply put me to shame. My 'doing' and my scheming were all so natural, so full of man. Something happened. I was brought to a place where I could say: 'Lord, my mind is set only on creaturely activities, but here is someone who is not out for them at all. Teach me to walk that way.' She had but one motive, one desire, and that was for God. Written in the front of her Bible were these words: 'Lord, I want nothing for myself.' Yes, she lived for God alone, and where that is the case you will find that such a one is bathed in light, and that that light illuminates others. That is real witness.[2]

Light has one law: it shines wherever it is admitted. That

---

[2] This is one of several references by the author to the late Miss Margaret E. Barber of Pagoda Anchorage, Foochow. —ED.

is the only requirement. *We* may shut it out of ourselves; it fears nothing else. If we throw ourselves open to God, He will reveal. The trouble comes when we have closed areas, locked and barred places in our hearts, where we think with pride that *we* are right. Our defeat then lies less in our being wrong than in our *not knowing that we are wrong*. Wrong may be a question of natural strength; ignorance of it is a question of light. You can see the natural strength in some but they cannot see it themselves. Oh, we need to be sincere and humble, and to open ourselves before God! Those who are *open* can see. God is light, and we cannot live in His light and be without understanding. Let us say again with the Psalmist: 'O send out thy light and thy truth: let them lead me' (Psalm 43. 3).

We praise God that today sin is being brought to the notice of Christians more than hitherto. In many places the eyes of Christians have been opened to see that victory over sin is important in Christian life, and in consequence many are walking closer to the Lord in seeking deliverance there. Praise the Lord for any movement towards Himself, any movement back to real holiness unto God! But that is not enough. There is one thing that must be touched, and that is the very life of the man, not merely his sins. The question of his soul power, his driving force, lies still at the heart of things. To make everything of sin, or even of the flesh in its more obvious manifestations, is still to be on the surface. You have not yet got to the root of the problem.

Adam did not let sin into the world by committing murder. That came later. Adam let in sin by choosing to have his soul developed to a place where he could go on by himself apart from God. When, therefore, God secures for His glory that race of men who will be the instrument of His purpose in the universe, they will be a people whose life—yea, whose very breath—is dependent upon Him. He will be the 'tree of life' to them.

What I more and more feel the need of in myself, and what I believe, as His Children, we all need to seek from God, is a real revelation of ourselves. I repeat that I do not mean we should be for ever looking within and asking: 'Now, is this soul or is it spirit?' That will never get us anywhere; it is darkness. No, Scripture shows us how the saints were brought to self-knowledge. It was always by light from God, and that light *is* God Himself. Isaiah, Ezekiel, Daniel, Peter, Paul, John, all came to a knowledge of themselves because the Lord flashed *Himself* upon them, and that flash brought revelation and conviction. (Isa. 6. 5; Ezek. 1. 28; Dan. 10. 8; Luke 22. 61, 62; Acts 9. 3–5; Rev. 1. 17.)

We can never know either the hatefulness of sin or the treachery of our self-nature until there is that flash of God upon us. I speak not of a sensation but of an inward revelation of the Lord Himself through His Word. Such a breaking in of divine light does for us what doctrine alone can never do.

Christ is our light; and He is the *living* Word. As we read the Scriptures, that life in Him brings revelation. 'The life was the light of men' (John 1. 4). Such illumination may not come to us all at once, but gradually; but it will be more and more clear and searching, until we see ourselves in the light of God and all our self-confidence is gone. For light is the purest thing in the world. It cleanses. It sterilizes. It kills what should not be there. In its radiance the 'dividing asunder of joints and marrow' becomes to us a fact and no mere teaching. We know fear and trembling as we recognize the corruption of our nature, the hatefulness of self, and the real threat to the work of God of our soul-life and energy, untamed and uncontrolled by His Holy Spirit. As never before, we see now how much of us needs God's drastic dealing if He is to use us, and we know that, apart from His dominion, as servants of God we are finished.

But here the Cross, in its widest meaning, will come to our help again, and we shall seek now to examine an aspect of its work which meets and deals with our problem of the human soul. For only a thorough understanding of the Cross can bring us to that place of dependence which the Lord Jesus Himself voluntarily took when He said: 'I can of myself do nothing: as I hear, I judge: and my judgment is righteous; because I seek not mine own will, but the will of him that sent me' (John 5. 30).

13

The Path of Progress: Bearing the Cross

I**N** our previous chapter we have touched several times upon the matter of service for the Lord. As we come now to look at the provision that God has made to meet the problem created by the soul-life of man, it will be helpful if we approach that problem by considering first the principles that regulate all such service. God has laid down spiritual laws which govern our world for Him and from which no one who tries to serve Him may deviate. The basis of our salvation, as we well know, is the fact of the Lord's death and resurrection; but the conditions of our service are no less definite. Just as the fact of the death and resurrection of the Lord is the ground of our acceptance with God, so the *principle* of death and resurrection is the basis of our life and service for Him.

The basis of all true ministry

No one can be a true servant of God without knowing the principle of death and the principle of resurrection. Even the Lord Jesus Himself served on that basis. You will find in

Matthew 3 that, before His public ministry ever began, our Lord submitted Himself to baptism. He was baptized not because He had any sin, or anything which needed cleansing. No, we know the meaning of baptism: it is a figure of death and resurrection. The ministry of the Lord did not begin until, in figure, He had taken His stand there. After He had been baptized and had voluntarily taken the ground of death and resurrection, the Holy Spirit came upon Him, and then He ministered.

What does this teach us? Our Lord was a sinless Man. None but He has trodden this earth and known no sin. Yet as Man He had a separate personality from His Father. Now we must tread very carefully when we touch our Lord; but remember His words: 'I seek not mine own will, but the will of him that sent me.' What does this mean? It certainly does not mean that the Lord had no will of His own. He had a will, as His own words show. As Son of man He had a will, but He did not do it; He came to do the will of the Father. So this is the point. That element in Him which is in distinction from the Father is the human soul, which He assumed when He was 'found in fashion as a man'. Being a perfect Man our Lord had a soul, and of course a body, just as you and I have a soul and a body, and it was thus possible for Him to act *from the soul*—that is, from Himself.

You remember that immediately after the Lord's baptism, and before His public ministry began, Satan came and tempted Him. He tempted Him to satisfy His essential needs by turning stones to bread; to secure immediate respect for His ministry by appearing miraculously in the temple court, to assume without delay the world dominion destined for Him; and you are inclined to wonder why he tempted Him to do such strange things. He might rather, you feel, have tempted Him to sin in a more thorough-going way. But Satan did not do that; he knew better. He only said to Jesus: 'If thou art the Son of God, command that these stones become bread.' What did it mean? The implication was this: 'If You are the Son of God You must do something to prove it. Here is a challenge. Some will certainly raise a question as to whether Your claim is real or not. Why do You not settle the matter finally now by coming out and proving it?'

The whole subtle object of Satan was to get the Lord to act for Himself—that is, from the soul—and, by the stand He took, Jesus absolutely repudiated such action. In Adam, man had acted from himself apart from God; that was the whole tragedy of the garden. Now in a similar situation the Son of man takes another ground. Later He defines it as His basic life-principle—and I like the word in the Greek: 'The Son can do nothing *out from* himself' (John 5. 19). That total denial of the supremacy of the soul-life was to govern all His ministry.

So we can safely say that all the work which the Lord Jesus did on earth, prior to His actual death on the cross, was done with the principle of death and resurrection as basis, even though as an actual event Calvary still lay in the future. Everything He did was on the ground. But if this is so—if the Son of man has to go through death and resurrection (in figure and in principle) in order to work, can we do otherwise? Surely no servant of the Lord can serve Him without himself knowing the working of that principle in his life. It is of course out of the question.

Jesus made this very clear to His disciples when He left them. He had died and was risen, and now He told them to wait in Jerusalem for power to come upon them. What is this power of the Holy Spirit, this 'power from on high' of which He spoke? It is nothing less than the virtue of His death, resurrection and ascension. To use another figure, the Holy Spirit is the Vessel in whom all the values of the death, resurrection and exaltation of the Lord are deposited, that they may be brought to us. He is the one who 'contains' those values and mediates them to men. That is why the Spirit could not be given until Jesus had been glorified. Then only could He rest upon men and women that they might witness; for without the values of the death and resurrection of Christ all such witness is empty.

If we turn to the Old Testament we find the same thing is there. I would refer you to a familiar passage in the seventeenth chapter of Numbers. The matter of Aaron's ministry has been contested. There is a question among the people as to whether Aaron is truly the chosen of God. They have entertained a suspicion, and have said in effect: 'Whether that man is ordained of God or not, we do not know!' and so God sets out to prove who is His servant and who is not. How does He do so? Twelve dead rods are laid before the Lord in the sanctuary over against the testimony, and are left there for a night. By the morning, the Lord has indicated His chosen minister by the rod which buds, blossoms and bears fruit.

We all know the meaning of that. The budding almond rod speaks of resurrection. It is death and resurrection that marks God-recognized ministry. Without that you have nothing. The budding of Aaron's rod proved him to be on a true basis, and God will only recognize as His ministers those who have come through death to resurrection ground.

We have seen the death of Christ working in different ways. We know how it has worked in regard to the forgiveness of our sins, and that without the shedding of Blood there is no remission. Further on, we have seen how His death works to deliver us from sin's power, and that our old man has been crucified with Him in order that henceforth we should not serve sin. Going further still, the question of human self-will arose, and our need of consecration became apparent; and we found death working that way to bring about in us a willingness to let go our own choices and obey Him. That indeed constitutes a starting-point for our ministry, but still it does not touch the core of the question. There may still be the lack of knowledge of what is meant by the soul.

Then another phase is presented to us in Romans 7 where the question of holiness of life is in view—a living, personal holiness. There you find a true man of God trying to please God in righteousness, and he comes under the law and the law finds him out. He is trying to please God by using his own carnal power, and the Cross has to bring him to the place where he says, 'I cannot do it. I cannot satisfy God with *my* powers; I can only trust the Holy Spirit to do that in me.' I believe some of us have passed through deep waters to learn this, and to discover the value of the death of the Lord working in this way.

Now mark you, there is still a great difference between 'the flesh', as spoken of in Romans 7 in relation to holiness of life, and the working of the natural energies of the soul-life in the service of the Lord. With all the above being known, and known in experience, there still remains this one sphere more which the death of the Lord must enter before we are truly of service to Him. For even with all these experiences, we are still unsafe for Him to use until this further thing is effected in us. How many of God's servants are used by Him, as we say in China, to build twelve feet of wall, only, when they have done so, to undo it all by themselves pulling down fifteen feet! We are used in a sense, but at the same time we destroy our own work, and sometimes that of others also, because of there being somewhat something undealt with by the Cross.

We now have to see how the Lord has set out to deal with the soul, and then, more particularly, how this touches the question of our service for Him.

The subjective working of the Cross

We must keep before us now four passages from the Gospels. They are: Matthew 10. 34–39; Mark 8. 32–35; Luke 17. 32–34; and John 12. 24–26. These four passages have something in common. In each you have the Lord Himself speaking to us concerning the soul-activity of man, and in each a different aspect or manifestation of the soul-life is touched upon. In these verses He makes it very plain that the soul of man can be dealt with in one way and in one way only, and that is by our bearing the cross daily and following Him.

As we have just seen, the soul-life or natural life that is here in view is something further than what we have in those passages which are concerned with the old man of the flesh. We have sought to make quite that, in respect of our old man, God emphasizes the thing He has done *once for all* in crucifying us with Christ on the Cross. We have seen that three times in the Epistle to the Galatians the 'crucifying' aspect of the Cross is referred to as a thing accomplished; and in Romans 6. 6 we have the clear statement that 'our old man was crucified', which, if the tense of the word means anything, we might well paraphrase: 'Our old man has been finally and for ever crucified.' It is something done, to be apprehended by divine revelation and then accepted by an act of simple faith.

But there is a further aspect of the Cross, namely that implied in the expression 'bearing his cross daily', which is before us now. The Cross has borne me; now I must bear it; and this bearing of the Cross is an inward thing. It is this that we mean when we speak of 'the subjective working of the Cross'. Moreover it is a continuous process, a step by step following after Him. It is this which is now brought before us in relation to the soul, and as we have just said, with an emphasis here that is not quite the same as with the old man. We do not have here the 'crucifixion' of the soul itself, in the sense that our natural gifts and faculties, our personality and our individuality, are to be put away altogether. Were it so it could hardly be said of us, as it is in Hebrews 10. 39, that we are to 'have faith unto the saving of the soul'. (Compare 1 Peter 1. 9; Luke 21. 19.) No, we do not lose our souls in this sense, for to do so would be to lose our individual existence completely. The soul is still there with its natural endowments, but the Cross is brought to bear upon it to bring those natural endowments into death—to put the mark of *His* death upon them—and thereafter, as God may please, to give them back to us in glorious resurrection.

It is in this sense that Paul, writing to the Philippians, expresses the desire 'that I may know him, and the power of his resurrection, and the fellowship of his sufferings, becoming conformed unto his death' (Phil. 3. 10). The mark of death is upon the soul all the time, to bring it to the place where it is always subordinate to the Spirit and never independently asserts itself. Only the Cross, working in such a way, could make a man of the calibre of Paul, and with the natural resources hinted at in Philippians 3, so distrust his own natural strength that he could write to the Corinthians: 'I determined not to know anything among you, save Jesus Christ, and him crucified. And I was with you in weakness, and in fear, and in much trembling. And my speech and my preaching were not in persuasive words of wisdom, but in demonstration of the Spirit and of power: that your faith should not stand in the wisdom of men, but in the power of God' (1 Cor. 2. 2, 3).

The soul is the seat of the affections, and what a great part of our decision and actions is influenced by these! There is nothing deliberately sinful about them, mind you. It is just that there is something in us which can go out in natural affection to another person, and which, ungoverned by the Spirit, can influence wrongly our whole course of action. So in the first of the four passages before us the Lord has to say: 'He that loveth father or mother more than me is not worthy of me; and he that loveth son or daughter more than me is not worthy of me. And he that doth not take his cross and follow after me, is not worthy of me' (Matt. 10. 37, 38). You note that to follow the Lord in the way of the Cross is set before us as His normal, His only way for us. What immediately follows? 'He that findeth his soul shall lose it; and he that loseth his soul for my sake shall find it' (Matt. 10. 39, mg.).

The secret danger lies in that subtle working of the affections to turn us away from the pathway of God; and the key to the matter is the soul. The Cross has to touch that. I have to 'lose' my soul in the sense in which the Lord meant those words, and which we are seeking here to explain.

Some of us know well what it means to lose our soul. We can no longer lightly fulfil its desire; we cannot just give in to it and gratify it: that is the 'loss' of the soul. We are going through a painful process to discourage what the soul is asking for. And many a time we have to confess that it is not any definite sin that is keeping us from following the Lord to the end. We are held up because of some secret love somewhere, some perfectly innocent natural affection diverting our course. Yes, human affection plays a great part in our lives, and the Cross has to come in there and do its purifying work.

Then we pass to the verses in Mark chapter 8. I think that is a most important passage. Our Lord had just taught His disciples at Cæsarea Philippi that He was going to suffer death at the hands of the elders of the Jews, and then Peter, with all his love for his Master, came up and protested, saying, 'Lord, do not do it; pity Thyself: this shall never come to Thee!' Out of his love for the Lord he appealed to Him to spare Himself; and the Lord had to rebuke Peter, as He would rebuke Satan, for caring for the things of men and not the things of God. And then, to the multitude that gathered to Him, the word was spoken once more: 'If any man would come after me, let him deny himself, and take up his cross, and follow me. For whosoever will save his soul shall lose it; and whosoever shall lose his soul for my sake and the gospel's shall save it' (Mark 8. 34, 35, mg.).

The whole question at issue is again that of the soul, and here it is particularly of the soul's desire for self-preservation. There is that subtle suggestion which says, 'If I could be allowed to live I would do anything, be willing for anything; but I must be kept alive!' There you have the soul almost crying out for help. 'Going to the Cross, being crucified—oh that is really too much! Have mercy on yourself; pity yourself! Do you mean to say you are going *against yourself* and *going with God*?' Some of us know well that, in order to go on with God, we have many a time to go against the voice of the soul—our own or other people's—and to let the Cross come in to silence that appeal for self-preservation.

Am I afraid of the will of God? The dear saint whom I have already mentioned as having had such an influence upon the course of my life, many times asked me the question: 'Do you like the will of God?' It is a tremendous question. She did not ask, 'Do you *do* the will of God?' she always asked, 'Do you *like* the will of God?' That question goes deeper than anything else. I remember once she was having a controversy with the Lord over a certain matter. She knew what the Lord wanted, and in her heart she wanted it too. But it was difficult, and I heard her pray like this: 'Lord I confess I don't like it, but please do not give in to me. Just wait, Lord—and *I* will give in to *Thee*.' She did not want the Lord to yield to her and to reduce His demands upon her. She wanted nothing but to please Him.

Many a time we have to come to the place where we are willing to let go to Him things we think to be good and precious—yes, and even, it may be, the very things of God themselves—that His will may be done. Peter's concern was for his Lord and was dictated by his natural love for Him. We might feel that Peter had a marvellous love for his Lord, sufficient even for him to dare to question Jesus. Only a strong love could bring one to attempt that! Yes, we think we understand Peter; but when there is purity of spirit without that mixture of soul, we shall not be so readily led into Peter's mistake. We shall more quickly recognize where the will of God lies, and shall discover there, and there alone, our heart's true delight.

Once again the Lord Jesus deals with the matter of the soul in Luke chapter 17, and now it is in relation to His return. Speaking of 'the day that the Son of man is revealed', He draws a parallel between that day and 'the day that Lot went out from Sodom' (verses 29, 30). A little later He speaks of the 'rapture' of the saints in the twice repeated words: 'One shall be taken, and the other shall be left' (verses 34, 35). But between His reference to the calling of Lot out of Sodom and this allusion to the gathering of the saints to Him, there come these remarkable words: 'In that day, he which shall be on the housetop, and his goods in the house, let him not go down to take them away: and let him that is in the field likewise not return back. Remember Lot's wife' (verses 31, 32). *Remember Lot's wife!* Why? Because 'whosoever shall seek to gain his soul shall lose it: but whosoever shall lose his soul shall save it alive' (verse 33, mg.).

If I mistake not, this is the one passage in the New Testament that tells of our reaction to the rapture call. We may have thought that, when the Son of man comes, we shall be gathered to Him automatically, as it were, because of what we read in 1 Corinthians 15. 51, 52: 'We shall all be changed, in a moment, in the twinkling of an eye, at the last trump.' Well, however we reconcile the two passages, this one in Luke's Gospel should at least make us pause and reflect; for the emphasis is here very strongly upon one being taken and the other left. It is a matter of our reaction to the call to go, and on the basis of this, a most urgent appeal is made to us to be ready (compare Matt. 24. 42).

There is surely a reason for this. Clearly that call is not going to produce a miraculous last-minute change in us out of all relation to our previous walk with the Lord. No, in that moment we shall discover our heart's real treasure. If it is the Lord Himself then there will be no backward look. A backward glance decides everything. It is so easy to become more attached to the gifts of God than to the Giver—and even, I should add, to the *work* of God than to God Himself.

Let me illustrate. At the present time[1] I am engaged in writing a book. I have finished eight chapters and I have another nine to write, about which I am very seriously exercised before the Lord. But if the call to 'Come up hither' should come and my reaction were to be, 'What about my book?' the answer might well be, 'All right, stay down and finish it!' That precious thing which we are doing downstairs 'in the house' can be enough to pin us down, a peg that holds us to earth.

It is all a question of our living by the soul or by the spirit. Here in this passage in Luke, we have depicted the soul-life in its engagement with the things of earth—and, mark you, not sinful things either. The Lord only mentioned marrying, planting, eating, selling—all perfectly legitimate activities,

[1] 1938.—ED.

with which there is nothing essentially wrong. But it is occupation with them, so that your heart goes out to them, that is enough to pin you down. The way out of that danger is by the losing of the soul. This is beautifully illustrated in the action of Peter when he recognized the risen Lord Jesus by the lake-side. Though, with the others, he was back for the moment in his former employment, there was now no thought of the ship, nor even of the net full of fishes so miraculously provided. When he heard John's cry of recognition: 'It is the Lord', we read that 'he cast himself into the sea' to go to Jesus.

That is true detachment. The question at issue is always, Where is my heart? The Cross has to work in us a true detachment in spirit from anything and anyone outside of the Lord Himself.

But, even here, we are as yet only dealing with the more outward aspects of the soul's activity. The soul giving rein to its affections, the soul asserting itself and trying to manipulate things, the soul becoming preoccupied with things on the earth: these are still small things, and do not yet touch the real heart of the matter. There is something deeper yet, which I will try now to explain.

The Cross and fruitfulness

Let us read again John 12. 24, 25. 'Verily, verily, I say unto you, Except a grain of wheat fall into the earth and die, it abideth by itself alone; but if it die, it beareth much fruit. He that loveth his life (Greek 'soul', as in the above passage) loseth it; and he that hateth his life ('soul') in this world shall keep it unto life eternal.'

Here we have the inward working of the Cross of which we have been speaking—the losing of the soul—linked with and likened to that aspect of the death of the Lord Jesus Himself which we have already seen depicted in the grain of wheat, namely, His death with a view to increase. The end in view is fruitfulness. There is a grain of wheat with life in it, but 'it abideth alone'. It has the power to impart its life to others; but to do so it must go down into death.

Now we know the way the Lord Jesus took. He passed into death, and, as we saw earlier, His life emerged in many lives. The Son died, and came forth as the first of 'many sons'. He let go His life that we might receive it. It is in this aspect of His death that we are called to die. It is here that He makes clear the value of conformity to His death, whereby we lose our own natural life in order that, in the power of His resurrection, we may become life-imparters, sharing thereafter with others the new life of God which is in us. This is the secret of ministry, the path of real fruitfulness to God. As Paul says: 'We which live are always delivered unto death for Jesus' sake, that the life of Jesus may be manifested in our mortal flesh. So then death worketh in us, but life in you' (2 Cor. 4. 11, 12).

We are coming to our point. In us who have received Christ, there is a new life. We all have that precious possession, the treasure in the vessel. Praise the Lord for the reality of His life within! But why is there so little expression of that life? Why is there an 'abiding alone'? Why is it not overflowing and imparting life to others? Why is it scarcely making itself apparent even in our own lives? The reason why there is so little sign of life where life is present is that the soul in us is enveloping and confining that life (as the husk envelops the grain of wheat) so that it cannot find out-let. We are living in the soul; we are working and serving in our own natural strength; we are not drawing from God. It is the *soul* that stands in the way of the springing up of life. Lose it; for that way lies fullness.

A dark night—a resurrection morn

So we come back to the almond rod, which was brought into the sanctuary for a night—a dark night in which there was nothing to be seen—and then in the morning it budded. There you have set forth the death and resurrection, the life yielded up and the life gained, and there you have the ministry attested. But how does this work out in practice? How do I recognize that God is dealing with me in this way?

First we must be clear about one thing: the soul, with its fund of natural energy and resource, will continue with us until our death. Till then there will be an unending, day-by-day need for the Cross to operate in us, dredging deeply that well-spring of nature. This is the life-long condition of service laid down by Jesus in the words: 'Let him deny himself, and take up his cross, and follow me' (Mark 8. 34). We never get past that. He who evades it 'is not worthy of me' (Matt. 10. 38); he 'cannot be my disciple' (Luke 14. 27). Death and resurrection must remain an abiding principle of our lives for the losing of the soul and the uprising of the Spirit of life.

Yet here too there may be a crisis that, once reached and passed, can transform our whole life and service for God. It is a wicket gate by which we may enter upon an entirely new pathway. Such a crisis occurred in the life of Jacob at

Peniel. It was the 'natural man' in Jacob that was seeking to attain God's end. Jacob well knew that God had said: 'The elder shall serve the younger', but he was trying to compass that end through is own ingenuity. God had to cripple that strength of nature in Jacob, and He did so when He touched the sinew of Jacob's thigh. Jacob continued to walk thereafter, but he continued to be lame. He was a different Jacob, as his change of name implies. He had his feet and he could use them, but the strength had been touched, and he limped from an injury from which he would never quite recover.

God must bring us to a point—I cannot tell you how it will be, but He will do it—where, through a deep and dark experience, our natural power is touched and fundamentally weakened, so that we no longer dare trust ourselves. He has had to deal with some of us very strangely, and take us through difficult and painful ways, in order to get us there. At length there comes a time when we no longer 'like' to do Christian work—indeed we almost dread to do things in the Lord's Name. But then at last it is that He can begin to use us.

I can tell you this, that for a year after I was converted I had a lust to preach. It was impossible for me to stay silent. It was as though there was something moving within me that drove me forward, and I had to keep going. Preaching had become my very life. The Lord may graciously allow you to go on for a long while like that, and to do so with a fair measure of blessing, until one day that natural force impelling you is touched, and from then on you no longer do it because you want to do it but because the Lord wants it. Before that experience you preached for the sake of the satisfaction you got from serving God in that way; and yet sometimes the Lord could not move you to do one thing that *He* wanted done. You were living by the natural life, and that life varies a great deal. It is the slave of your temperament. When emotionally you are set on His way you go ahead at full speed, but when your emotions are directed the other way you are reluctant to move at all, even when duty calls. You are not pliable in the Lord's hands. He has therefore to weaken that strength of preference, of like and dislike, in you, until you will do a thing because He wants it and not because you like it. You may enjoy it or you may not, but you will do it just the same. It is not that you can derive a certain satisfaction from preaching or from doing this or that work for God, and therefore you do it. No, you do it now because it is the will of God, and regardless of whether or not it gives you conscious joy. The true joy you know in doing His will lies deeper than your fluctuating emotions.

God is bringing you to the place where He has but to express a wish and you respond instantly. That is the spirit of the Servant (Psalm 40. 7, 8), but such a spirit does not come *naturally* to any of us. It comes only when our soul, the seat of our natural energy and will and affections, has been brought, by the touch of the Cross, under His sway. Yet such a servant spirit is what He seeks, and will have in us all. The way to it may be long-drawn, or it may be just one stroke; but God has His ways and we must have regard for them.

Every true servant of God must know at some time that disabling from which he can never recover; he can never be quite the same again. There must be that established in you which means that from henceforth you will *really* fear yourself. You will fear to move out on the impulse of your soul, for you know what a bad time you will have in your own heart before the Lord if you do. You have known something of the chastening hand of a loving God upon you, a God who 'dealeth with you as with sons' (Heb. 12. 7). The Spirit Himself bears witness in your spirit to that relationship, and to the inheritance and glory that are ours 'if so be that we suffer with him' (Rom. 8. 16, 17); and your response to the Father of our spirits is: 'Abba, Father.'

But when this is really established in you, you have come to a new place which we speak of as 'resurrection ground'. Death, in principle, may have had to be wrought out to a crisis in your natural life, but when it has, then you find God releases you into resurrection. You discover that what you have lost is being given back, though not quite as before. The principle of life is at work in you now: something that directs and empowers you, animating you with fresh divine life. From henceforth what you have lost will be brought back, but touched now with new values because under heaven's control.

Let me again make this quite clear. If we want to be spiritual people, there is no need for us to amputate our hands or feet: we can still have our body. In the same way we have can our soul, with the full use of its faculties; and yet the soul is not now our life-spring. We are no longer living in it, we are no longer drawing from it and living by it; we use it. When the body becomes our life we live like beasts. When the soul becomes our life we live as rebels and fugitives from God—gifted, cultured, educated, no doubt, but alienated from the life of God. But when we come to live our life in the Spirit and by the Spirit, though we still use our soul faculties just as we do our physical faculties, *they are now the servants of the Spirit*; and when we have reached that point God can really use us.

But the difficulty with many of us is that dark night. The Lord graciously laid me aside once in my life for a number of months and put me, spiritually, into utter darkness. It was almost as though He had forsaken me, almost as though nothing was going on and I had really come to the end of everything. And then by degrees He brought things back again. The temptation is always to try to help God by taking things back ourselves; but remember, there must be a full night in the sanctuary—a full night in darkness. It cannot be hurried; He knows what He is doing.

We would like to have death and resurrection put together within one hour of each other. We cannot face the thought that God will keep us aside for so long a time; we cannot bear to wait. And of course I cannot tell you how long He will take, but in principle I think it is quite safe to say this, that there will be a definite period when He will keep you there. It will seem as though nothing is happening; as though everything you valued is slipping from your grasp. There confronts you a blank wall with no door in it. Seemingly everyone else is being blessed and used, while you yourself have been passed by and are losing out. Lie quiet. All is in darkness, but it is only for a night. It must indeed be a full night, but that is all. Afterwards you will find that everything is given back to you in glorious resurrection; and nothing can measure the difference between what was before and what now is!

I was sitting one day at supper with a young brother to whom the Lord had been speaking on this very question of our natural energy. He said to me, 'It is a blessed thing when you know the Lord has met you and touched you in that fundamental way, and that disabling touch has been received.' There was a plate of biscuits between us on the table, and I picked one up and broke it half as though to eat it. Then, fitting the two pieces together again carefully, I said, 'It looks all right, but it is never quite the same again, is it? When once your back is broken, you will yield ever after to the slightest touch from God.'

That is it. The Lord knows what He is doing with His own, and He has left no aspect of our need unmet in His Cross, that the glory of the Son may be manifested in the sons. Disciples who have gone this way can, I believe, truly echo the words of the apostle Paul, who could claim to serve God 'in my spirit in the gospel of his Son' (Rom. 1. 9). They have learned, as he had, the secret of such a ministry: 'We . . . worship by the Spirit of God, and glory in Christ Jesus, and have no confidence in the flesh' (Phil. 3. 3).

Few can have led a more active life than Paul's. To the Romans he puts it on record that he has preached the Gospel from Jerusalem to Illyicum (Rom. 15. 19) and that he is ready now to go on to Rome (1. 10) and thence, if possible, to Spain (15. 24, 28). Yet in all this service, embracing as it does the whole Mediterranean world, his heart is set on one object only—the uplifting of the One who has made it all possible. 'I have therefore my glorying in Christ Jesus in things pertaining to God. For I will not dare to speak of any things save those which Christ wrought through me, for the obedience of the Gentiles, by word and deed' (Rom. 15. 17, 18). That is spiritual service.

May God make each one of us, as truly as he was, 'a bondservant of Jesus Christ'.

14

The Goal of the Gospel

FOR our final chapter we will take as our starting-point an incident in the Gospels that occurs under the very shadow of the Cross—an incident that, in its details, is at once historic and prophetic. 'While he was in Bethany in the house of Simon the leper, as he sat at meat, there came a woman having an alabaster cruse of ointment of spikenard very costly; and she brake the cruse, and poured it over his head. . . . Jesus said . . . Verily I say unto you, Wheresoever the gospel shall be preached throughout the whole world, that also which this woman hath done shall be spoken of for a memorial of her' (Mark 14. 3, 6, 9).

Thus the Lord ordained that the story of Mary anointing Him with that costly ointment should always accompany the story of the Gospel; that what Mary has done should always be coupled with what the Lord has done. That is His own statement. What does He intend that we should understand by it?

I think we all know the story of Mary's action well. From the details given in John chapter 12, where the incident follows not long after her brother's restoration to life, we may gather that the family was not a specially wealthy one. The sisters had to work in the house themselves, for we are told that at this feast 'Martha also served' (John 12. 2 and compare Luke 10. 40).[1] No doubt every penny mattered to them. Yet one of those sisters, Mary, having among her treasures an alabaster cruse containing three hundred pence worth of ointment, expended the whole thing on the Lord. Human reasoning said this was really to much: it was giving the Lord more than his due. That is why Judas took the lead, and the other disciples supported him, in voicing a general complaint that Mary's action was a wasteful one.

Waste

'But there were some that had indignation among themselves saying, To what purpose hath this waste of the ointment been made? For this ointment might have been sold for above three hundred pence and given to the poor. And they murmured against her' (Mark 14. 4, 5). These words bring us to what I believe the Lord would have us consider finally together, namely, that which is signified by the little word 'waste'.

What is waste? Waste means, among other things, giving more than is necessary. If a shilling will do and you give a pound, it is a waste. If two grams will do and you give a kilogram, it is a waste. If three days will suffice to finish a

---

[1] The author here takes the fairly common view that the 'house of Simon the leper' was the home of Mary, Martha and Lazarus, Simon presumably also being a relative of the two sisters.—ED.

task well enough and you lavish five days or a week on it, it is a waste. Waste means that you give something too much for something too little. If someone is receiving more than he is considered to be worth, then that is waste.

But remember, we are dealing here with something which the Lord said was to go out with the Gospel, wherever that Gospel should be carried. Why? Because He intends that the preaching of the Gospel should issue something along the very lines of the action of Mary here, namely, that people should come to Him and waste themselves on Him. This is the result that He is seeking.

We must look at this question of wasting on the Lord from two angles: that of Judas (John 12. 4–6) and that of the other disciples (Matt. 26. 8, 9); and for our present purpose we will run together the parallel accounts.

All the twelve thought it a waste. To Judas of course, who had never called Jesus 'Lord', everything that was poured out upon Him was waste. Not only was ointment waste: even water would have been waste. Here Judas stands for the world. In the world's estimation the service of the Lord, and our giving ourselves to Him for such service, is sheer waste. He has never been loved, never had a place in the hearts of the world, so any giving to Him is a waste. Many say: 'Such-and-such a man could make good in the world if only he were not a Christian!' Because a man has some natural talent or other asset in the world's eyes, they count it a shame for him to be serving the Lord. They think such people are really too good for the Lord. 'What waste of a useful life!' they say.

Let me give a personal instance. In 1929 I returned from Shanghai to my home town of Foochow. One day I was walking along the street with a stick, very weak and in broken health, and I met one of my old college professors. He took me into a teashop where we sat down. He looked at me from head to foot and from foot to head, and then he said: 'Now look here; during your college days we thought a good deal of you, and we had hopes that you would achieve something great. *Do you mean to tell me that this is what you are?*' Looking at me with penetrating eyes, he asked that very pointed question. I must confess that, on hearing it, my first desire was to break down and weep. My career, my health, everything had gone, and here was my old professor who taught me law in the school, asking me: 'Are you still in this condition, with no success, no progress, nothing to show?'

But the very next moment—and I have to admit that in all my life it was the first time—I really knew what it meant to have the 'Spirit of glory' resting upon me. The thought of being able to pour out my life for my Lord flooded my soul with glory. Nothing short of the Spirit of glory was on me then. I could look up and without a reservation say, 'Lord, I praise Thee! This is the best thing possible; it is the right course that I have chosen!' To my professor it seemed a total waste to serve the Lord; but that is what the Gospel is for— to bring each one of us to a true estimate of His worth.

Judas felt it a waste. 'We could manage better with the money by using it in some other way. There are plenty of poor people. Why not rather give it for charity, do some social service for their uplift, help the poor in some practical way? Why pour it out at the feet of Jesus?' (see John 12. 4–6.) That is always the way the world reasons. 'Can you not find a better employment for your life? Can you not do something better with yourself than this? It is going a bit too far to give yourself altogether to the Lord!'

But if the Lord is worthy, then how can it be a waste? He is worthy to be so served. He is worthy for me to be His prisoner. He is worthy for me just to live for Him. *He is worthy!* What the world says about this does not matter. The Lord says: 'Do not trouble her.' So let us not be troubled. Men may say what they like, but we can stand on this ground, that the Lord said, 'It is a good work. Every true work is not done on the poor; every true work is done to Me.' When once our eyes have been opened to the real worth of our Lord Jesus, *nothing* is too good for Him.

But I do not want to dwell too much on Judas. Let us go on to see what was the attitude of the other disciples, because their reaction affects us even more than does his. We do not greatly mind what the world is saying; we can stand that, but we do very much mind what other Christians are saying who ought to understand. And yet we find that they said the same thing as Judas; and they not only said it but they were very upset, very indignant about it. 'When the disciples saw it, they had indignation, saying, To what purpose is this waste? For this ointment might have been sold for much, and given to the poor' (Matt. 26. 8, 9).

Of course we know that the attitude of mind is all too common among Christians which says, 'Get all you can for as little as possible.' That however is not what is in view here, but something deeper. Let me illustrate. Has someone been telling you that you are wasting your life by sitting still and not doing much? They say, 'Here are people who ought to get out into this or that kind of work. They could be used to help this or that group of people. Why are they not more active?'—and in saying so, their whole idea is *use*. Everything ought to be used to the full in ways they understand.

There are those who have been very concerned with some dear servants of the Lord on this very ground, that they are apparently not *doing* enough. They could do so much more, they think, if they could secure an entry somewhere and enjoy a greater acceptance and prominence in certain circles. They could then be used in a far greater way. I have spoken already of a sister whom I knew for a long time and who, I think, is the one by whom I have been helped most. She was used of the Lord in a very real way during those years when I was associated with her, though to some of us at the time this was not so apparent. The one concern in my heart was this: 'She is not used!' Constantly I said to myself, 'Why does she not get out and take some meetings, go somewhere, do something? It is a waste for her to be living in that small village with nothing happening!' Sometimes, when I went to see her, I almost shouted at her. I said, 'No one knows the Lord as you do. You know the Book in a most living way. Do you not see the need around? Why don't you *do* something? It is a waste of time, a waste of energy, a waste of money, a waste of everything, just sitting here and doing nothing!'

But no, brethren, that is not the first thing with the Lord. He wants you and me to be used, certainly. God forbid that I should preach inactivity, or seek to justify a complacent attitude to the world's need. As Jesus Himself says here, 'the gospel shall be preached throughout the whole world'. But the question is one of emphasis. Looking back today, I realize how greatly the Lord was in fact using that dear sister to speak to a number of us who, as young men, were at that

time in His training school for this very work of the Gospel.
I cannot thank God enough for her and for the influence of
her life upon me.

What, then, is the secret? Clearly it is this, that in approving Mary's action at Bethany, the Lord Jesus was laying
down one thing as a basis of all service: that you pour out
all you have, your very self, *unto Him;* and if that should be
all He allows you to do, that is enough. It is not first of all a
question of whether 'the poor' have been helped or not.
That will follow, but the first question is: Has the Lord been
satisfied?

There is many a meeting we might address, many a convention at which we might minister, many a Gospel campaign in which we might have a share. It is not that we are
unable to do it. We could labour and be used to the full; but
the Lord is not so concerned about our ceaseless occupation
in work for Him. That is not His first object. The service of
the Lord is not to be measured by tangible results. No, my
friends, the Lord's first concern is with our position at His
feet and our anointing of His head. Whatever we have as an
'alabaster box': the most precious thing, the thing dearest in
the world to us—yes, let me say it, *the outflow from us of a life
that is produced by the very Cross itself*—we give that all up *to
the Lord*. To some, even of those who should understand, it
seems a waste; but that is what He seeks above all. Often
enough the giving to Him will be in tireless service, but He
reserves to Himself the right to suspend the service for a
time, in order to discover to us whether it is that, or Himself, that holds us.

Ministering to His pleasure

'Wheresoever the gospel shall be preached . . . that also which this woman hath done shall be spoken of' (Mark 14. 9).

Why did the Lord say this? Because the Gospel is meant to produce this. It is what the Gospel is for. The Gospel is not just to satisfy sinners. Praise the Lord, sinners will be satisfied! but their satisfaction is, we may say, a blessed by-product of the Gospel and not its primary aim. The Gospel is preached in the first place so that *the Lord* may be satisfied.

I am afraid we lay too much emphasis on the good of sinners and we have not sufficiently appreciated what the Lord has in view as His goal. We have been thinking how the sinner will fare if there is no Gospel, but that is not the main consideration. Yes, Praise God! the sinner has his part. God meets his need and showers him with blessings; but that is not the most important thing. The first thing is this, that everything should be to the satisfaction of the Son of God. It is only when He is satisfied that we shall be satisfied and the sinner will be satisfied. I have never met a soul who has set out to satisfy the Lord and has not been satisfied himself. It is impossible. Our satisfaction comes unfailingly when we satisfy Him first.

But we have to remember this, that He will never be satisfied without our 'wasting' ourselves upon Him. Have you ever given too much to the Lord? May I tell you something? One lesson some of us have come to learn is this, that in divine service the principle of waste is the principle of power. The principle which determines usefulness is the very principle of scattering. Real usefulness in the hand of

God is measured in terms of 'waste'. The more you think you can *do*, and the more you employ your gifts up to the very limit (and some even go over the limit!) in order to do it, the more you find that you are applying the principle of the world and not of the Lord. God's ways with us are all designed to establish in us this other principle, namely, that our work *for* Him springs out of our ministering *to* Him. I do not mean that we are going to do nothing; but the first thing for us must be the Lord Himself, not His work.

But we must come down to very practical issues. You say: 'I have given up a position; I have given up a ministry; I have foregone certain attractive possibilities of a bright future, in order to go on with the Lord in this way. Now I try to serve Him. Sometimes it seems that the Lord hears me, and sometimes He keeps me waiting for a definite answer. Sometimes He uses me, but sometimes it seems that He passes me by. Then, when this is so, I compare myself with that other fellow who is in a certain big system. He too had a bright future, but he has never given it up. He continues on and he serves the Lord. He sees souls saved and the Lord blesses his ministry. He is successful—I do not mean materially, but spiritually—and I sometimes think he looks more like a Christian than I do, so happy, so satisfied. After all, what do I get out of this? He has a good time; I have all the bad time. He has never gone this way, and yet he has much that Christians today regard as spiritual prosperity, while I have all sorts of complications coming to me. What is the meaning of it all? Am I wasting my life? Have I really given too much?'

So there is your problem. You feel that were you to follow in that other brother's steps—were you, shall we say, to consecrate yourself enough for the blessing but not enough for the trouble, enough for the Lord to use you but not enough for Him to shut you up—all would be perfectly all right. But would it? You know quite well that it would not.

Take your eyes off that other man! Look at your Lord, and ask yourself again what it is that *He* values most highly. The principle of waste is the principle that He would have govern us. 'She is doing this *for Me*.' True satisfaction is brought to the heart of God when we are really, as people would think, 'wasting' ourselves upon Him. It seems as though we are giving too much and getting nothing—and *that* is the secret of pleasing God.

Oh, friends, what are we seeking? Do we seek for 'use' as those disciples did? They wanted to make every penny of those three hundred pence go to its full length. The whole question was one of obvious 'usefulness' to God in terms that could be measured and put on record. The Lord waits to hear us say: 'Lord, I do not mind about that. If I can only please *Thee*, it is enough.'

Anointing Him beforehand

'Let her alone; why trouble ye her? she hath wrought a good work on me. For ye have the poor always with you, and whensoever ye will ye can do them good: but me ye have not always. She hath done what she could: she hath anointed my body aforehand for the burying' (Mark 14. 6–8).

In these verses the Lord Jesus introduces a time-factor with the word 'beforehand', and this is something of which we can have a new application today, for it is as important

to us now as it was to her then. We all know that in the age
to come we shall be called to a greater work—not to inactivity. 'Well done, good and faithful servant: thou hast been
faithful over a few things, I will set thee over many things:
enter thou into the joy of thy lord' (Matthew 25. 21; and
compare Matthew 24. 47 and Luke 19. 17). Yes, there will
be a greater work; for the work of God's house will go on,
just as in the story the care of the poor went on. The poor
would always be with them, but they could not always have
Him. There was something, represented by this pouring out
of the ointment, which Mary had to do *beforehand* or she
would have no later opportunity. I believe that in that day
we shall all love Him as we have never done now, but yet
that it will be most blessed for those who have poured out
their all upon the Lord today. When we see Him face to
face, I trust that we shall all break and pour out everything
for Him. But *today*—what are we doing *today*?

Several days after Mary broke the alabaster box and
poured the ointment on Jesus' head, there were some
women who went early in the morning to anoint the body
of the Lord. Did they do it? Did they succeed in their purpose on that first day of the week? No, there was only one
soul who succeeded in anointing the Lord, and it was Mary,
who anointed Him beforehand. The others never did it, for
He had risen. Now I suggest that, in just such a way, the
matter of time may be supremely important to us also, and
that for us the question above all questions is: *What am I
doing to the Lord today.*

Have our eyes been opened to see the preciousness of the
One whom we are serving? Have we come to see that nothing less than the dearest, the costliest, the most precious, is

fit for Him? Have we recognized that working for the poor, working for the benefit of the world, working for the souls of men and for the eternal good of the sinner—all these so necessary and valuable things—are right only if they are in their place? In themselves, as things apart, they are as nothing compared with work that is done *to the Lord*.

The Lord has to open our eyes to His worth. If there is in the world some precious art treasure, and I pay the high price asked for it, be it one thousand, ten thousand, or even fifty thousand pounds, dare anyone say it is a waste? The idea of waste only comes into our Christianity when we underestimate the worth of our Lord. The whole question is: How precious is He to us now? If we do not think much of Him, then of course to give Him anything at all, however small, will seem to us a wicked waste. But when He is really precious to our souls, nothing will be too good, nothing too costly for Him; everything we have, our dearest, our most priceless treasure, we shall pour out upon Him, and we shall not count it a shame to have done so.

Of Mary the Lord said: 'She hath done what she could.' What does that mean? It means that she had given up her all. She had kept nothing in reserve for a future day. She had lavished on Him all she had; and yet on the resurrection morning she had no reason to regret her extravagance. And the Lord will not be satisfied with anything less from us than that we too should have done 'what we could'. By this, remember, I do not mean the expenditure of our effort and energy in trying to do something for Him, for that is not the point here. What the Lord Jesus looks for in us is a life laid at His feet, and that in view of His death and burial and of a future day. His burial was already in view that day in the home in Bethany. Today it is His crowning that is in view, when He shall be acclaimed in glory as the Anointed One, the Christ of God. Yes, then we shall pour out our all upon Him! But it is a precious thing—indeed it is a far more precious thing to Him—that we should anoint Him now, not with any material oil but with something costly, something from our hearts.

That which is merely external and superficial has no place here. It has already been dealt with by the Cross, and we have given our consent to God's judgment upon it and learnt to know in experience its cutting off. What God is demanding of us now is represented by that flask of alabaster: something mined from the depths, something turned and chased and wrought upon, something that, because it is so truly of the Lord, we cherish as Mary cherished that flask, and we would not, we dare not break it. It comes now from the heart, from the very depth of our being; and we come to the Lord with that, and we break it and pour it out and say: 'Lord, here it is. It is all Yours, because You are worthy!'—and the Lord has got what He desired. May He receive such an anointing from us *today*.

Fragrance

'And the house was filled with the odour of the ointment' (John 12. 3). By the breaking of that flask and the anointing of the Lord Jesus, the house was pervaded with the sweetest fragrance. Everyone could smell it and none could be unaware of it. What is the significance of this?

Whenever you meet someone who has really suffered— someone who has gone through experiences with the Lord that have brought limitation, and who, instead of trying to break free in order to be 'used', has been willing to be imprisoned by Him and has thus learned to find satisfaction in the Lord and nowhere else—then immediately you become aware of something. Immediately your spiritual senses detect a sweet savour of Christ. Something has been crushed, something has been broken in that life, and so you smell the odour. The odour that filled the house that day in Bethany still fills the Church today; Mary's fragrance never passes. It needed but one stroke to break the flask for the Lord, but her action—that unreserved giving and the fragrance of that anointing—abides.

We are speaking here of what we are; not of what we do or what we preach. Perhaps you may have been asking the Lord for a long time that He will be pleased to use you in such a way as to impart impressions of Himself to others. That prayer is not exactly for the gift of preaching or teaching. It is rather that you might be able, in your touch with others, to impart God, the presence of God, the sense of God. Let me tell you, dear friends, you cannot produce such impressions of God upon others without the breaking of everything, even your most precious possessions, at the feet of the Lord Jesus.

But if once that point is reached, you may or may not seem to be much used in an outward way, but God will begin to use you to create a hunger in others. People will scent Christ in you. The most unlikely people will detect that. They will sense that here is one who has gone with the Lord, one who has suffered, one who has not moved freely, independently, but who has known what it is to subject everything to Him. That kind of life creates impressions, and impressions create hunger, and hunger provokes men to go on seeking until they are brought by divine revelation into fullness of life in Christ.

God does not set us here first of all to preach or to do work for Him. The first thing for which He sets us here is to create in others a hunger for Himself. That is, after all, what prepares the soil for the preaching.

If you set a delicious cake in front of two men who have just had a heavy meal, what will be their reaction? They will talk about it, admire its appearance, discuss the recipe, argue about the cost—do everything in fact but eat it! But if they are truly hungry it will not be very long before that cake is gone. And so it is with the things of the Spirit. No true work will ever begin in a life without first of all a sense of need being created. But how can this be done? We cannot inject spiritual appetite by force into others; we cannot compel people to be hungry. Hunger has to be created, and it can be created in others only by those who carry with them the impressions of God.

I always like to think of the words of that 'great woman' of Shunem. Speaking of the prophet, whom she had observed but whom she did not know well, she said: 'Behold now, I perceive that this is an holy man of God, which passeth by us continually' (2 Kings 4. 9). It was not what Elisha said or did that conveyed that impression, but what he was. By his merely passing by she could detect something; she could *see*. What are people sensing about us? We may leave many kinds of impressions: we may leave the impression that we are clever, that we are gifted, that *we* are this or that or the other. But no, the impression left by Elisha was an impression of God Himself.

This matter of our impact upon others turns upon one thing, and that is the working of the Cross in us with regard to the pleasure of the heart of God. It demands that I seek His pleasure, that I seek to satisfy Him only, and I do not mind how much it costs me to do so. The sister of whom I have spoken came once into a situation that was very difficult for her; I mean, it was costing her everything. I was with her at the time, and together we knelt down and prayed with wet eyes. Looking up she said: 'Lord, I am willing to break my heart in order that I may satisfy Thy heart!' To talk thus of heart-break might with many of us be merely romantic sentiment, but in the particular situation in which she was, it meant to her just that.

There must be something—a willingness to yield, a breaking and a pouring out of everything to Him—which gives release to that fragrance of Christ and produces in other lives an awareness of need, drawing them out and on to know the Lord. This is what I feel to be the heart of everything. The Gospel has as its one object the producing in us sinners of a condition that will satisfy the heart of our God. In order that He may have that, we come to Him with all we have, all we are—yes, even the most cherished things in our spiritual experience—and we make known to Him: 'Lord, I am willing to let go all of this for You: not just for Your work, not for Your children, not for anything else at all, but altogether and only for Yourself!'

Oh, to be wasted! It is a blessed thing to be wasted for the Lord. So many who have been prominent in the Christian world know nothing of this. Many of us have been used to the full—have been used, I would say, too much—but we do not know what it means to be wasted on God' We like to be always 'on the go': the Lord would sometimes prefer to have us in prison. We think in terms of apostolic journeys: God dares to put His greatest ambassadors in chains.

'But thanks be unto God, which always leadeth us in triumph in Christ, and maketh manifest through us the savour of his knowledge in every place' (2 Cor. 2. 14).

'And the house was filled with the odour of the ointment' (John 12. 3).

The Lord grant us grace that we may learn how to please Him. When, like Paul, we make this our supreme aim (2 Cor. 5. 9), the Gospel will have achieved its end.

SIT, WALK, STAND

Sit
Walk
Stand

WATCHMAN NEE

Preface to the Fourth Edition

Compiled from the spoken ministry of Mr Watchman Nee (Nee To-sheng) of Foochow and first published in Bombay, *Sit, Walk, Stand* continues to stir the hearts of readers with its arousing message. Although through successive editions the book has been slightly expanded, all the source material dates from a single period—the spacious days of evangelistic witness in China just prior to the Japanese war, when the author and his fellow Christians enjoyed a liberty in the service of God that is rare today. A message which expresses at once their triumphant assurance in the finished work of Christ and their humble sense of the high qualities called for in His servants has a fresh relevance for us now, when Christian work everywhere is on trial. May God give us grace not only to heed its challenge but to find ways, while there is time, of applying its lessons in our own sphere of opportunity.

ANGUS I. KINNEAR
London, 1962

Introduction

If the life of a Christian is to be pleasing to God it must be properly adjusted to Him in all things. Too often we place the emphasis in our own lives upon the application of this principle to some single detail of our behaviour or of our work for Him. Often we fail therefore to appreciate either the extent of the adjustment called for or, at times even, the point from which it should begin. But God measures everything, from start to finish, by the perfections of His Son. Scripture clearly affirms that it is God's good pleasure 'to sum up all things in Christ . . . in whom also we were made a heritage' (Eph. 1. 9–11). It is my earnest prayer that, in the discussion that follows, our eyes may be opened afresh to see that it is only by placing our entire emphasis *there* that we can hope to realise the divine purpose for us, which is that 'we should be unto the praise of his glory' (1. 12).

We shall take as a background to our thoughts the Epistle of Paul to the Ephesians.

Like so many of the apostle's letters, this Epistle falls naturally into two sections, a doctrinal and a practical. The doctrinal section (chapters 1 to 3) is concerned mainly with the great facts of the redemption which God has wrought for us in Christ. The practical section (chapters 4 to 6) then goes on to present us with the demands, in terms of Christian conduct and zeal, that God is making upon us in the light of that redemption. The two halves are closely related, but it will be seen that the emphasis in each is different.

Then, further, the second and more obviously practical half of the letter may again conveniently be subdivided according to its subject-matter into a first long section from chapter 4. 1 to 6. 9 and a second and much shorter section from chapter 6. 10 to the end. The first part deals with our life in the midst of the world; the second with our conflict with the devil.

Thus we have, in all, three sub-divisions of the Epistle to the Ephesians, setting forth the believer's position in Christ (1. 1–3. 21), his life in the world (4. 1–6. 9), and his attitude to the enemy (6. 10–24). We may summarise these as follows:

EPHESIANS

A. Doctrinal (Chapters 1 to 3)

1. OUR POSITION IN CHRIST (1. 1–3. 21)

B. Practical (Chapters 4 to 6)

2. OUR LIFE IN THE WORLD (4. 1–6. 9)

3. OUR ATTITUDE TO THE ENEMY (6. 10–24)

Of all Paul's epistles, it is in Ephesians that we find the highest spiritual truths concerning the Christian life. The letter abounds with spiritual riches, and yet at the same time it is intensely practical. The first half of the letter reveals our life in Christ to be one of union with Him in the highest heavens. The second half shows us in very practical terms how such a heavenly life is to be lived by us down here on the earth. We do not here propose to study the letter in detail. We shall, however, touch on a few principles lying at its heart. For this purpose we shall select one key-word in each of the above three sections to express what we believe to be its governing idea.

In the first section of the letter we note the word *sit* (2. 6) which is the key to that section and the secret of a true Christian experience. God has made us to sit with Christ in the heavenly places, and every Christian must begin his spiritual life from that place of rest. In the second part we select the work *walk* (4. 1) as expressive of our life in the world, which is its subject. We are challenged there to display in our Christian walk conduct that is in keeping with our high calling. And finally, in the third part we find the key to our attitude towards the enemy contained in the one word *stand* (6. 11), expressive of our place of triumph at the end. Thus we have:

KEY WORDS IN EPHESIANS

1. Our Position in Christ—'SIT' (2. 6)
2. Our Life in the World—'WALK' (4. 1)
3. Our Attitude to the Enemy—'STAND' (6. 11)

The life of the believer always presents these three aspects—to God, to man, and to the Satanic powers. To be useful in God's hand a man must be properly adjusted in respect of all three: his position, his life, and his warfare. He falls short of God's requirements if he under-estimates the importance of any one of them, for each is a sphere in which God would express 'the glory of his grace, which he freely bestowed on us in the Beloved' (1. 6).

We will take, then, these three words—'Sit', 'Walk', 'Stand'—as guides to the teaching of the Epistle, and as the text for its present message to our hearts. We shall find it most instructive to note both the order and the connection in which they come.

1

Sit

'*The God of our Lord Jesus Christ, . . . raised him from the dead, and made him to sit at his right hand in the heavenly places, far above all rule, and authority, and power, and dominion, and every name that is named, not only in this world, but also in that which is to come*' (Eph. 1. 17–21).

'*And raised us up with him, and made us to sit with him in the heavenly places, in Christ Jesus: . . . for by grace have ye been saved through faith; and that not of yourselves: it is the gift of God: not of works, that no man should glory*' (Eph. 2. 6–9).

'God . . . made him to sit . . . and made us to sit with him.' Let us first consider the implications of this word 'sit'. As we have said, it reveals the secret of a heavenly life. Christian life does not begin with walking; it begins with sitting. The Christian era began with Christ, of whom we are told that, when He had made purification of sins, He 'sat down on the right hand of the Majesty on high' (Heb. 1. 3). With equal truth we can say that the individual Christian life begins with a man 'in Christ'—that is to say, when by faith we see ourselves seated together with Him in the heavens.

Most Christians make the mistake of trying to walk in order to be able to sit, but that is a reversal of the true order. Our natural reason says, If we do not walk, how can we ever reach the goal? What can we attain without effort? How can we ever get anywhere if we do not move? But Christianity is a queer business! If at the outset we try to do anything, we get nothing; if we seek to attain something, we miss everything. For Christianity begins not with a big DO, but with a big DONE. Thus Ephesians opens with the statement that God *has* 'blessed us with every spiritual blessing in the heavenly places in Christ' (1. 3) and we are invited at the very outset to sit down and enjoy what God has done for us; not to set out to try and attain it for ourselves.

Walking implies effort, whereas God says that we are saved, not by works, but 'by grace . . . through faith' (2. 8). We constantly speak of being 'saved through faith', but what do we mean by it? We mean this, that we are saved by reposing in the Lord Jesus. We did nothing whatever to save ourselves; we simply laid upon Him the burden of our sin-sick souls. We began our Christian life by depending not upon our own doing but upon what He had done. Until a man does this he is no Christian; for to say: 'I can do nothing to save myself; but by His grace God *has done* everything for me in Christ', is to take the first step in the life of faith. The Christian life from start to finish is based upon this principle of utter dependence upon the Lord Jesus. There is no limit to the grace God is willing to bestow upon us. He will give us everything, but we can receive none of it except as we rest in Him. 'Sitting' is an attitude of rest. Something has been finished, work stops, and we sit. It is paradoxical, but true, that we only advance in the Christian life as we learn first of all to sit down.

What does it really mean to sit down? When we walk or stand we bear on our legs all the weight of our own body, but when we sit down our entire weight rests upon the chair or couch on which we sit. We grow weary when we walk or stand, but we feel rested when we have sat down for a while. In walking or standing we expend a great deal of energy, but when we are seated we relax at once, because the strain no longer falls upon our muscles and nerves but upon something outside of ourselves. So also in the spiritual realm, to sit down is simply to rest our whole weight—our load, ourselves, our future, everything—upon the Lord. We let Him bear the responsibility and cease to carry it ourselves.

This was God's principle from the beginning. In the creation God worked from the first to the sixth day and rested on the seventh. We may truthfully say that for those first six days He was very busy. Then, the task He had set Himself completed, He ceased to work. The seventh day became the sabbath of God; it was God's rest.

But what of Adam? Where did he stand in relation to that rest of God? Adam, we are told, was created on the sixth day. Clearly, then, he had no part in those first six days of work, for he came into being only at their end. God's seventh day was, in fact, Adam's first. Whereas God worked six days and then enjoyed His sabbath rest, Adam began his life with the sabbath; for God works before He rests, while man must first enter into God's rest, and then alone can he work. Moreover it was because God's work of creation was truly complete that Adam's life could begin with rest. And here is the Gospel: that God has gone one stage further and has completed also the work of redemption, and that we need do nothing whatever to merit it, but can enter by faith directly into the values of His finished work.

Of course we know that between these two historic facts, between God's rest in creation and God's rest in redemption, there lies the whole tragic story of Adam's sin and judgment, of man's unceasing, unprofitable labour, and of the coming of the Son of God to toil and to give Himself until the lost position was recovered. 'My Father worketh even until now, and I work,' He explained as He pursued His way. Only with the atoning price paid could He cry: 'It is finished!'

But because of that triumphant cry, the analogy we have drawn is a true one. Christianity indeed means that God has done everything in Christ, and that we simply step by faith into the enjoyment of that fact. Our keyword here is not of course, in its context, a command to 'sit down' but to see ourselves as 'seated' in Christ. Paul prays that the eyes of our heart may be enlightened (1. 18) to understand all that is contained for us in this double fact, that God has first by mighty power 'made him to sit', and then by grace 'made us to sit with him'. And the first lesson we must learn is this, that the work is not initially ours at all, but His. It is not that we work for God, but that He works for us. God *gives* us our position of rest. He brings His Son's finished work and presents it to us, and then He says to us, 'Please sit' (*ch'eng tso*). His offer to us cannot, I think, be better expressed than in the words of the invitation to the great banquet: 'Come; for all things are now ready' (Luke 14. 17). Our Christian life begins with the discovery of what God has provided.

The range of His finished work

From this point onwards Christian experience proceeds as it began, not on the basis of our own work but always on that of the finished work of Another. Every new spiritual experience begins with an acceptance by faith of what God has done—with a new 'sitting down', if you like. This is a principle of life, and one which God Himself has appointed; and from beginning to end, each successive stage of the Christian life follows on the same divinely determined principle.

How can I receive the power of the Spirit for service? Must I labour for it? Must I plead with God for it? Must I afflict my soul by fastings and self-denials to merit it? Never! That is not the teaching of Scripture. Think again: How did we receive the forgiveness of our sins? Paul tells us that it was 'according to the riches of his grace', and that this was 'freely bestowed on us in the Beloved' (1. 6, 7). We did nothing to merit it. We have our redemption through His blood, that is, on the ground of what *He* has done.

What, then, is God's basis for the outpouring of the Spirit? It is the exaltation of the Lord Jesus (Acts 2. 33). Because Jesus died on the Cross my sins are forgiven; because He is exalted to the throne I am endued with power from on high. The one gift is no more dependent than the other upon what I am or what I do. I did not merit forgiveness, and neither do I merit the gift of the Spirit. I receive everything not by walking but by sitting down, not by doing but by resting in the Lord. Hence, just as there is no need to wait for the initial experience of salvation, so there is no need to wait for the Spirit's outpouring. Let me assure you that you need not plead with God for this gift, nor agonize, nor hold 'tarrying meetings'. It is yours not because of your doing but because of the exaltation of Christ, 'in whom, having also believed, ye were sealed with the Holy Spirit of promise'. This, no less than the forgiveness of sins, is contained in 'the gospel of your salvation' (1. 13).

Or consider another subject, one that is a special theme of Ephesians. How do we become members of Christ? What fits us to be parts of that Body which Paul speaks of as 'the fulness of him'? Certainly we never arrive there by walking. I am not joined to Him by effort of my own. 'There is one body and one Spirit, even as also ye were called in one hope of your calling' (4. 4). Ephesians sets forth what *is*. It starts with Jesus Christ, and with the fact that God chose us *in Him* before the foundation of the world (1. 4). When the Holy Spirit shows us Christ and we believe on Him, then at once, with no further act on our part, there begins for us a life in union with Him.

But if all these things become ours by faith alone, what then of the now very urgent and practical matter of our sanctification? How can we know present deliverance from sin's reign? How is our 'old man', who has followed us and troubled us for years, to be 'crucified' and put away? Once again the secret is not in walking but in sitting; not in doing but in resting in something done. 'We *died* to sin.' We '*were baptized* . . . unto his death'. 'We *were buried* with him.' 'God . . . *quickened* us together with Christ.' (Rom. 6. 2, 3, 4; Eph. 2. 5.) All these statements are in the past (aorist) tense. Why is this? Because the Lord Jesus was crucified outside Jerusalem nearly two thousand years ago, and *I was crucified with Him*. This is the great historic fact. By it His experience has now become my spiritual history, and God can speak of me as already having everything 'with Him'. All that I now have I have 'with Christ'. In the Scriptures we never find these things spoken of as in the future, nor even to be desired in the present. They are historic facts of Christ, into which all we who have believed have entered.

'With Christ'—crucified, quickened, raised, set in the heavenlies: to the human mind these ideas are no less puzzling than were the words of Jesus to Nicodemus in John 3. 3. There it was a question of how to be born again. Here it is something even more improbable—something not only to be effected in us, as new birth, but to be seen and accepted as ours because it *has already been effected* long ago in Someone else. How could such a thing be? We cannot explain. We must receive it from God as something He has done. We were not born with Christ, but we were crucified with Him (Gal. 2. 20). Our union with Him began therefore with His death. God included us in Him there. We were 'with Him' because we were 'in Him'.

But how can I be sure that I am 'in Christ'? I can be sure because the Bible affirms that it is so, and that it was God who put me there. 'Of him [God] are ye in Christ Jesus' (1 Cor. 1. 30). 'He that stablisheth us with you in Christ . . . is God' (2 Cor. 1. 21). It is something accomplished by Him in His sovereign wisdom, to be seen, believed, accepted, and rejoiced in by us.

If I put a pound note between the pages of a magazine, and then burn the magazine, where is the pound note? It has gone the same way as the magazine—to ashes. Where the one goes the other goes too. Their history has become one. But, just as effectively, God has put us in Christ. What happened to Him happened also to us. All the experiences He met, we too have met *in Him*. 'Our old man was crucified with him, that the body of sin might be done away, that so we should no longer be in bondage to sin' (Rom. 6. 6). That is not an exhortation to struggle. That is history: our history, written in Christ before we were born. Do you believe that? It is true! Our crucifixion with Christ is a glorious historic fact. Our deliverance from sin is based, not on what we can do, nor even on what God is going to do for us, but on what He has already done for us in Christ. When that fact dawns upon us and we rest back upon it (Rom. 6. 11), then we have found the secret of a holy life.

But it is true that we know all too little of this in experience. Consider an example. If someone makes a very unkind remark about you in your presence, how do you meet the situation? You compress your lips, clench your teeth, swallow hard, and take a firm grip upon yourself; and if with a great effort you manage to suppress all sign of resentment and be reasonably polite in return, you feel you have gained a great victory. But the resentment is still there; it has merely been covered up. And at times you do not even succeed in covering it. What is the trouble? The trouble is that you are trying to walk before you have sat down, and that way lies sure defeat. Let me repeat: no Christian experience begins with walking, but always with a definite sitting down. The secret of deliverance from sin is not to *do* something but to rest on what God has done.

An engineer living in a large city in the West left his homeland for the Far East. He was away for two or three years, and during his absence his wife was unfaithful to him and went off with one of his best friends. On his return home he found he had lost his wife, his two children and his best friend. At the close of a meeting which I was addressing, this grief-stricken man unburdened himself to me. 'Day and night for two solid years my heart has been full of hatred,' he said. 'I am a Christian, and I know I ought to forgive my wife and my friend, but though I try and try to forgive them, I simply cannot. Every day I resolve to love them, and every day I fail. What can I do about it?' 'Do nothing at all,' I replied. 'What do you mean?' he asked, startled. 'Am I to continue to hate them?' So I explained: 'The solution of your problem lies here, that when the Lord Jesus died on the Cross He not only bore your sins away but He bore *you* away too. When He was crucified, your old man was crucified in Him, so that that unforgiving "you", who simply cannot love those who have wronged you, has been taken right out of the way in His death. God has dealt with the whole situation in the Cross, and there is nothing left for you to deal with. Just say to Him, "Lord, I cannot love and I give up trying, but I count on Thy perfect love. I cannot forgive, but I trust Thee to forgive instead of me, and to do so henceforth in me." '

The man sat there amazed and said, 'That's all so new, I feel I must *do* something about it.' Then a moment later he added again, 'But what can I *do*?' 'God is waiting till you cease to do,' I said. 'When you cease doing, then God will begin. Have you ever tried to save a drowning man? The trouble is that his fear prevents him trusting himself to you. When that is so, there are just two ways of going about it. Either you must knock him unconscious and then drag him to the shore, or else you must leave him to struggle and shout until his strength gives way before you go to his rescue. If you try to save him while he has any strength left, he will clutch at you in his terror and drag you under, and both he and you will be lost. God is waiting for your store of strength to be utterly exhausted before He can deliver you. Once you have ceased to struggle, He will do everything. God is waiting for you to despair.'

My engineer friend jumped up. 'Brother,' he said, 'I've seen it. Praise God, it's all right now with me! There's nothing for me to do. *He* has done it all!' And with radiant face he went off rejoicing.

God the giver

Of all the parables in the Gospels, that of the prodigal son affords, I think, the supreme illustration of the way to please God. The father says: 'It was meet to make merry and be glad' (Luke 15. 32), and in these words Jesus reveals what it is that, in the sphere of redemption, supremely rejoices His Father's heart. It is not an elder brother who toils incessantly for the father, but a younger brother who lets the father do everything for him. It is not an elder brother who always wants to be the giver, but a younger brother who is always willing to be the receiver. When the prodigal returned home, having wasted his substance in riotous living, the father had not a word of rebuke for the waste nor a word of inquiry regarding the substance. He did not sorrow over all that was spent; he only rejoiced over the opportunity the son's return afforded him for spending more.

God is so wealthy that His chief delight is to give. His treasure-stores are so full that it is pain to Him when we refuse Him an opportunity of lavishing those treasures upon us. It was the father's joy that he could find in the prodigal an applicant for the robe, the ring, the shoes, and the feast; it was his sorrow that in the elder son he found no such applicant. It is a grief to the heart of God when we try to provide things for Him. He is so very, very rich. It gives Him true joy when we just let Him give and give and give again to us. It is a grief to Him, too, when we try to *do* things for Him, for He is so very, very able. He longs that we will just let Him do and do and do. He wants to be the Giver eternally, and He wants to be the Doer eternally. If only we saw how rich and how great He is, we would leave all the giving and all the doing to Him.

Do you think that if you cease trying to please God your good behaviour will cease? If you leave all the giving and all the working to God, do you think the result will be less satisfactory than if you do some of it? It is when we seek to do it ourselves that we place ourselves back again under the Law. But the works of the Law, even our best efforts are 'dead works', hateful to God because ineffectual. In the parable, both sons were equally far removed from the joys of the father's house. True, the elder son was not in the far country, yet he was only at home in theory. 'These many years do I serve thee, and yet . . .': his heart had not found rest. His theoretical position could never, as did the prodigal's, come to be enjoyed by him while he still clung to his own good works.

Just you stop 'giving', and you will prove what a Giver God is! Stop 'working', and you will discover what a Worker He is! The younger son was all wrong, but he came home and he found rest—and that is where Christian life

begins. 'God, being rich in mercy, for his great love wherewith he loved us . . . made us to sit with him in the heavenly places, in Christ Jesus' (Eph. 2. 4, 6). 'It was meet to
make merry and be glad!' (Luke 15. 32).

2

Walk

We have sought to make it clear that Christian experience does not begin with walking but with sitting. Every time we reverse the divine order the result is disaster. The Lord Jesus has done everything for us, and our need now is to rest confidently in Him. He is seated in the throne, so we are carried through in His strength. It cannot be too strongly emphasised that all true spiritual experience begins from rest.

But it does not end there. Though the Christian life begins with sitting, sitting is always followed by walking. When once we have been well and truly seated and have found our strength in sitting down, then we do in fact begin to walk. Sitting describes our position with Christ in the heavenlies. Walking is the practical out-working of that heavenly position here on earth. As a heavenly people we are required to bear the stamp of that heavenliness upon us in our earthly conduct, and this raises new problems. What then, we must now ask, has Ephesians to say to us about walking? We shall find that the Epistle urges upon us two things. We will look now at the first of them.

'I therefore, the prisoner in the Lord, beseech you to walk worthily of the calling wherewith ye were called, with all lowliness and meekness . . .' (4. 1, 2).

'This I say . . . that ye no longer walk as the Gentiles also walk, in the vanity of their mind . . . But . . . that ye be renewed in the spirit of your mind' (4. 17, 23).

'Walk in love, even as Christ also loved you, and gave himself up for you' (5. 2, mg.).

'Walk as children of light, . . . proving what is well-pleasing unto the Lord' (5. 8, 10).

Eight times in Ephesians the word 'walk' is used. It means literally 'to walk around', and is used here figuratively by Paul to mean 'to deport oneself', 'to order one's behaviour'. It brings immediately before us the subject of Christian conduct, and the second section of the letter is largely taken up with this. But we saw earlier that the Body of Christ, the fellowship of Christian believers, is another great theme of Ephesians. Now, here in chapter 4, it is in view of such fellowship that we find this matter of a holy walk arises. Paul proceeds, in the light of our heavenly calling, to challenge us upon the whole field of our relationships, both domestic and public, addressing himself to neighbours, to husbands and wives, to parents and children, employers and employed, all in a most realistic way.

Let us be clear that the Body of Christ is not something remote and unreal, to be expressed only in heavenly terms. It is very present and practical, finding the real test of our conduct in our relations with others. For while it is true we are a heavenly people, it is no use just to talk of a distant heaven. Unless we bring heavenliness into our dwellings and offices, our shops and kitchens, and practise it there, it will be without meaning. May I suggest this, dear friends, that those who are parents and those who are children look through the New Testament to see what parents should be and children should be? We may be surprised, for I fear many of us who say we are seated in the heavenlies in Christ display a very questionable walk in our homes. And husbands too, and wives; there are quite a number of passages for them. Read Ephesians 5, and then turn to 1 Corinthians 7. It would do every husband and every wife good to read the latter chapter carefully to discover what a real married life—a spiritual one before God and not just in theory—demands. You dare not theorise about a thing that is so practical.

Look now, in the field of Christian relationships, how forthright are the commands of God in the section here before us. 'Walk . . . with longsuffering, forbearing one another.' 'Putting away falsehood, speak ye truth each one with his neighbour.' 'Be ye angry, and sin not.' 'Steal no more.' 'Let all bitterness . . . be put away from you.' 'Be ye kind . . . forgiving each other.' 'Subjecting yourselves to one another.' 'Provoke not.' 'Be obedient.' 'Forbear threatening.' Nothing could be more realistic than this list of imperatives.

Let me remind you that the Lord Jesus Himself begins His teaching on this very note. Notice carefully the wording of this passage from His Sermon on the Mount:

'Ye have heard that it was said, An eye for an eye, and a tooth for a tooth: but I say unto you, Resist not him that is evil: but whosoever smiteth thee on thy right cheek, turn to him the other also. And if any man would go to law with thee, and take away thy coat, let him have thy cloke also. And whosoever shall compel thee to go one mile, go with him twain. Give to him that asketh thee, and from him that would borrow of thee turn not thou away. Ye have heard that it was said, Thou shalt love thy neighbour, and hate thine enemy: but I say unto you, Love your enemies, and pray for them that persecute you; that ye may be sons of your Father which is in heaven: for he maketh his sun to rise on the evil and the good, and sendeth rain on the just and the unjust. For if ye love them that love you, what reward have ye? do not even the publicans the same? And if ye salute your brethren only, what do ye more than others? do not even the Gentiles the same? Ye therefore shall be perfect, as your heavenly Father is perfect.' (Matt. 5. 38–48.)

'But,' you say, 'I cannot do it. These are impossible demands.' Maybe, like my engineer friend, you feel you have been wronged—perhaps terribly wronged—and you cannot bring yourself to forgive. *You* were in the right, and your enemy's action has been wholly unjust. To love him may be ideal, but it is impossible.

The perfection of the Father

Since the day that Adam took the fruit of the tree of knowledge, man has been engaged in deciding what is good and what is evil. The natural man has worked out his own standards of right and wrong, justice and injustice, and striven to live by them. Of course as Christians we are different. Yes, but in what way are we different? Since we were converted a new sense of righteousness has been developed in us, with the result that we too are, quite rightly, occupied with the question of good and evil. But have we realized that for us the starting point is a different one? Christ is for us the Tree of Life. We do not begin from the matter of ethical right and wrong. We do not start from that other tree. We begin from *Him*; and the whole question for us is one of Life.

Nothing has done greater damage to our Christian testimony than our trying to be right and demanding right of others. We become preoccupied with what is and what is not right. We ask ourselves, Have we been justly or unjustly treated? and we think thus to vindicate our actions. But that is not our standard. The whole question for us is one of cross-bearing. You ask me, 'Is it right for someone to strike my cheek?' I reply, 'Of course not! But the question is, do you only want to be right?' As Christians our standard of living can never be 'right or wrong', but the Cross. The principle of the Cross is our principle of conduct. Praise God that He makes His sun to shine on the evil and the good. With Him it is a question of His grace and not of right or wrong. But that is to be our standard also: 'Forgiving each other, even as God also in Christ forgave you' (4. 32). 'Right or wrong' is the principle of the Gentiles and tax gatherers. My life is to be governed by the principle of the Cross and of the perfection of the Father: 'Ye therefore shall be perfect, as your heavenly Father is perfect.'

A brother in South China had a rice field in the middle of the hill. In time of drought he used a water-wheel, worked by a tread-mill, to lift water from the irrigation stream into his field. His neighbour had two fields below his, and, one night, made a breach in the dividing bank and drained off all his water. When the brother repaired the breach and pumped in more water his neighbour did the same thing again, and this was repeated three or four times. So he consulted his brethren. 'I have tried to be patient and not to retaliate,' he said, 'but *is it right?*' After they had prayed together about it, one of them replied, 'If we only try to do the right thing, surely we are very poor Christians. We have to do something more than what is right.' The brother was much impressed. Next morning he pumped water for the two fields below, and in the afternoon pumped water for his own field. After that the water stayed in his field. His neighbour was so amazed at his action that he began to inquire the reason, and in course of time he too became a Christian.

So, my brethren, don't stand on your right. Don't feel that because you have gone the second mile you have done what is just. The second mile is only typical of the third and the fourth. The principle is that of conformity to Christ. We have nothing to stand for, nothing to ask or demand. We have only to give. When the Lord Jesus died on the Cross, He did not do so to defend our 'rights'; it was grace that took Him there. Now, as His children, we try always to give others what is their due and more.

We have to remind ourselves that we are often *not* right. We fail, and it is always good to learn from our failures—to be ready to confess and willing to go beyond what is necessary in doing so. The Lord wants this. Why? 'That ye may be sons of your Father which is in heaven' (Matt. 5. 45). The question is one of practical sonship. True, God has 'foreordained us unto adoption as sons through Jesus Christ' (1. 5), but we make the mistake of thinking that we have already 'come of age'—that we are already mature sons. The Sermon on the Mount teaches us that the children attain to the responsibility of sons in the measure in which they manifest kinship of spirit and of attitude with their Father. We are called to be 'perfect' in love, showing forth His grace. So Paul also writes: 'Be ye therefore imitators of God, as beloved children; and walk in love, even as Christ also loved you, and gave himself up for you' (5. 1, 2, mg.).

We are faced with a challenge. Matthew 5 sets a standard that we may well feel is impossibly high, and Paul in this section of Ephesians endorses it. The trouble is that we just do not find in ourselves by nature the means to attain to that standard—to walk 'as becometh saints' (5. 3). Where, then, lies the answer to our problem of God's exacting demands?

The secret is, in the words of Paul, 'the power that worketh in us' (3. 20). In a parallel passage (Col. 1. 29) he says: 'I labour also, striving according to his working, which worketh in me mightily.'

We are back again in the first section of Ephesians. What is the secret strength of the Christian life? Whence has it its power? Let me give you the answer in a sentence: *The Christian's secret is his rest in Christ.* His power derives from his God-given position. All who sit can walk, for in the thought of God the one follows the other spontaneously. We sit for ever with Christ that we may walk continuously before men. Forsake for a moment our place of rest in Him, and immediately we are tripped and our testimony in the world is marred. But abide in Christ, and our position there ensures the power to walk worthy of Him here. If you desire an illustration of this kind of progress, think, first of all, not of a runner in a race but of a man in a car, or better still, of a cripple in a power-driven invalid carriage. What does he do? He *goes*—but he also *sits*. And he keeps going because he remains sitting. His progress follows from the position in which he has been placed. This, of course, is a far-from-perfect picture of the Christian life, but it may serve to remind us that our conduct and behaviour depend fundamentally upon our inward rest in Christ.

This explains Paul's language here. He has first learned to sit. He has come to a place of rest in God. As a result his walking is not based on his efforts but on God's mighty inward working. There lies the secret of his strength. Paul has seen himself seated in Christ; therefore his walk before men takes its character from Christ dwelling in him. Small wonder that he prays for the Ephesians: 'That Christ may dwell in your hearts through faith' (3. 17).

How does my wrist-watch go? By moving first, or by being moved? Of course it goes because first it is moved by a power outside itself. Then only will it do the work for which it was designed. And there are works for which we too are designed. 'We are his workmanship, created in Christ Jesus for good works, which God afore prepared that we should walk in them' (2. 10). 'Work out your own salvation with fear and trembling,' writes Paul to the Philippians, 'for it is God which worketh in you both to will and to work, for his good pleasure.' God is working it in; work it out! That is the secret. But until we are willing for God to work it in, it is useless for us to try to work it out. Often we try to be meek and gentle without knowing what it means to let God work in us the meekness and gentleness *of Christ*. We try to show love, and, finding we have none, we ask the Lord for love. Then we are surprised that He does not seem to give it to us.

Let me take up again an earlier illustration. Perhaps there is a certain brother whom you find very trying and with whom you are constantly getting into difficulties. Whenever you meet him he says or does something calculated to arouse in you resentment. This troubles you. You say: 'I am a Christian and ought to love him. I want to love him; indeed I am *determined* to love him!' And so you pray very earnestly: 'Lord, increase my love for him. O God, give me love!' Then, taking a firm grip on yourself and summoning all your will-power, you set out with a genuine desire to display to him that love for which you have prayed. But alas, when you get into his presence something happens to bring all your good intentions to nought. His response to you is not in the least encouraging but rather the reverse, and immediately your old resentment flares up, and once again the utmost you can do is to be polite to him. Why is this? You were surely not *wrong* in seeking love from God? No, but you were wrong in seeking that love as something in itself, a kind of package-commodity, when what God desires is to express through you the love of His Son.

God has given us Christ. There is nothing now for us to receive outside of Him. The Holy Spirit has been sent to produce what is of Christ in us; not to produce anything that is apart from or outside of Him. We are 'strengthened with power through his Spirit in the inward man; . . . to know the love of Christ' (3. 16, 19). What we show forth outwardly is what God has first put within.

Recall once again the great words of 1 Corinthians 1. 30. Not only did God set us 'in Christ'. By Him also 'Christ Jesus . . . was made unto us wisdom from God, and righteousness and sanctification, and redemption.' This is one of the grandest statements in Scripture. *He* 'was made unto us . . .'. If we believe this, we can put in there anything we need, and can know that God has made it good; for, through the Holy Spirit within us, the Lord Jesus is Himself made unto us whatever we lack. We have been accustomed to look upon holiness as a virtue, upon humility as a grace, upon love as a gift to be sought from God. But the Christ of God is *Himself* everything that we shall ever need.

Many a time in my need I used to think of Christ as a Person apart, and failed to identify Him in this practical way with the 'things' I felt so strongly the lack of. For two whole years I was groping in that kind of darkness, seeking to amass the virtues that I felt sure should make up the Christian life, and getting nowhere in the effort. And then one day—it was in the year 1933—light broke from heaven for me, and I saw Christ ordained of God to be made over to me in His fulness. What a difference! Oh the emptiness of 'things'! Held by us out of relation to Christ they are dead. Once we see this it will be the beginning of a new life for us. Our holiness will be spelled thereafter with a capital H, our love with a capital L. *He Himself* is revealed as the answer in us to all God's demands.

Go back now to that difficult brother, but this time, before you go, address God thus: 'Lord, it is clear to me at last that in myself I cannot love him at all; but I know now that there is a life within me, the life of Thy Son, and that the law of that life is to love. It cannot but love him.' There is no need to exert yourself. Repose in Him. Count upon His life. Dare thus to go and see that brother and to speak to him—and here is the amazing thing! Quite unconsciously (and I would emphasise the word 'unconsciously', for the consciousness only comes afterwards) you find yourself speaking most pleasantly to him; quite unconsciously you love him; quite unconsciously you know him as your brother. You converse with him freely and in true fellowship, and on your return you find yourself saying with amazement: 'Why, I did not exercise the least bit of anxious care just now, and yet I did not become in the least bit irritable! In some unaccountable way the Lord was with me and His love triumphed.'

The operation of His life in us is in a true sense spontaneous, that is to say, it is without effort of ours. The all-important rule is not to 'try' but to 'trust', not to depend upon our own strength but upon His. For it is the flow of life which reveals what we truly are 'in Christ'. It is from the Fountain of life that the sweet water issues.

Too many of us are caught *acting* as Christians. The life of many Christians today is largely a pretence. They live a 'spiritual' life, talk a 'spiritual' language, adopt 'spiritual' attitudes, but they are doing the whole thing themselves. It is the effort involved that should reveal to them that something is wrong. They force themselves to refrain from doing this, from saying that, from eating the other, and how hard they find it all! It is just the same as when we Chinese try to talk a language that is not our own. No matter how hard we try, it does not come spontaneously; we have to force ourselves to talk that way. But when it comes to speaking our own language, nothing could be easier. Even when we forget all about what we are doing, we still speak it. It flows. It comes to us perfectly naturally, and its very spontaneity reveals to everyone *what we are.*

Our life *is* the life of Christ, mediated in us by the indwelling Holy Spirit Himself, and the law of that life *is* spontaneous. The moment we see that fact we shall end our struggling and cast away our pretence. Nothing is so hurtful to the life of a Christian as acting; nothing so blessed as when our outward efforts cease and our attitudes become natural—when our words, our prayers, our very life, all become a spontaneous and unforced expression of the life within. Have we discovered how good the Lord is? Then *in us* He is as good as that! Is His power great? Then *in us* it is no less great! Praise God, His life is as mighty as ever, and in the lives of those who dare to believe the Word of God the divine life will be manifest in a power not one whit less mighty than was manifest of old.

What does our Lord mean when He says: 'Except your righteousness shall exceed the righteousness of the scribes and Pharisees, ye shall in no wise enter into the kingdom of heaven'? (Matt. 5. 20). We have seen above how He goes on to set the contrast between the requirements of the Law of Moses and His own tremendous demands, by His repeated use of the words: 'Ye have heard that it was said . . . but I say unto you . . .'. But since already, over many centuries, men had sought to attain to the first standard and had failed, how could the Lord dare to raise the standard higher still? He could do so only because He believed in His own life. He is not afraid of making the most exacting demands upon Himself. Indeed we may well find comfort in reading the laws of the kingdom as set forth in Matthew chapters 5 to 7, for they show what utter confidence the Lord has in His own life *made available to His children*. These three chapters set forth the divine taxation of the divine life.

The greatness of His demands upon us only shows how confident He is that the resources He has put within us are fully enough to meet them. God does not command what He will not perform; but we must throw ourselves back on Him for the performance.

Does some difficult situation confront us? Is it a problem of right or wrong, good or evil? We do not need to look for wisdom. We need no longer apply to the tree of knowledge. We have Christ, and *He* is made unto us wisdom from God. The law of the Spirit of life in Christ Jesus continually communicates to us His standards of right and wrong, and, with them, the attitude of spirit with which the difficult situation should be met.

More and more things will turn up to hurt our Christian sense of righteousness and to test what our reactions are going to be. We need to learn the principle of the Cross— that our standard is not now the old but the new man 'which after God hath been created in righteousness and holiness of truth' (4. 22–24). 'Lord, I've got no rights to defend. Everything I have is through Thy grace, and everything is in Thee!' I knew of an old Japanese Christian woman who was disturbed by a thief who had broken into her house. In her simple but practical faith in the Lord, she cooked the man a meal—then offered him her keys. He was shamed by her action and God spoke to him. Through her testimony that man is a brother in Christ today.

Too many Christians have all the doctrine but live lives that are a contradiction of it. They know all about chapters 1 to 3 of Ephesians but they do not put chapters 4 to 6 into practice. It were better to have no doctrine than to be a contradiction. Has God commanded something? Then throw yourself back on God for the means to do what He has commanded. May the Lord teach us that the whole principle of the Christian life is that we go beyond what is right to do that which is well-pleasing to Him.

Redeeming the time

But there remains something further to be added to the above on the subject of our Christian walk. The word 'walk' has, as must already be obvious, a further meaning. It suggests first conduct or behaviour, but it also contains in it the idea of progress. To 'walk' is to 'proceed', to 'follow on', and we want to consider briefly now this further matter of our progress towards a goal.

> *'Look therefore carefully how ye walk, not as unwise, but as wise; redeeming the time, because the days are evil. Wherefore be ye not foolish, but understand what the will of the Lord is'* (5. 15–17).

You will notice that in the above verses there is an association between the idea of Time and the difference between wisdom and foolishness. 'Walk . . . as wise; redeeming the time. . . . Be ye not foolish.' This is important. I want now to remind you of two other passages in which these things are similarly brought together:

> 'Then shall the kingdom of heaven be likened unto ten virgins. . . . Five of them were foolish, and five were wise. For the foolish, when they took their lamps, took no oil with them. . . . But at midnight there is a cry, Behold, the bridegroom! Come ye forth to meet him. Then all those virgins arose, and trimmed their lamps. And the foolish said, . . . Our lamps are going out. . . . And while they went away to buy, the bridegroom came;

and they that were ready went in with him to the marriage feast: and the door was shut. Afterward come also the other virgins . . .' (see Matt. 25. 1–13).

'And I saw, and behold, the Lamb standing on the mount Zion, and with him a hundred and forty and four thousand, having his name and the name of his Father, written on their foreheads. . . . These are virgins. These are they which follow the Lamb whithersoever he goeth. These were purchased from among men, to be the first-fruits unto God and unto the Lamb. And in their mouth was found no lie: they are without blemish' (see Rev. 14. 1–5).

There are many passages of Scripture that assure us that what God has begun He will finish. Our Saviour is a Saviour to the uttermost. No Christian believer will be 'half-saved' at the end, even if now that might be said of us in any sense. God will perfect every man who has faith in Him. That is what we believe, and we must keep it in mind as a background for what we are going to say next. With Paul, we are 'confident of this very thing, that he which began a good work in you will perfect it until the day of Jesus Christ' (Phil. 1. 6). There are no limits to God's power. He 'is able . . . to set you before the presence of his glory without blemish' (Jude 24; and see: 2 Tim. 1. 12; Eph. 3. 20).

It is, however, when we turn to the subjective aspect of this—to its practical outworking in our lives here and now on the earth—that we encounter the question of Time. In Revelation 14 there are firstfruits (verse 4) and there is a harvest (verse 15). What is the difference between harvest and firstfruits? It is certainly not one of quality, for the whole crop is one. Their difference lies only in the time of their ripeness. Some fruits reach maturity before others and thus they become 'firstfruits'.

My home town in Fukien province is famous for its oranges. I would say (and no doubt I am prejudiced!) that there are none like them anywhere in the world. As you look out on the hills at the beginning of the orange season, all the groves are green. But if you look more carefully you will see, sprinkled here and there on the trees, golden oranges already showing up. It is a beautiful sight to see the flecks of gold dotted among the dark green trees. Later the whole crop will ripen and the groves will turn to gold, but now it is these firstfruits that are gathered. They are carefully hand-picked, and it is they that fetch the top market-prices—often three times the price of the harvest.

All will reach ripeness, somehow. But the Lamb is seeking firstfruits. The 'wise' in the parable are not those who have done better, but those who have done well *at an earlier hour*. The others, be it noted, were also virgins—'foolish', no doubt, but not false. Along with the wise, they had gone out to meet the Bridegroom. They too had oil in their lamps, and their lamps were burning. But they had not reckoned on His tarrying, and now that their lamps burned low they had no reserve of oil in their vessels, nor had the others enough to spare them.

Some are troubled at this point by the Lord's words to the foolish ones: 'I know you not.' How, they feel, could He say this of them if they represent His true children, 'espoused . . . as a pure virgin to Christ'? (2 Cor. 11. 2). But we must recognize the whole point of the teaching of this parable, which is surely that there is some privilege of serving Him in the future which His children may miss by being unprepared. It says that the five came to the door and said: 'Lord, Lord, open to us.' What door? Certainly not the door of salvation. If you are lost, you cannot come to the door of heaven and knock. When therefore the Lord says: 'I know you not,' He surely uses these words in some such limited sense as in the following illustration.

In Shanghai the son of a police-court magistrate was taken up for careless driving. He was brought to court and found his father sitting on the magistrate's bench. Court procedure is more or less the same the world over, and so the boy was asked: 'What is your name? What is your address? What is your occupation?' and so on. Astonished, he turned to his father: 'Father, do you mean to say you don't know me?' Rapping on his desk the father answered sternly: 'Young man, I do not know you. What is your name? What is your address?' He did not of course mean by this that he did not know him at all. In the family and in the home he knew him, but *in that place and at that time* he did not know him. Though still his father's son, the boy must go right through the court procedure and pay his fine.

Yes, all ten virgins had oil in their lamps. What distinguished the foolish was that they had no reserve in their vessels. As true Christians, they have life in Christ, and they have a testimony before men. But theirs is a fitful testimony for they live a hand-to-mouth existence. They have the Spirit, but they are not, we may say, 'filled with the Spirit'. When the crisis comes they must go out to buy more oil. In the end, of course, all the ten had enough. But the difference lay in the fact that the wise had sufficient oil in time, while the foolish, when at length they did have sufficient, had missed the purpose for which it was intended. It is all a question of time, and this is the point which the Lord seeks to drive home when, at the end of the parable, he urges his disciples not just to be disciples but to be watchful disciples.

'Be not drunken with wine, wherein is riot, but be filled with the Spirit' (5. 18). In Matthew 25 it is not a question of the initial reception of Jesus Christ, nor yet of the coming of the Holy Spirit upon His servants for spiritual gifts. It is a question of the extra oil in the vessel—of the light being sustained, through however long a time of waiting, by means of the continual miraculous supply of the Spirit within (for whereas in the parable there is both a lamp and a vessel, in reality we are the lamp and we are the vessel). What Christian could possibly live in eternity in heaven without knowing this inner fulness? Surely not one virgin can escape this? And so the Lord is taking all possible steps to bring us to the knowledge of that fulness now. 'Watch therefore, for ye know not the day nor the hour.'

'Be being filled' (*plerousthe*) is the unusual expression used here in relation to the Holy Spirit. 'Allow yourselves to be continually made full.' It is not a crisis, as at Pentecost, but a state we are to be in all the time. And it is not something external, but internal; not a question of spiritual gifts and manifestations outwardly but of the personal presence and activity of the Holy Spirit within our spirits, guaranteeing that the light in the vessel will burn undimmed, long after midnight if need be.

And moreover, it is not wholly a personal thing. As the next verse (5. 19) surely indicates, it is something which we share with other Christians in mutual dependence. For to be 'filled with the Spirit' means, in the language of that verse, not merely 'singing and making melody with your heart to the Lord' but *speaking one to another* in psalms and hymns and spiritual songs'. Some of us may well find it easy to sing solos, but much harder to sing in time and harmony as a quartet or even as a duet. Yet this message of oneness in the Spirit lies at the heart of our second section of Ephesians (see 4. 3, 15, 16). The fulness of the Spirit is given to us that we should sing *together* a new song before the throne (Rev. 14. 3).

But, to keep to our main emphasis, let me repeat that folly or wisdom hinges on this one point alone, that if you are wise you will seek this fulness sooner, but if you are foolish you will put it off till later. Some of us are parents and have children. How greatly those children can differ in temperament! One will obey at once; another will think that by procrastination he can avoid the need to do so. If that is indeed the case, and you are weak enough to allow him a loophole for escape, then the one who procrastinates is in fact the wise one, for he succeeds in doing nothing. But if your word holds, if your command cannot be evaded and ultimately *must* be obeyed, then he is certainly the wiser who faces the issue squarely at once.

Get clear about the will of God. If God's words can be discounted, then you might not be foolish to try to escape their implications; but if God is an unchanging God with an unchanging will, then be wise; redeem the time. Seek above all things to have that extra supply of oil in the vessel, 'that ye may be filled unto all the fulness of God' (3. 19).

The parable does not answer all our questions. How do the foolish buy? We are not told. We are nowhere told what further steps God may have to take to bring all His children eventually to maturity. That is not our concern. We are concerned here with firstfruits. We are being urged to press on; not to speculate on what may happen if we don't.

You cannot, by dodging the issue, avoid reaching maturity—or paying the price of it. But wisdom is connected with time. Those who are wise redeem the time. Just as my fountain pen is now filled and ready to my hand for immediate use, so, by co-operating with the Lord, the wise provide God with what He wants: handy tools, instantly available to Him.

Look at the apostle Paul. He is consumed with a burning passion. He has seen that God's purpose for us is bound up with the 'fulness of the times' (1. 10). He is one of those who have 'before hoped in Christ' by resting in a salvation that is yet to be fully revealed 'in the ages to come' (1. 12; 2. 7). And in view of all this, what does he do? He walks. And he not only walks; he runs. 'I therefore so run, as not uncertainly' (1 Cor. 9. 26). 'I press on toward the goal unto the prize of the high calling of God in Christ Jesus' (Phil. 3. 14).

Often when souls come into an understanding of spiritual things and begin to go on with the Lord, the feeling in my heart is: 'Oh, if only they had come to see this five years earlier!' The time is so short, even if we *are* going on. There is such need for urgency. For remember, it is not a question of what we get out of it. It is a question of *what the Lord must have now*. The Lord's need today is for ready instruments. Why? 'Because the days are evil.' The situation is desperate among the Christian public. Oh that we might see it!

The Lord may have to deal drastically with us. Paul had to say 'I am an abortive child'. He had passed through tremendous crises to bring him to the point where he then was—and still he pressed on. It is always a question of time.

God may have to do something in us swiftly, compressing it into a short space; but He *has* to do that much. May the eyes of our heart be enlightened to know what is 'the hope of his calling', and then may we walk—nay, run—as those who 'understand what the will of the Lord is' (1. 18; 5. 17). The Lord always loved desperate souls.

3

Stand

'*Finally, be strong in the Lord, and in the strength of his might. Put on the whole armour of God, that ye may be able to stand against the wiles of the devil. . . . That ye may be able to withstand in the evil day, and, having done all, to stand. Stand therefore, having girded your loins . . . having put on the breast-plate . . . having shod your feet . . . taking up the shield . . . and the helmet . . . and the sword . . . praying . . . and watching*' (Eph. 6. 10–11, 13–18).

Christian experience begins with sitting and leads to walking, but it does not end with these. Every Christian must learn also to stand. Each one of us must be prepared for the conflict. We must know how to sit with Christ in heavenly places and we must know how to walk worthy of Him down here, but we must also know how to stand before the foe. This matter of conflict now comes before us in the third section of Ephesians (6. 10–20). It is what Paul calls 'our wrestling with wicked spirits'.

But let us first remind ourselves once again of the order in which Ephesians presents us with these things. It is: 'sit . . . walk . . . stand'. For no Christian can hope to enter the warfare of the ages without learning first to rest in Christ and in what He has done, and then, through the strength of the Holy Spirit within, to follow Him in a practical, holy life here on earth. If he is deficient in either of these he will find that all the talk about spiritual warfare remains only talk; he will never know its reality. Satan can afford to ignore him for he does not count for anything. Yet the very same Christian can be made strong 'in the Lord, and in the strength of his might' by knowing the values first of His exaltation and then of His indwelling (compare 6. 10 with 1. 19 and 3. 16). It is with these two lessons well and truly learned that he comes to appreciate the third principle of the Christian life now summed up in the word 'Stand'.

God has an arch-enemy, and under his power are countless demons and fallen angels seeking to overrun the world with evil and to exclude God from His own kingdom. This is the meaning of verse 12. It is an explanation of things taking place around us. *We* see only 'flesh and blood' ranged against us—that is to say, a world system of hostile kings and rulers, sinners and evil men. No, says Paul, our wrestling is not against these, 'but against the principalities, against the powers, against the world-rulers of this darkness, against the spiritual hosts of wickedness in the heavenly places'—in short against the wiles of the devil himself. Two thrones are at war. God is claiming the earth for His dominion, and Satan is seeking to usurp the authority of God. The Church is called to displace Satan from his present realm and to make Christ Head over all. What are we doing about it?

I want now to deal with this matter of our warfare first in general terms in relation to our personal Christian lives and

then in a more special sense in relation to the work of the
Lord entrusted to us. There are many direct assaults of
Satan upon God's children. Of course we must not attribute
to the devil those troubles that are the result of our own
breach of divine laws. We should, by now, know how to put
these right. But there are physical attacks upon the saints,
attacks of the evil one upon their bodies and minds, of
which we must take serious account. Surely, too, there are
few of us who do not know something of the enemy's
assaults upon our spiritual life. Are we going to let these
pass unchallenged?

We have our position with the Lord in the heavenlies,
and we are learning how to walk with Him before the
world; but how are we to acquit ourselves in the presence
of the adversary—His adversary and ours? God's word is:
'Stand!' 'Put on the whole armour of God that you may be
able to stand against the wiles of the devil.' The Greek verb
'stand' with its following preposition 'against' in verse 11
really means 'hold your ground'. There is a precious truth
hidden in that command of God. It is not a command to
invade a foreign territory. Warfare, in modern parlance,
would imply a command to 'march'. Armies march into
other countries to occupy and to subdue. God has not told
us to do this. We are not to march but to stand. The word
'stand' implies that the ground disputed by the enemy is
really His, and therefore ours. We need not struggle to gain
a foothold on it.

Nearly all the weapons of our warfare described in Ephesians are purely defensive. Even the sword can be used as
well for defence as for offence. The difference between
defensive and offensive warfare is this, that in the former I

have got the ground and only seek to keep it, whereas in the latter I have not got the ground and am fighting in order to get it. And that is precisely the difference between the warfare waged by the Lord Jesus and the warfare waged by us. His was offensive; ours is, in essence, defensive. He warred against Satan in order to gain the victory. Through the Cross He carried that warfare to the very threshold of Hell itself, to lead forth thence his captivity captive (4. 8, 9). Today we war against Satan only to maintain and consolidate the victory which He has already gained. By the resurrection God proclaimed His Son Victor over the whole realm of darkness, and the ground Christ won He has given to us. We do not need to fight to obtain it. We only need to hold it against all challengers.

Our task is one of holding, not of attacking. It is a matter not of advance but of sphere, the sphere of Christ. In the person of Jesus Christ, God has already conquered. He has given us His victory to *hold*. Within the sphere of Christ the enemy's defeat is already a fact, and the Church has been put there to keep him defeated. Satan is the one who must do the counter-attacking in his efforts to dislodge us from that sphere. For our part we need not struggle to occupy ground that is already ours. In Christ we *are* conquerors— nay, 'more than conquerors' (Rom. 8. 37). In Him, therefore, we *stand*. Thus today we do not fight *for* victory; we fight *from* victory. We do not fight in order to win but because in Christ we have already won. Overcomers are those who rest in the victory already given to them by their God.

When you fight *to get* the victory, then you have lost the battle at the very outset. Suppose Satan sets out to assault you in your home or in your business. Difficulties mount

up, misunderstandings arise, a situation that you can neither deal with nor escape threatens to overwhelm you. You
pray, you fast, you struggle and resist for days, but nothing
happens. Why? You are trying to fight into victory, and in
doing so are relinquishing to the enemy the very ground
that is yours. For victory is still for you a distant thing,
somewhere ahead of you, and you cannot reach it. I was in
just such a situation once myself, and God brought to my
mind the word in 2 Thessalonians concerning the man of
sin, whom the Lord Jesus 'shall slay with the breath of his
mouth'. The thought came: It will need but a breath from
my Lord to finish him off, and here am I trying to raise a
hurricane! Was not Satan once for all defeated? Then this
victory too is already won.

Only those who sit can stand. Our power for standing, as
for walking, lies in our having first been made to sit
together with Christ. The Christian's walk and warfare alike
derive their strength from his position there. If he is not sitting before God he cannot hope to stand before the enemy.

Satan's primary object is not to get us to sin, but simply
to make it easy for us to do so by getting us off the ground
of perfect triumph on to which the Lord has brought us.
Through the avenue of the head or of the heart, through
our intellect or our feelings, he assaults our rest in Christ or
our walk in the Spirit. But for every point of his attack
defensive armour is provided, the helmet and the breast-
plate, the girdle and the shoes, while over all is the shield of
faith to turn aside his fiery darts. Faith says: Christ is
exalted. Faith says: We are saved by His grace. Faith says:
We have access through Him. Faith says: He indwells us by
His Spirit (see 1.20; 2. 8; 3. 12, 17).

Because victory is His, therefore it is ours. If only we will not try to gain the victory but simply to maintain it, then we shall see the enemy utterly routed. We must not ask the Lord to enable *us* to overcome the enemy, nor even look to *Him* to overcome, but praise Him because He has already done so; He *is* Victor. It is all a matter o faith in Him. If we believe the Lord, we shall not pray so much but rather we shall praise Him more. The simpler and clearer our faith in Him, the less we shall pray in such situations and the more we shall praise.

Let me say again: In Christ we *are already* conquerors. Is it not obvious then that, since this is so, for us merely to pray for victory—unless that prayer is shot through with praise—must be to court defeat by throwing away our fundamental position? Let me ask you: Has defeat been your experience? Have you found yourself hoping that one day you will be strong enough to win? Then my prayer for you can go no further than that of the apostle Paul to his Ephesian readers. It is that God may open your eyes anew to see yourself seated with Him who has Himself been made to sit 'far above all rule, and authority, and power, and dominion, and every name that is named' (1. 20, 21). The difficulties around you may not alter; the lion may roar as loudly as ever; but you need no longer *hope* to overcome. In Christ Jesus you *are* victor in the field.

In His name

But this is not all. Ephesians 6 is concerned with more than the personal side of our warfare. It has to do too with the work of God entrusted to us—the utterance of the mystery of the Gospel of which Paul has already had much to say (see 3. 1–13). For this it arms us now with the sword of the Word and its companion weapon, prayer.

> *'Take . . . the sword of the Spirit, which is the word of God: with all prayer and supplication praying at all seasons in the Spirit, and watching thereunto in all perseverance and supplication for all the saints, and on my behalf, that utterance may be given unto me in opening my mouth, to make known with boldness the mystery of the gospel, for which I am an ambassador in chains; that in it I may speak boldly, as I ought to speak' (6. 17–20).*

I want to say something more about this warfare in its relation to our work for God, for here we may encounter a difficulty. It is true, on the one hand, that our Lord Jesus is seated 'far above all rule, and authority', and that all things have been put 'in subjection under his feet' (1. 21, 22). Clearly it is in the light of this completed victory that we are to 'give thanks always for all things *in the name of Jesus Christ*' (5. 20). Yet on the other hand we have to admit that we do not yet see all things subject to Him. There are still, as Paul says, hosts of wicked spirits in the heavenly places, dark, evil powers behind this world's rulers, occupying territory that is rightly His. How far are we correct in calling this a defensive warfare? We do not want to be falsely presumptive. When, therefore, and under what conditions are we justified in occupying territory that is outwardly the enemy's and holding it in the name of the Lord Jesus?

Let us 'take . . . the word of God' to help us here. What does it tell us about prayer and action 'in the name'? Consider first the following two passages:

> 'Verily I say unto you, What things soever ye shall bind on earth shall be bound in heaven: and what things soever ye

shall loose on earth shall be loosed in heaven. Again I say unto you, that if two of you shall agree on earth as touching any-thing that they shall ask, it shall be done for them . . . For where two or three are gathered together in my name, there am I. . . .' (Matt. 18. 18–20).

'In that day ye shall ask me nothing. Verily, verily, I say unto you, If ye shall ask anything of the Father, he will give it you in my name. Hitherto have ye asked nothing in my name: ask, and ye shall receive, that your joy may be fulfilled. . . . In that day ye shall ask in my name' (John 16. 23, 24, 26).

None can be saved without knowing the name of Jesus, and none can be effectively used of God without knowing the authority of that name. The apostle Paul makes it clear that the 'name' to which Jesus alludes in the above passages is not simply the name by which He was known while here among men. To be sure, it *is* that very self-same name of His humanity, but it is that name invested now with the title and authority given to Him by God after He had become obedient to death (Phil. 2. 6–10). It is the outcome of His sufferings, the name of His exaltation and glory; and today it is in *that* 'name which is above every name' that we gather and that we ask of God.

This distinction is made not by Paul alone but already by Jesus Himself in the second passage quoted above: 'Hitherto ye have asked nothing . . . In that day ye shall ask' (verses 24, 26). For the disciples 'that day' will differ greatly from the 'now' of verse 22. Something they do not have now they will receive then, and having received it they will use it. That something is the authority that goes with His name.

Our eyes must be opened to see the mighty change wrought by the ascension. The name of Jesus certainly establishes the identity of the One in the throne with the Carpenter of Nazareth, but it goes further than that. It represents now the power and dominion given to Him by God, a power and a dominion before which every knee in heaven and earth and beneath the earth must bow. Even the Jewish leaders recognized that there could be this kind of significance in a mere name, when they inquired of the disciples concerning the healing of the lame man: 'By what power, or in what name, have ye done this?' (Acts 4. 7).

Today the name tells us that God has committed all authority to His Son, so that in the very name itself there is power. But further, we must note in Scripture the recurring expression 'in the name'—that is to say, the use to which the apostles in fact put that name. It is not only that He *has* such a name, but that we are to *use* it. In three passages in His last discourse the Lord Jesus repeats the words 'ask in my name' (see John 14. 13, 14; 15. 16; 16. 23–26). He has placed that authority in our hands for us to use. Not only is it His, but it is 'given among men' (Acts 4. 12). If we do not know our part in it we suffer great loss.

The power of His name operates in three directions. In our preaching it is effective to the salvation of men (Acts 4. 10–12) through the remission of their sins, and through their cleansing, justification, and sanctification to God (Luke 24. 47; Acts 10. 43; 1 Cor. 6. 11). In our warfare it is mighty against the Satanic powers, to bind and bring them into subjection (Mark 16. 17; Luke 10. 17–19; Acts 16. 18). And as we have already seen, in our asking it is effective towards God, for twice we are told: 'Whatsoever ye shall ask . . .', and twice: 'If ye shall ask anything . . .' (John 14. 13, 14; 15. 16; 16. 23). Faced with these challenging words, well might we reverently say: 'Lord, Your courage is very great!'

For God thus to commit Himself to His servants is indeed a tremendous thing. Glance now with me at three incidents in the Acts which serve to illustrate this further: 'Peter said, . . . In the name of Jesus Christ of Nazareth, walk' (Acts 3. 6). 'Paul . . . turned and said to the spirit, I charge thee in the name of Jesus Christ to come out of her. And it came out that very hour' (Acts 16. 18). 'Certain . . . exorcists, took upon them to name over them which had the evil spirits the name of the Lord Jesus, saying, I adjure you by Jesus whom Paul preacheth. . . . And the evil spirit answered and said unto them, Jesus I know, and Paul I know; but who are ye?' (Acts 19. 13, 15).

Observe first the action of Peter in dealing with the crippled man at the gate. He does not kneel and pray and ask the mind of the Lord first. At once he says: 'Walk.' He uses the name as if it were his to use, not something far away in heaven. With Paul at Philippi it is the same. He senses in his spirit that the Satanic activity has gone far enough. We are not told that thereupon he pauses to pray. No, his is a true walk before God, and because this is so he can, as a custodian of the name, take action almost as though the power were in himself. He commands, and the evil spirit flees 'that very hour'.

What is this? It is an example of what I shall call God's 'committal' of Himself to man. God has committed Himself to His servants to act through them, as they take action 'in the name'. And they, what do they do? It is clear that they do nothing of themselves. They use the name. Equally clearly no other name, whether their own or that of another apostle, will have the same effect. All that takes place results from the impact of the name of the Lord Jesus on the situation, and *they are authorized to use that name*.

God looks at His Son in the glory, not at us here on the earth. It is because He sees us seated with Him *there* that His name and His authority can be entrusted to us here. A simple illustration will help to make this clear. Some time ago my fellow-worker sent to me for a sum of money. I read his letter, prepared what he had asked, and gave the sum to the messenger. Was I right? Yes, certainly. The letter bore my friend's signature, and to me that was sufficient. Should I instead have asked the messenger *his* name and age and employment and native place, and then perhaps sent him away because I objected to what *he* was? No, by no means; for he had come in my friend's name, and I honoured that name.

The divine self-committal

It is a mighty thing that God has done in thus committing Himself to His Church. In so doing He has entrusted to His servants the greatest possible power; that of One whose dominion is 'above every name that is named, not only in this world, but also in that which is to come' (1. 21). Jesus is now exalted in heaven, and all His work of saving men, speaking to their hearts, and working for them miracles of His grace, is done through the medium of His servants as they act *in His name*. Thus the Church's work is His work.

The name of Jesus is in fact God's greatest legacy to her, for where such a self-committal of God is really operative, He Himself takes responsibility for what is done in that name. And God *desires* so to commit Himself, for He has allowed Himself no other means for completing His task.

No work is worthy to be called a work of God if God is not, in this sense, committing Himself to it. It is the authorisation to use His name that counts. We must be able to stand up and speak *in His name*. If not, our work lack spiritual impact. But let me tell you, this is not something that can be 'worked up' at a time of crisis. It is a fruit of obedience to God and of a resulting spiritual position known and maintained. It is something we must have already if it is to be available in a time of need.

'Jesus I know, and Paul I know.' Praise God for the second! The evil powers recognize the Son; the Gospels give us plenty of evidence of this. But there are those also who are in union with the Son, and they too count in Hades. The question is, *Can* God commit Himself thus to you?

Let me illustrate again. If something is to be done in my name, it means that, subject to certain conditions, I give my name to another to use, and that I am then prepared to take responsibility for what he does with it. It may mean, for example, that I give him my cheque book and my signature. Of course, if I am poor, with no personal standing and no bank account, my name is of little moment. I well remember how, as a student, I used to be fond of stamping my name everywhere, on books, papers, and anything that came to hand. But when I first had a cheque book and a bank account—fourteen pounds in the Post Office—I became very careful over the use of my personal seal, for fear someone else should counterfeit it and use it.* My name had become important to me.

How powerful and how wealthy is our Lord Jesus! How precious to Him is His name! If, therefore, He is to take responsibility for everything that happens in consequence, how careful must He be as to how that name is used! I ask you again: *Can* God commit Himself—His 'bank balance', His 'cheque book', His 'signature'—to *you*? That question must be settled first. Then only can you use His name freely. Then only 'what things soever ye shall bind on earth shall be bound in heaven'. Then, because of the reality of His committal to you, you can move as a true representative of Him in this world. That is the fruit of union with Him.

Are we in such a union with the Lord that He *will* thus commit Himself to what we are doing? It seems often that we shall be running a big risk in stepping into a situation with only the promises of God to back up our stand. The point is, will God—*can* God—back us up?

Briefly let me outline four essential features of a work to which God can fully commit Himself. The first vital need is of a true revelation to our hearts of the eternal purpose of God. We cannot do without this. If I am working on a building, even as an unskilled labourer, I must know whether the objective is a garage or an aeroplane hangar or a palace.

---

* The Chinese custom is for everyone to have his own personal *tu-cheng*, a seal or die bearing the characters of his name carved in wood, stone or ivory in an individual design. The impression is usually made with an opaque red ink. This is felt to be less easily forged than a handwritten signature, and the seal is kept under lock and key and used for signing cheques and other personal documents.—ED.

I must see the plan or I cannot be an intelligent worker. Today evangelism is assumed by most Christians to be *the* work of God. But evangelism can never be an unrelated thing. It must be integrated with God's whole plan, for it is in fact but a means to an end. That end is the pre-eminence of the Son of God, and evangelism is bringing in the sons among whom He shall stand pre-eminent.

In Paul's generation every believer had a specific relation to the eternal purpose of God (see especially chapter 4. 11–16). That should be no less true of us today. The eyes of God are turning towards His coming kingdom. What we know as organized Christianity will shortly have to make way for something else—the sovereign rule of Christ. But as with the kingdom of Solomon, so now, there is first a period of spiritual warfare represented by the reign of David. God is seeking those who will co-operate with Him today in that preparatory warfare.

It is a question of the identification of my purpose with the eternal purpose of God. All Christian work that is not so identified is fragmentary and unrelated, and it does not ultimately get anywhere. We have to seek from God a revelation to our hearts by His Holy Spirit of 'the counsel of his will' (see 1. 9–12) and then to ask ourselves concerning the work to which we are going back after reading this: 'Is it directly related to that?' When that is settled, all the small questions of daily guidance will solve themselves.

Secondly, all work that is going to be effective in the divine purpose must be conceived by God. If *we* plan work and then ask God to bless it, we need not expect God to commit Himself to it. God's name can never be a 'rubber-stamp' to authorize work that is ours in conception. True, there may be blessing upon such work, but it will be partial and not full. There can be no 'in His name' there; only, alas, our name!

'The Son can do nothing of himself.' How often in the book of the Acts we find the Holy Spirit's prohibitions! We read in chapter 16 how Paul and those with him were 'forbidden of the Holy Ghost to speak the word in Asia'. And again: 'The Spirit of Jesus suffered them not.' Yet this book is the book of the *acts* of the Holy Spirit, not of His 'inactivities'. Too often we think that the actual doing is what matters. We have to learn the lesson of not doing—of keeping quiet for Him. We have to learn that if God does not move we dare not move. When we have learned this, then it is that He can safely send us forth to speak for Him.

I must have, therefore, a knowledge of God's will in my particular sphere of work. Out of that knowledge only should the work be initiated. The abiding principle of all true Christian work is: 'In the beginning God . . .'

Thirdly, all work to be effective must depend for its continuance upon the power of God alone. What is power? We often use the word loosely. We say of a man, 'He is a very powerful speaker', but we have to ask ourselves the question: What power is he using? Is it spiritual power or is it natural power? There is today all too much place given to the power of nature in the service of God. We have got to learn that, even where God has initiated a work, if we are trying to accomplish it in our own power God will never commit Himself to it.

You ask me what I mean by natural power. Put very simply, it is what we can do without the help of God. We give a man the task of organizing something—of planning a Gospel campaign or some other Christian activity—because he is naturally a good organizer. But if that is so, how hard will he pray? If he is accustomed to depend on his natural gifts, he may feel no need to cry to God. The trouble with us all is that there are so many things we can do without relying upon God. We must be brought to the place where, naturally gifted though we may be, we dare not act, we dare not speak, except in conscious and continual dependence on Him.

Stephen described Moses, after his Egyptian education, as a man 'mighty in his words and works'. Yet, after God had dealt with him, Moses had to say: 'Oh Lord, I am not eloquent, neither heretofore nor since thou hast spoken to thy servant: for I am slow of speech, and of a slow tongue.' When a born orator comes to the place of saying 'I can't speak', then he has learned a fundamental lesson and is on the road to real usefulness for God. That discovery involves a crisis and then a lifelong process, both of them implied, surely, in Luke's expression 'baptised into the name' (Acts 8. 16; 19. 5). That expression points every new believer to the necessity for a fundamental knowledge of the death and resurrection of Christ in its relation to his entire natural man. Somehow, in our history with God, we must experience that initial crippling touch of His hand to weaken our natural strength, so that we stand forth on the ground of resurrection life in Christ alone, where death has no longer any claim. After that the circle goes on widening, as fresh areas of our own self-energy are brought under the working of the Cross. The way is a costly one, but it is God's sure way to fruitfulness of life and ministry, for it provides Him with the ground He requires in order that He may give His backing to what we do in the name of His Son.

In the work of God today things are often so constituted that we have no need to rely upon God. But the Lord's verdict upon all such work is uncompromising: 'Apart from me ye can do nothing.' Such work as man can do apart from God is wood, hay, stubble, and the test of fire will prove it so. For divine work can only be done with divine power, and that power is to be found in the Lord Jesus alone. It is made available to us in Him on the resurrection side of the Cross. That is to say, it is when we have reached the point where in all honesty we cry: 'I cannot speak,' that we discover God *is* speaking. When we come to an end of our works, His work begins. Thus the fire in the days to come and the Cross today effect the same thing. What cannot stand the Cross today will not survive the fire later. If *my* work, which is done in *my* power is brought to death, how much comes out of the grave? Nothing! Nothing ever survives the Cross but what is wholly of God in Christ.

God never asks us to do anything we *can* do. He asks us to live a life which we can never live and to do a work which we can never do. Yet, by His grace, we *are* living it and doing it. The life we live is the life of Christ lived in the power of God, and the work we do is the work of Christ carried on through us by His Spirit whom we obey. Self is the only obstruction to that life and to that work. May we each one pray from our hearts: 'O Lord, deal with *me*!'

Finally, the end and object of all work to which God can commit Himself must be His glory. This means that we get nothing out of it for ourselves. It is a divine principle that the less we get of personal gratification out of such a work the greater is its true value to God. There is no room for glory to man in the work of God. True, there is a deep, precious joy in any service that brings Him pleasure and that opens the door to His working, but the ground of that joy is His glory and not man's. Everything is 'to the praise of the glory of his grace' (1. 6, 12, 14).

It is when these questions are truly settled between us and God that God will commit Himself—and indeed I believe He will allow us to say that then He *has* to do so. Experience in China has taught us this, that if there is ground for doubt whether our work is of God, then sure enough we find God is reluctant to answer prayer in relation to it. But when it is wholly of Him, He will commit Himself in wonderful ways. Then it is that, in utter obedience to Him, you can use His name, and all Hell will have to recognise your authority to do so. When God commits Himself to a thing, then He comes out in power to prove that He is in it and is Himself its Author.

The God of Elijah

Let me give you in closing an experience of my own. A few years after the beginning of our work we entered upon a period of severe testing. They were days of disappointment and near-despair. We had come in for a great deal of criticism and discredit on account of the stand we were taking, resulting in coolness and estrangement, even on the part of the Lord's true people. We had honestly faced and examined the charges made against us, for it is essential always to take criticism seriously and examine it, and not to pass it off with 'Oh! he's just *criticizing* me!' Yet we had reason to believe that the Lord was with us, for, as a particularly difficult year drew to its close, we were able to reckon that within that period He had given us several hundreds of real conversions. Then, at the year's end, it seemed that a climax was reached.

Annually for several years it had been our custom at the New Year public holiday to hold a convention in the city for believers of different connections from throughout the province. This year the sponsors of the convention asked me not to attend. The request came as a shock to us. It was, I now realize, an attempt by the Evil One to draw me and my brethren off our ground of rest in Christ. The question was, how would we react?

The New Year holiday is a long one, lasting fully fifteen days, and besides being a suitable period for a convention, it is also the best time for Gospel preaching. After seeking the Lord's will we became clear that He would have us use it for the latter purpose, so I planned to take with me five brothers for a fifteen-day preaching visit to an island off the South China coast. At the last moment another young brother whom I shall call 'brother Wu' joined the party. He was only sixteen years of age and had been expelled from school, but he had just lately been born again and there was a marked change in his life. Moreover he was very eager to come, so after some hesitation I agreed to take him. This made us seven in all.

The island was a fairly large one with a big main village of 'six thousand stoves'. An old school-mate of mine was there as headmaster of the village school, and I wrote to him in advance asking for a room in which we might lodge during our stay from January 1st to 15th. When however we arrived, late and in darkness, and when he discovered we had come for Gospel preaching, he refused us accommodation.

So we sought through the village for somewhere to lodge, until eventually a Chinese herbalist had pity on us and took us in, making us quite comfortable on planks and straw in his attic.

It was not long before the herbalist became our first convert. But though we laboured systematically and hard, and though we found the people of the village most courteous, we had very little fruit from the island, and we began to wonder why this was.

On January 9th we were outside preaching. Brother Wu with some others was in one part of the village and suddenly asked publicly: 'Why will none of you believe?' Someone in the crowd replied at once: 'We have a god—*one* god—Ta-wang,* and he has never failed us. He is an effective god.' 'How do you know that you can trust him?' asked Wu. 'We have held his festival procession every January for 286 years. The chosen day is revealed by divination beforehand, and every year without fail his Day is a perfect one without rain or cloud,' was the reply. 'When is the procession this year?' 'It is fixed for January 11th at eight in the morning.' 'Then,' said brother Wu impetuously, 'I promise you that it will certainly rain on the 11th.' At once there was an outburst of cries from the crowd: 'That is enough! We don't want to hear any more preaching. If there is rain on the 11th, then your God is God!'

I was elsewhere in the village when this occurred. As soon as I heard of it I saw that it was most serious. The news had spread like wildfire, and before long over twenty

---

* Pronounced with a long *a* as in 'car' and with the final *ng* very lightly sounded. The name means 'Great King'.—Ed.

thousand people would know about it. What were we to do? We stopped our preaching at once, and gave ourselves to prayer. We asked the Lord to forgive us if we had over-stepped ourselves. I tell you, we were in deadly earnest. What had we done? Had we made a terrible mistake, or dare we ask God for a miracle?

The more you want an answer to prayer from God, the more you desire to be clear with Him. There must be no doubt about fellowship—no shadow between. If your faith were in coincidence you could afford to have a controversy with Him, but not otherwise. We did not mind being thrown out if we had done something wrong. After all, you can't drag God into a thing against His will! But, we reflected, this would mean an end to the Gospel testimony in the island, and Ta-wang would reign supreme for ever. What should we do? Should we leave now?

Up to this point we had feared to pray for rain. Then, like a flash, there came the word to me: 'Where is the God of Elijah?' It came with such clarity and power that I knew it was from God. Confidently I announced to the brothers: 'I have the answer. The Lord will send rain on the 11th.' Together we thanked Him, and then, full of praise, we went out—all seven of us—and told everyone. We could accept the devil's challenge in the name of the Lord, and we would broadcast our acceptance.

That evening the herbalist made two very pointed obser-vations. Undoubtedly, he said, Ta-wang *was* an effective god. The devil was with that image. Their faith in him was not groundless. Alternatively, if you preferred a rationalis-tic explanation, here was a whole village of fishermen. For two or three months on end the men were at sea, and on the 15th they would be out again. They, of all people, should know by long experience when it would not rain for two or three days ahead.

This disturbed us. As we went to our evening prayer, we all began once more to pray for rain—*now*! Then it was that there came to us a stern rebuke from the Lord: 'Where is the God of Elijah?' Were we going to fight our way through this battle, or were we going to rest in the finished victory of Christ? What had Elisha done when he spoke those words? He had laid claim in his own personal experience to the very miracle that his lord Elijah, now in the glory, had himself performed. In New Testament terms, he had taken his stand by faith on the ground of a finished work.

We confessed our sins again. 'Lord,' we said, 'we don't need rain until the 11th morning.' We went to bed, and next morning (the 10th) we set off for a neighbouring island for a day's preaching. The Lord was very gracious, and that day three families turned to Him, confessing Him publicly and burning their idols. We returned late, tired out but rejoicing. We could afford to sleep late tomorrow.

I was awakened by the direct rays of the sun through the single window of our attic. 'This isn't rain!' I said. It was already past seven o'clock. I got up, knelt down and prayed. 'Lord,' I said, 'please send the rain!' But once again, ringing in my ears came the word: 'Where is the God of Elijah?' Humbled, I walked downstairs before God in silence. We sat down to breakfast—eight of us together, including our host—all very quiet. There was no cloud in the sky, but we knew God was committed. As we bowed to say grace before the food I said, 'I think the time is up. Rain must come now. We can bring it to the Lord's remembrance.' Quietly we did so, and this time the answer came with no hint whatever of rebuke in it.

'Where is the God of Elijah?' Even before our Amen we heard a few drops on the tiles. There was a steady shower as we ate our rice and were served with a second bowl. 'Let us give thanks again,' I said, and now we asked God for heavier rain. As we began on that second bowl of rice the rain was coming down in buckets-full. By the time we had finished, the street outside was already deep in water and the three steps at the door of the house were covered.

Soon we heard what had happened in the village. Already, at the first drop of rain, a few of the younger generation had begun to say openly: 'There is God; there is no more Ta-wang! He is kept in by the rain.' But he wasn't. They carried him out on a sedan chair. Surely he would stop the shower! Then came the downpour. After only some ten or twelve yards, three of the coolies stumbled and fell. Down went the chair and Ta-wang with it, fracturing his jaw and his left arm. Still determined, they carried out emergency repairs and put him back in the chair. Somehow, slipping and stumbling, they dragged or carried him half-way round the village. Then the floods defeated them. Some of the village elders, old men of 60 to 80 years, bare-headed and without umbrellas as their faith in Ta-wang's weather required, had fallen and were in serious difficulties. The procession was stopped and the idol taken into a house. Divination was made. 'Today was the wrong day,' came the answer. 'The festival is to be on the 14th with the procession at six in the evening.'

Immediately we heard this there came the assurance in our hearts: 'God will send rain on the 14th.' We went to prayer: 'Lord, send rain on the 14th at 6-00 p.m. and give us four good days until then.' That afternoon the sky cleared, and now we had a good hearing for the Gospel. The Lord gave us over thirty converts—real ones—in the village and in the island during those three short days. The 14th broke, another perfect day, and we had good meetings. As the evening approached we met, and again, at the appointed hour, we quietly brought the matter to the Lord's remembrance. Not a minute late, His answer came with torrential rain and floods as before.

The next day our time was up and we had to leave. We have not been back. Other workers asked for those islands and we never question anyone's claim to a field. But for us the essential point was that Satan's power in that idol had been broken, and that is an eternal thing. Ta-wang was no more 'an effective god'. The salvation of souls would follow, but was in itself secondary to this vital and unchanging fact.

The impression on us all was a lasting one. God had committed Himself. We had tasted the authority of the name that is above every name—the name that has power in heaven and earth and hell. In those few days we had known what it is to be, as we say, 'in the very centre of the will of God'. Those words were no longer something vague or visionary to us. They described an experience we had ourselves been through. Together we had been granted a brief glimpse of 'the mystery of his will' (1. 9; 3. 10). We would go softly all our days. Years later I met 'brother Wu'. I had lost touch with him, and in the interval he had become a pilot in the Airways. When I asked him whether he still followed the Lord, 'Mr Nee!' he said, 'do you mean to say that after all we went through I could ever forsake Him?'

Do you see what it means to 'stand'? We do not try to gain ground; we merely stand on the ground which the Lord Jesus has gained for us, and resolutely refuse to be moved from it. When our eyes are really opened to see Christ as our victorious Lord, then our praise flows forth freely and without restraint. Singing with melody in our hearts to the Lord, we give thanks for all things in His name (5. 19–20). Praise that is the outcome of effort has a laboured and discordant note, but praise that wells up spontaneously from hearts at rest in Him has always a pure, sweet tone.

The Christian life consists of sitting with Christ, walking by Him and standing in Him. We begin our spiritual life by resting in the finished work of the Lord Jesus. That rest is the source of our strength for a consistent and unfaltering walk in the world. And at the end of a gruelling warfare with the hosts of darkness we are found standing with Him at last in triumphant possession of the field.

'Unto him . . . be the glory . . . for ever.'